Changing Social Science

Changing Social Science

CRITICAL THEORY AND OTHER CRITICAL PERSPECTIVES

Edited by
Daniel R. Sabia, Jr.
and Jerald Wallulis

State University of New York Press
ALBANY

For
Nancy and Annie

Published by State University of New York Press, Albany

©1983 State University of New York

All rights reserved

Printed in the United States of America

For information, address State University of New York Press, State University Plaza, Albany, N.Y., 12246

Library of Congress Cataloging in Publication Data

Main entry under title:

Changing social science.

Includes bibliographical references and index.

Contents: The idea of a critical social science / Daniel R. Sabia, Jr. and Jerald Wallulis—The ontological presuppositions and political consequences of a social science / Terence Ball—Mutual knowledge / John O'Neill—[etc.]

1. Sociology—Philosophy—Addresses, essays, lectures. 2. Social sciences—Philosophy—Addresses, essays, lectures. 3. Criticism (Philosophy)—Addresses, essays, lectures. 4. Habermas, Jürgen—Addresses, essays, lectures. I. Sabia, Daniel R., 1947-   . II. Wallulis, Jerald, 1947-   .

HM24.C44 1983   300'.1   82-10454

ISBN 0-87395-679-6

ISBN 0-87395-680-X (pbk.)

Contents

v

Contents

Preface

The essays in this volume describe, develop, and evaluate or defend a form of critical inquiry for the social sciences. They are addressed primarily to graduate students and to specialists in the fields of political science, sociology, and the philosophy of the social sciences. Integration is provided through the idea of a critical social science developed in the introductory first essay and then elaborated and evaluated in succeeding chapters. Because critical inquiry is not the prevailing approach in the disciplines addressed by the contributors, the title *Changing Social Science* has suggested itself in both its descriptive and prescriptive senses.

The major stimulus for compiling *Changing Social Science* was an interdisciplinary conference on "Critical Theory: Contributors and Criticisms," held at the University of South Carolina in 1980. Three of the chapters which appear here were delivered in a preliminary form at the conference. Three other original essays, and an article specially revised for the volume, were subsequently commissioned by the editors.

The philosophers, sociologists, and political scientists who have collaborated on and contributed to the volume deserve our special thanks for their support and perseverance. We want also to acknowledge and thank the Departments of Philosophy and of Government and International Studies for co-sponsoring the conference at the University of South Carolina. Finally, we wish to thank Chester W. Bain, Dean of the College of Humanities and Social Sciences at the University, for his encouragement and support for this project.

Dan Sabia, Political Science
Jerry Wallulis, Philosophy
University of South Carolina, April 1982

The Contributors

Terence Ball
Associate Professor of Political Science, University of Minnesota
Ph.D., University of California, Berkeley
Professor Ball is the author of *Civil Disobedience and Civil Deviance* and editor of *Political Theory and Praxis*; his articles, reviews and translations have appeared in such journals as *Philosophy of the Social Sciences, American Political Science Review, Political Theory, American Journal of Political Science,* and *Review of Politics.*

David R. Dickens
Assistant Professor of Sociology, University of Kentucky
Ph.D., University of Kansas
Professor Dickens is the author of "Phenomenology," published in *Theoretical Perspectives in Sociology.*

Brian Fay
Associate Professor of Philosophy, Wesleyan University
Ph.D., Oxford
Professor Fay is the author of *Social Theory and Political Practice* and of essays published in anthologies and in *Philosophy of the Social Sciences.*

Richard W. Miller
Associate Professor of Philosophy, Cornell University
Ph.D., Harvard University
Professor Miller is the author of numerous articles appearing in such journals as *American Philosophical Quarterly, Philosophical Review, Philosophy of Science, Mind, Philosophy and Public Affairs,* and *Journal of the History of Philosophy.*

J. Donald Moon
Associate Professor of Government, Wesleyan University
Ph.D., University of Minnesota
Professor Moon, who has authored essays appearing in such journals as the *American Journal of Political Science, Political Theory, Philosophy of the Social Sciences,* and *Journal of Politics,* is also the author of "The Logic of Political Inquiry" in Volume I of the *Handbook of Political Science.*

John O'Neill
Professor of Sociology, York University
Ph.D., Stanford University
Professor O'Neill has authored numerous essays and reviews, as well as *Perception, Expression and History, Sociology as a Skin Trade,* and *Making Sense Together.* He is also the editor of *On Critical Theory* and *Modes of Individualism and Collectivism.*

Daniel R. Sabia, Jr.
Assistant Professor of Political Science, University of South Carolina
Ph.D., University of Minnesota
Professor Sabia is the author of numerous reviews and of an article in *Journal of Political Science.* He is also a co-editor of, and contributor to, *Dissent and Affirmation: Essays in Honor of Mulford Q. Sibley.*

Jerald Wallulis
Assistant Professor of Philosophy, University of South Carolina
Ph.D., University of Notre Dame
Professor Wallulis has contributed to *Indiana Academy Proceedings* and to a recent volume of *Anelecta Husserliana.*

Stephen K. White
Assistant Professor of Political Science, Virginia Polytechnic Institute and State University
Ph.D., Graduate School of the City University of New York
Professor White is the author of articles published in *American Political Science Review, Journal of Politics,* and *Review of Politics.*

PART ONE
Reflexivity

CHAPTER ONE
The Idea of a Critical Social Science
Daniel R. Sabia, Jr.
Jerald Wallulis

Brought together in this volume are essays by philosophers, sociologists, and political scientists who advocate changing the way social science is conceived and practiced. They contend that the ethical responsibilities of those who seek to produce sociological and political knowledge in contemporary societies cannot be escaped—and so must be directly confronted. For this reason they confront the political implications of theories in their disciplines, and go on to argue that the limitations of social scientific practice are neither properly respected nor adequately understood. The methodological assumptions underlying current research are objects of their criticism, and new directions are offered for the way work should and should not proceed. In all cases a more critical form of social scientific inquiry, especially in sociology and political science, is advocated and defended.

The idea of a critical social science does not spring newborn from the heads of our seven contributors. Accusations of bias in social science theory, criticisms of social science methodology, calls for a more practical, relevant or critical social science—contentions of this sort are expressed with periodic regularity by disenchanted practioners of virtually every discipline of the social sciences. More important, however, are demands for change of a more programmatic kind associated with various traditions of thought and with critical scholars on whom our contributors draw and to whom they are often indebted. Included among these critics and advocates are hermeneuticists from Dilthey to Gadamer, *verstehen* and reflexive sociologists from Weber to Gouldner, phenomenologists and ethnomethodologists from Schutz to Garfinkel, recent political theorists such as Oakeshott, Arendt, Strauss, and Wolin, and philosophers like Taylor, Winch, and MacIntyre.

Another school of thought which has demanded fundamental change in the social sciences, and which has developed an explicitly critical program of its own, is the Frankfurt School. Influenced by the thought of Hegel and Marx, members of the Frankfurt Institute for Social Research such as Max Horkheimer, Theodor Adorno, and Herbert Marcuse have sought since the twenties to tie social theory to an interest in human emancipation.[1] The basic idea of their "critical theory" is that since persons cannot be free from that about which they are ignorant, liberation depends in the first instance on recognition of that which imprisons the human mind or dominates the human person.

Like Marx in the nineteenth century, critical theorists in the twentieth believe that men and women suffer various forms of domination about which they are unaware. Like Marx, they have accordingly attempted to develop a critical theory of society which would contribute to the realization of individual autonomy and freedom. In order to accomplish this, such a theory would have to be efficacious, that is, it would have to have practical effect. Of course there is the further demand that the theory would have to be true, which leads the Frankfurt School to a critique of social science. For the critical theorist needs to ask whether the social sciences are capable of providing the kind of knowledge requisite to a critical theory of society. Marx asked this question of nineteenth-century social thinkers and economists, and argued that their methods of inquiry were confused or mistaken. Worse yet, they produced theories of society or political economy that contributed to domination by implicitly (and sometimes explicitly) justifying socio-economic and political structures and practices that alienated individuals. Horkheimer and other Institute members have similarly criticized the now traditional conception of social inquiry both for the inadequacy of its methods and the, albeit unwitting, social and political conservatism of its consequences.[2]

In recent years the Frankfurt School has gained in recognition and popularity due largely to the work of Jürgen Habermas. For students and scholars unfamiliar with his work, the review by David Dickens in Chapter Six (and also the contributions by Stephen White and J. Donald Moon) will be most helpful in understanding the many reasons why the attention is deserved.[3] Habermas quite naturally knows the thought of earlier members of the Frankfurt School, but he is equally conversant in the methods and theories currently employed in the social sciences. He is also highly versed in other traditions of social philosophy such as phenomenology and hermeneutics which have stressed the importance of interpretation for understanding social action and historical traditions.[4] Consequently Habermas has found himself in a better position than his predecessors to articulate a comprehensive and systematic account of what a critical theory of the social sciences should be.

With this considerable background in mind, Habermas has developed a philosophical argument to the effect that the traditional goals and methodological assumptions of the social sciences are undergirded or informed by a particular kind of human interest—a "knowledge-constitutive interest." Analyzed more fully by Dickens and Moon, Habermas's argument involves the claim that the adoption of the goals of prediction and explanation in the social sciences is itself explained by a knowledge-guiding interest in achieving technical control over objectified processes, whether natural or human. This interest, culturally derived and socially useful, is "knowledge-constitutive" because it informs and constitutes the goals and methods of those who embrace it.

Habermas wants social scientists to reflect critically on this argument for at least two reasons. First, such reflection might indicate to them that the interest in technical control, however important and useful in the natural sciences, is but one possible interest social science could serve. Habermas maintains that there are other constitutive interests guiding other approaches to social and political inquiry. For example, whereas the interest in technical control, and hence the focus on causal explanation and theory, informs the many variants of naturalist or "positivist" social science, historical disciplines, often termed the *Geisteswissenschaften*, are undergirded by a practical interest in communication or understanding. Habermas, of course, advocates a third aproach: a critical social science constituted by an interest in human emancipation. Methodologically, this form of inquiry synthesizes elements of the explanatory stance characteristic of naturalist social science with an historically based hermeneutic or phenomenological approach *and* a Marxist critique of ideology.

The interest in emancipation introduces the second reason for Habermas's appeal to knowledge-constitutive interests. Once social scientists come to recognize the connection between their naturalist science (its goals and methods) and their society (from which their "interest" is derived), they will also become sensitive to the ethical problems arising out of this connection. In particular, any claim to ethical neutrality on their part will be put into question and may even be abandoned in favor of the emancipatory goals of a critical social science. Thus, in place of a doctrine of ethical neutrality, Habermas insists that social scientists ought to be committed to the ideal of human liberation;

ought to be willing to critique those facets of contemporary culture which prevent or retard progress in this direction; and ought to seek to develop the knowledge and theories which would facilitate its realization.

Few of the contributors to *Changing Social Science* consider themselves to be critical theorists of either early or recent vintage. Indeed many openly criticize certain features of the Habermasian/critical program. In Part Three, for example, crucial objections are raised against the justification Habermas gives for the normative foundation of the interest in human emancipation. This facet of his work is the central topic of discussion in the essays by Moon and White and is also elaborated on below with respect to its normative implications for the general prospect of critical inquiry.

Nevertheless, the problematic and arguments of the essays collected here do share important affinities to the Habermasian project. *Changing Social Science* advances, as Habermas has advanced, a set of philosophical arguments intended to explain how the attitudes, methods, and goals of social scientists may be conceived in a more critically responsible manner. There is a similar concern for the political implications of both the methods and theories of the social sciences, although in our case this concern encompasses critical approaches to social and political inquiry as well. In addition, the role of value judgments in social theorizing is considered and the doctrine of ethical neutrality attacked, but so too is Habermas's own theory of normative justification. Underlying assumptions of traditional and critical approaches to social inquiry are also explored, although the emphasis in *Changing Social Science* is on the models of man presupposed by these approaches and not on the knowledge-constitutive interests which may inform them. Finally, the central and unavoidable problems of methodology, such as the role of causality, the need for interpretation, and the relationship between the social and natural sciences, are examined from different philosophical viewpoints that lay open the options available for a critical form of social science.

Our goal in this initial chapter is to sketch and amplify these arguments by indicating how they justify a reconstruction of social science, particularly of sociology and political science, in accord with the idea of a critical social science. In our view such a science is characterized by three central features: an emphasis on reflexivity, the acceptance of a methodological and ontological orientation distinct from the naturalist paradigm, and a commitment to social criticism and advocacy. Reflexivity involves the demand from the practicing social scientist for a critical self-awareness of his or her goals and methods, of the role of the social sciences in contemporary society, of the values and political biases implicit in social science method and theory, and of the limits and unresolved difficulties intrinsic to any science of man and society (including a critical science). Methodologically, critical social science questions the naturalist orientation dominant in contemporary social science and develops alternative stances appropriate to both the subject matter and goals of critical social inquiry. Finally, a critical social science, while committed to the search for knowledge of man and society, is equally dedicated to the political task of enlightenment; it willingly embraces and defends, therefore, ethical ideals appropriate to social criticism and advocacy. These three aspects make up the idea of a critical social science; its attractiveness and tenability are explored throughout *Changing Social Science*.

Politics and Science

A recurring criticism of contemporary social science theories is that they too often embody, usually in tacit or hidden ways, political biases and values.[5] As briefly explained above, Habermas has expanded this criticism by arguing that the social sciences necessarily embody such biases and values in their very goals and methods. Historically, this connection has led to what Habermas terms the "scientization of politics," described by Dickens as referring to the "illegitimate extension of technological reason into the sphere of politics" (p. 138). Habermas hopes with this historical account to draw attention, as Max Weber had earlier in the century, to the tendency in modern Western culture to reduce all problems of human existence to technical solutions. Rooted in the rise of industrialization, of capitalist organization, and of bureaucratic government, modern societies are characterized in Weberian fashion as evincing an "escalating scale of continually expanded technical control over nature and a continually refined administration of human beings and their relations to each other by means of social organization."[6]

As technology comes to dominate social existence and as technocratic elites come to dominate public policy direction and discussion, the threat to human freedom and democratic practice becomes obvious. The role of the social sciences in this process—when viewed from a critical perspective—is equally clear. Neither separate nor immune from the needs and attitudes of contemporary society, social scientists often support and maintain the status quo by producing information and knowledge that are of value to those who pay their salaries and fund their research. More fundamentally, Habermas points out that the contemporary social sciences are heirs of modern Western culture and thought; their very approaches to social inquiry are therefore rooted in the dominant impulses of a technological culture.

In our next chapter, "The Ontological Presuppositions and Political Consequences of a Social Science," Terence Ball continues and deepens the exercise in political self-awareness through historical reflections on the roots of modern political science. Directing his attention primarily to American political science, Ball argues that the naturalist perspective dominant in this discipline, as well as its leading theories of politics, are historically, practically, and conceptually linked to a familiar form of political life—one in which political activity is understood in instrumental terms as the pursuit of interests of a broadly economic kind. That politics *is* "the pursuit of private interests through public channels," no contemporary American, whether citizen or academic, is likely to deny; the conception permeates everyday language and typically underlies both lay and academic explanations of political behavior and processes.

In Ball's view, however, this familiar understanding of politics, and the form of life which it genuinely reflects, is the product of history. Consequently, neither the conception, nor the corresponding practice, are sacrosanct, normal, or natural. In order to demonstrate this thesis, Ball turns to "conceptual history" exemplified in the work of Hannah Arendt. Arendt's elucidation of the Greek conception of politics discloses one of many possible "alternative" conceptions of political activity, "and in so doing exposes the time-bound character of our own" (p. 37). In the Greek view, citizens were public actors, not private individuals; they were expected to participate, through speech and deed, in the public affairs of the community; and the focus of the community was on "the moral development and well-being of its citizens, not their physical protection or economic welfare" (p. 39).

To this conception of Greek politics Ball contrasts the beliefs underlying and informing the United States Constitution. Based on the premises that individuals naturally seek their self-interest, and that self-interest can be scientifically engineered to counteract or check other self-interest, the Framers in Philadelphia constructed a set of political and governmental institutions the efficacy of which required precisely the kind of behavior they presupposed. As every schoolboy knows, the success of the Framers' science of politics can be measured in terms of the longevity of the republican institutions they created. But Ball suggests that their success needs also to be measured in terms of the

8

kind of society those institutions encouraged and legitimized: a society in which the pursuit of private interests through public channels is equally expected and accepted. Or a society in which this kind of behavior is believed to be, if not sacrosanct, then certainly normal and natural.

American political science, Ball wants to argue, is also rooted in this history. Not only do American political scientists typically construct explanations and theories of politics in terms of the kind of behavior conventional in their society and rooted in its past; their science also presupposes, even requires, this behavior. It is this latter fact which provides the conceptual link between self-interested behavior and the naturalist perspective endemic to contemporary political science. Drawing on Albert Hirschman, Ball argues that the rise of an ethic of self-interest, intertwined with the rise of capitalist society, was promoted by various thinkers in the form of the "theory of countervailing passions." Briefly put, this theory asserted that avarice or greed, long regarded as a natural vice of mankind, was potentially a socially useful trait and, for that reason, was better regarded as a natural virtue. Since avarice was a "natural" trait or disposition of men, it could *if encouraged* be depended on to produce predictable and therefore controllable behavior—a desideratum of both a science of man and of emerging societies threatened by growing numbers of citizens whose traditional forms of life were disintegrating. What Ball's conceptual history illuminates is that self-interested behavior was in thought and practice deliberately legitimized on the supposition that, since it was a behavioral regularity rooted in man's unchanging nature, the political theorists who sought to explain and predict behavior, as well as the statesmen who sought to control it, could achieve their ends by grasping this eternal verity and using it to their advantage.

The point can be further illustrated by a recently popular research program in both sociology and political science which makes "rational self-interest" or utility maximization the centerpiece of theories which seek to explain the behavior of individuals, groups and organizations. This program—variously termed "game theory," "positive theory," "exchange theory," "rational man modelling," "the public choice paradigm"—is novel only in its explicit borrowing from economics.[7] But that it borrows from economics is, in light of Ball's critical reflections, telling. For it is this social science, proceeding on Adam Smith's proclamation of a "propensity in human nature . . . to truck, barter, and exchange" in order to satisfy self-interest, that is most obviously indebted to the intellectual and cultural heritage Ball describes.[8] Because modern industrial societies suppose with Smith that self-interest is a permissible and natural rather than a pernicious and conventional "propensity," economic and kindred sociological and political theories contribute to the legitimation, not just of the pursuit of self-interest, but of the institutions, practices, and processes which this behavior produces. Thus, for example, theories which explain political apathy in terms of rational self-interest effectively justify such behavior. Similarly, theories which maintain that individuals join large groups on the basis of selective incentives which appeal to their rational self-interest, do more than explain the appearance of group leaders or "entrepreneurs" who "need" to provide and manipulate such incentives in order to gain and maintain group members. Rather, the explanation appears to justify such behaviors precisely on the ground that it is "necessary" for "rational" persons to act in this way, that this is the "logical" consequence of perfectly acceptable, because rationally self-interested, behavior.

If it is protested that, biased or not, theories of this type do happen to be "successful" in explaining and predicting behaviors and processes, we offer the following response for consideration. The predictive success of these theories, when applied to individuals in contemporary industrial societies, should be thoroughly expected since they do little more than identify the "logical" consequences of an historically contingent, institutionally reinforced, conventional form of social behavior. When applied, as Ball says, to "other peoples in other places"—or to domains of social interaction such as friendship, courtship, and worship, or to behaviors and processes based on guilt, zeal, love, patriotism, or revolutionary fervor—the utility of these theories rapidly diminishes. Yet it is precisely the limitations of such theories—restricted to particular societies, contingent interests, and culturally dominant views of human motivation—that are too often ignored or overlooked by social and political theorists. Instead, there is a tendency in social science theorizing to confuse the conventional with the natural—to suppose, for example, that the pursuit of self-interest characterizes the political behavior of all people or even that it characterizes all forms of human behavior. This tendency is not only theoretically, but *politically*, dangerous. To confuse the conventional with the natural is to reify the former; and to reify convention is, as Brian Fay explains in Chapter Five, to engage in

> a form of ideological distortion. For in such cases the social scientist is illicitly transforming the generalizations which account for one particular way of doing things into purported general laws which

supposedly govern human life as such. The effect of this concealed ideological transformation can be particularly oppressive, for it can reinforce the social actors' acceptance of a status quo which may be deeply frustrating to them. It can do this both by giving them reason to believe that their social life must be as it is, and by failing to provide them with an analysis of their situation which might help them to change it. . . . (pp. 126–127)

The Ontological Foundation of a Critical Social Science

The tendency towards reification in the social sciences is, as both Ball and Fay point out, the direct result of a basic commitment to the discovery of invariant or universal laws of human behavior and social interaction. According to naturalism, this commitment is a prerequisite for science. As a prescription for practice, naturalism maintains that social scientific inquiry ought to be governed by the methodological principles operative in the natural sciences. The argument for the adoption of the naturalist stance toward social objects and processes is twofold: first, that since the natural sciences have been most successful in producing knowledge, the social sciences need to imitate the natural sciences; second, that a naturalist social science can discover immutable knowledge directly applicable to the organization and control of society and polity. The first basis of argumentation rests on a belief in scientism, the doctrine that science alone produces knowledge; its origins have been traced in impressive attacks on its plausibility by both Edmund Husserl and Habermas.[9] The second basis is what directly concerns us here. Its adequacy rests on one of two assumptions: either the objects of the social and natural sciences do not differ in any qualitatively important sense; or the differences between social and natural objects are methodologically irrelevant.

A critical social science rejects these assumptions. It maintains that the objects of the social and natural sciences *do* differ in a qualitatively important sense, and that this difference has methodological consequences. Ball suggests that we describe the qualitative difference in ontological terms. Naturalism, he argues, implicitly presupposes a particular ontology of man and society which is seriously flawed. The ontology in question is essentially Hobbesian. It supposes that individuals are objects in nature sharing a fixed and similar constitution. When these like objects are subjected to similar stimuli or to similar circumstances, they will behave in similar ways. Their fixed nature, in other words, guarantees behavioral regularities. Society, in turn, is understood

11

to be constituted by these objects; it is moved hither and thither by them as their collective behaviors and interactions manifest themselves, under given conditions, in macro events and tendencies.[10]

That something like this ontology of man and society is presupposed by a naturalist social science is clear, for without it the conception of knowledge and the attendant methodology embraced by most social scientists would have neither sense nor utility. The goal of a naturalist social science is to discover causal regularities on the individual and social levels, recast them in the form of laws, account for them by incorporating them into theories, and use them to explain and predict human behavior and social processes and events.

Since a naturalist orientation to social inquiry presupposes a Hobbesian ontology, a rejection or qualification of the latter would seem to require a corresponding rejection or qualification of the former. In virtually all of the essays which follow, the Hobbesian conception of man and society is implicitly or explicitly qualified. In this section of our remarks, we will sketch the nonnaturalist ontology of man and society presupposed or discussed by the contributors. Toward the end of this section, and in the next, we shall describe the implications of this alternative ontology for social science methodology.

None of our contributors would deny the Hobbesian contention that man is an object in nature. But they would emphasize that man is also a "self-interpreting animal" capable of action.[11] Action consists of the things people intentionally do and which typically capture, therefore, the attention of social scientists, as "voting" captures the attention of political scientists, "consuming" the attention of economists, and "praying" the attention of sociologists of religion. That people do these things intentionally reflects their ability to form purposes and goals and to embody these in their behavior. Purposes and goals, in turn, are rooted in the understandings people have of themselves. For example, a person able to conceive of herself as having community-relevant preferences and as being (actually or potentially) a participant in a collective decision-making procedure can conceive of herself as being a voter. Such conceptions or self-understandings constitute in large part a person's self: as a voter with preferences, as a consumer with wants, as a Christian with a soul.

An attentiveness to changes in the self-understandings of human beings indicates, in addition, their historical nature. The historicity of man is not due merely to the fact that people change their behavior over time, for even Hobbesian men, given changing conditions, do that. Rather, men are historical animals because, within limits, they can change themselves. Just as the individual, from childhood to old age, can change by internalizing new conceptions of self and new possibilities of action, so can generations change themselves as they seek to cope with, understand, and participate in changing social and natural environments; as they develop the arts and sciences; and as they reflect on their self-images, their experiences, and their society and culture. Brian Fay puts this point particularly well on p. 117 when he explains that human "life is essentially historical, not because changes in how it is lived have occurred, but because parts of these changes have been authored by the participants themselves in this historical process."

The self-understandings which give shape to purposes and direction to history are socially mediated. A person cannot conceive of herself as a voter unless she has been exposed to a society in which there are such things as collective decision-making procedures and in which a vocabulary exists for identifying and conceptualizing such procedures, their functions, the roles of participants in these, the character of the participants (for instance, that they have community-relevant preferences), and so on. In other words, the elements constitutive of an individual's self-understandings are *identified and understood* in terms of a socially shared language and therefore in terms of intersubjective (not simply subjective) meanings.

The social mediation of human identity and action suggests that man must be conceived as a social animal, and society as constituted by shared meanings. Not just the actions of social actors, but the relations between individuals and groups, social institutions and practices, social processes and events—all these are typically endowed with, *and* are identified and understood in terms of, the meanings shared by a social group. As John O'Neill expounds in Chapter Three, shared meanings, including "unarticulated" meanings or knowledge, provide the basis for social cohesion and mutual understanding and interaction. Similarly, Ball points out that the conception of politics shared by American citizens and political scientists enables them to identify, describe, and explain political behaviors, institutions, and processes in a certain way; and these features of political life in turn embody that conception in the sense that they would not be what they are were they conceived differently. The same point is made by Fay when, in describing the emergence of new conceptions of politics, he indicates how these new conceptions "altered the very nature" of political relationships and institutions. Such fundamental change can and does occur, not simply because ideas affect social reality, but because ideas are constitutive of social reality.

In his essay on "Mutual Knowledge," O'Neill develops the methodological import of this perspective by contending that the "primacy of the everyday world as a self-interpreted structure of practical knowledge and values is fundamental" (p. 56). Since the meaningfulness of the social world has been constructed by the social actors who inhabit and interact in it, the social scientist will not be able to ignore the structure of meanings which permeate and shape it. This can be brought out by recognizing that social scientists must interpret (name, categorize, describe) social phenomena before they can explain them. Interpretation is usually accomplished by implicitly presupposing or (more rarely) by explicitly postulating what the phenomenologist Alfred Schutz termed a "typification."

Very briefly, a typification is a mental construct which identifies the characteristic features (qualities, propensities, location, etc.) of some social entity, be it a person, a class of persons (e.g., politicians, businessmen, priests), or a collectivity or institution (the government, a corporation, a church). Schutz maintains that people interact with one another and act more generally in the world on the basis of more or less elaborate and, as O'Neill emphasizes, corrigible typifications. Schutz also maintains that social scientists do the same thing whenever they construct explanations of social behavior, institutions and processes.[12] Sometimes this is done explicitly—Weber's ideal types and the rational man models mentioned earlier are examples. Nevertheless, whenever an explanation or theory is proferred by a social scientist, it will implicitly presuppose typifications or, in another idiom, a "model of man" that makes at least rudimentary assumptions about "human motivation, sociality, and rationality."[13]

O'Neill claims that the naturalist orientation to social inquiry hides the role of typifications from social scientists and, at the same time, makes them either hostile to or unaware of the need for an interpretive approach to social inquiry. In this respect the ontological difference between the Hobbesian and Schutzian "model of man" is seen to have methodological consequences. The ontological basis for a critical social science culminates in the view that individual action and social phenomena are literally constituted by humanly established and socially shared meanings, the content of which can and does vary over time and space. O'Neill is therefore correct to insist that such an ontological foundation carries with it methodological implications:

The purely methodological issue is that the social sciences, while aspiring to the practice of the natural sciences in their operations of definition and generalization, lack an analogously dumb material of reference. That is to say, while the natural sciences benefit from the indifference of natural and physicial processess to scientific formulation, the social sciences are not similarly privileged in their encounters with persons and institutions. (p. 54)

O'Neill uses this observation to develop an interesting criticism of naturalist and even critical approaches to social inquiry. The criticism will occupy us in the concluding section of this essay, but the question for immediate attention is: How might a critical social science incorporate this insight into a coherent methodology?

Methodology and the Problem of Explanation

The naturalist account of social science identifies knowledge with the ability to explain and predict as is clearly demonstrated by the "covering-law" model of explanation.[14] According to this model (which is allegedly based on the practice of natural science), explanation consists in the subsumption of that which is to be explained under one or more general laws. A general law is a well-confirmed causal generalization which asserts that, under specified conditions, some class or type of event or result will *always* occur, or will occur *always* with some specified degree of probability. Since general laws are in this respect unrestricted, the covering-law model of explanation necessarily presupposes the existence of causal regularities independent of the apparent flux and uniqueness we ordinarily associate with human life and culture.

Is the covering-law model of explanation either accurate or acceptable from the viewpoint of a critical social science? To pose the question in this manner might be construed as an act of impertinence, since many philosophers of science have proclaimed the unacceptability of critical attempts at explanation precisely because they did not fulfill the requirements prescribed by the covering-law model. Recently, however, there has been a recognition by "post-empiricists" of the substantive and methodological diversity characteristic of the sciences, and a related commitment to describing rather than prescribing methodological principles and practices. Post-empiricism is not an especially well-defined or distinct "school" in the philosophy of science, but it does tend to emphasize certain themes.[15] There is the rejection of any so-called neutral observational vocabulary against which the explanatory hypotheses of science can be tested and conclusively falsified. Instead, so-called "facts" are always "interpreted" or "theory-laden," with the result that the processes of confirmation and disconfirmation become complex activities involving not singular hypotheses but a whole network of hypotheses, assumptions, and generalizations. The background network constitutes a more or less well-defined theory or research program and enables the scientist to select and give meaning to the "data" against which hypothesis-testing takes place. To further complicate matters, the involved process of confirmation takes place in the context of rival networks of hypotheses and competing theories or research programs.

The insights of post-empiricism have led many to question the adequacy of the covering-law model or to supplement it with other explanatory models. One option open to the critically minded social theorist is to follow the spirit and principles of post-empiricism in attempting to make room for explanations which involve such factors as interpretation and objective interests. This option is in fact taken up by Richard Miller in the essay, "Fact and Method in the Social Sciences." Miller's approach contrasts with the arguments of Brian Fay in "General Laws and Explaining Human Behavior," since Fay chooses to defend the covering-law model under Miller's attack. Nevertheless Fay, too, is pursuing a critical option insofar as he stresses the differences in types of explanation between the natural and social sciences and accounts for these differences by virtue of the human capabilities for critical self-reflection and historical change described in our last section on ontological assumptions. Therefore both Miller and Fay seek to demonstrate, albeit through different strategies, that the social sciences can and should be interpretive and critical in addition to being explanatory.

Miller enjoins social scientists and philosophers to take up the problem of explanation, and indeed all methodological issues, in an empirical, nonprescriptive spirit. As he announces in his introduction on p. 73, "methodology does not stand above social science," since "it includes principles governing science that might be changed in light of changes in science." By this Miller means that most of the principles regulating scientific practice are and ought to be viewed as *empirical* principles, as rules and guidelines subject to change and dispute on empirical grounds. These empirical grounds include the competing theories and prototheories, the hypotheses, assumptions, and generalizations, the dominant biases and tacit beliefs, available instruments and data, and techniques of analysis and interpretation which are present at any given time in a scientific community.

16

The principles of post-empiricism are also in evidence when Miller inveighs against the contention that there is only one genuine form of scientific explanation. He argues to the contrary that what counts as a valid explanation in both the natural and social sciences is rarely subsumable under a general law, and that what *is* accepted as an adequate explanation is typically field- and theory-dependent. As a consequence, judgments of explanatory adequacy within any social science cannot be based on some logical model allegedly derived from the natural sciences; rather, such judgments will be based on empirical considerations "specific, say, to the study of power structures or investment decisions." (p. 86) Since questions of explanatory adequacy are dependent on controversial questions of fact and theoretical perspective, Miller is able to question an important general argument used to support the covering-law model. The assertion that an event does not merely precede another but also explains it, is often said to be unverifiable except by the testing of an implicit covering law. Miller contends, however, that this perspective is plausible only if "we view verification as the direct confrontation of a proposed explanation and a body of data." The problem with such a perspective is that it fails to conform to reality, wherein "there are many other actors in the drama of explanation-testing" which "may make acceptance or rejection rational without supporting or overturning a law-like part of the explanation" (p. 90).

Miller includes among these actors "auxiliary principles" which guide "the interpretation of data." Such principles, he says, "are usually crucial"; and among them he includes, for the social sciences, interpretive principles of the sort "given prominence in the hermeneutic tradition." Thus, although Miller does not direct his attention to the ontological differences between the social and natural sciences, he does recognize the role of interpretation in the social sciences. In one place, for instance, an example is provided of a historian who explains, in causal but ideographic fashion, a counterrevolutionary uprising in the Vendée region of France in 1793. By covering-law criteria, the historian would have to abandon his explanation if it were discovered that a similar situation prevailed in another society but a counterrevolution failed to materialize. Against this picture, Miller points out that what counts as a "similar situation" is an empirical question: for instance, an alleged example from ninth-century Japan would be dismissed, whereas "a counterexample from seventeenth-century England cannot simply be ignored" because here the societies are in fact "quite similar." Our point is that this "empirical question" is actually a hermeneutical question, since one cannot decide whether Japan, France, and England are similar in the relevant respects without engaging in the process of (in this case, historical) interpretation.

Further developing his themes in a nonprescriptive spirit, Miller proposes, in an admittedly "sketchy and tentative" fashion, his own account of the logic of explanation. This account, believed by Miller to reflect actual practice, retains the concept of causality but in such a way as to ensure a role for empirical considerations. Indeed, the central purpose of the sketch is to demonstrate to social scientists "how their explanations depend on a variety of controversial empirical principles." An example is the principle of causal sufficiency which demands that any explanation identify causal factors sufficient to bring about the phenomena in question. This principle is empirical because no general rule exists for deciding when, in fact, a causal factor is sufficient; instead, particular rules of causal sufficiency are embedded in specific theoretical frameworks, themselves "subject to empirical debate." Another proposed principle requires that the causal factors identified in an explanation be "underlying" factors; here too, the principle is subject to empirical considerations since what is or is not a sufficiently "deep" or underlying factor will vary among different, often competing, theoretical frameworks. One theoretical framework enjoying Miller's own favor is the Marxist theory of ideology which employs the notion of objective interests and encourages social investigation of deep-seated material interests as the underlying factors of historical change. But again Miller is consistent even in the adoption of his critical stance: his use of the theory of ideology is only an illustration, whose truth must stand the trial of empirical testing.

Fay, by contrast, adopts a qualified defense of the covering-law model. The context in which he presents his defense concerns those philosophers who have contested the very possibility of achieving causal explanations of human action. Against this position, Fay argues that purported explanations of human action must rest at least implicitly on causal generalizations or laws. For example, "reason explanations" which purportedly explain an action without recourse to causal notions (by demonstrating that the action was "rational" or "appropriate" given the agent's beliefs and situation) are in Fay's view either implicit causal accounts, or they do not explain at all. This is because, with respect to any particular reason explanation, we must always ask whether, out of all the contending sets of beliefs and desires which can rationalize a particular action, the presence of the particular one offered in the explanation was in fact the cause of the behavior in question. This question cannot be answered in the absence of a generalization or law which specifies and explains the relation between the preferred "set" and the action.

Another argument often used to defeat the claim that causal generalizations or laws are necessary in the social sciences rests on the undeniable fact that social scientists often accept causal accounts of phenomena which, if recast in the form of a causal law, they deny. For example, acceptance of the causal generalization that, in some (specified) societies declining birth rates are under certain conditions due to declining family income, does not guarantee acceptance of an alleged law to the effect that, under these conditions, birth rates are always linked to family income. In fact, no social scientist would accept this alleged law. Such examples seem to show that causal laws are not needed in the social sciences, but Fay argues that this conclusion is unwarranted. What such examples demonstrate, he argues, is that social scientists are ignorant of such laws and that they are ignorant because the laws which, in principle, would explain their generalizations are of a different kind altogether. Specifically, they would be statable only in an entirely different vocabulary (as, for instance, generalizations linking poisons to death are undergirded by laws linking chemical compounds and reactions to physiological processes). Generalizations that are actually or potentially undergirded by laws with a "conceptually dissimilar" vocabulary are "heteronomic" generalizations. Fay's position is that social science generalizations are heteronomic in character.

Having defended the necessity of causal explanation, Fay nevertheless contends that there is "a deep difference between the sciences of intentional action and the sciences of nature" (p. 115). The basis for this contention is that the heteronomic generalizations of the social sciences will never achieve the status of genuine laws. This limitation of the social sciences is due to ontological features: Fay argues that socially mediated self-understandings and meanings "constitute social and psychological objects and events" and that this, in turn, implies the historicity of man and society. With respect to historicity, Fay emphasizes the constantly changing character of social and psychological phenomena that results from "the various conceptual innovations which a group's members introduce and come to accept" (pp. 116–117). Given this mutability of social reality, Fay concludes that:

> The objects of social science are open-ended in a practically unpredictable way. Social institutions and practices, as well as the beliefs and desires of the members of particular social groups, are

19

continually in a state of flux and evolution which will always appear
to be indeterminate to those who wish to study them. (p. 120)

Since the world about which social scientists theorize is constantly
changing in pragmatically unpredictable ways, social scientists cannot
develop genuine causal laws. Instead, they can produce only heteronomic
causal generalizations.

Thus, although Fay defends, contrary to Miller, a covering-law or at
least a deductive model of explanation, he agrees with Miller on a
number of other points. Both conclude that generalizations rather than
"general laws properly so called" will undergird social science explanations of causal processes (see Fay p. 103 and compare Miller p. 91).
In addition, Fay's heteronomic generalizations are neither "universal,
nor well confirmed; their boundary conditions are not well articulated;
and their capacity to support counterfactuals is limited to a quantifiably
unspecified range of events" (p. 199n.). Consequently, he would almost
surely endorse Miller's view that the actual testing of causal hypotheses
is subject to a number of quite different kinds of "empirical" disputes.
Finally, both Fay and Miller emphasize the role of theory in the social
sciences in order to insure genuinely causal explanations.

Fay concludes his essay by pointing out that if social scientists fail
to grasp the intentional and mutable character of social reality, they
will reify their causal explanations and theories, inviting the political
dangers this entails. From this perspective, the inability of social scientists to frame genuine laws and wide-ranging theories—a serious flaw
from a naturalist point of view—is desirable because instructive. Such
a "flaw" reflects the constitutive role beliefs play in a mutable social
reality. In particular, they reflect the ability of human beings to educate,
and so transform, themselves and their world. Fay's discussion of social
scientific explanation and theory points to the plausibility and desirability of critical theory since, according to it, social scientific theories
not only must self-consciously recognize that their limitations are
grounded in the transformable character of human life, but they must
make this feature their cornerstone. That is,

> critical theory insists that social science ought to . . . isolate in
> the lives of a group of people those causal conditions that depend
> for their power on the ignorance of those people as to the nature
> of their collective existence, and that are frustrating them. The
> intention here is to enlighten this group of people about these
> causal conditions and the ways in which they are oppressive, so

that, *being enlightened, these people might change these conditions and so transform their lives . . .* (p. 127) (italics in original).

For Fay, as for most of the proponents of the idea of a critical social science in this volume and elsewhere, the issues of social scientific ontology, methodology, and aspiration are inextricably connected.

Criticism and Ethical Neutrality

The commitment of a critical social science to enlightenment mandates that social scientists seek to develop the kind of knowledge on which human beings might draw in order to improve their individual and collective existence. Should social scientists accept such a commitment? Should critical research, practical criticism, and political advocacy be engaged in with the intent of enlightening individuals as to their present condition and suggesting how it might be improved? And if, in principle, these aims are adopted, how might a critical social science go about fulfilling them? That is, how might social scientists identify, and how can they justify, the ethical norms needed to orient and support both critical research and practical criticism?

To contend that social scientists ought to be critical and prescriptive, and to suppose that such a position can be rationally justified, involves adopting positions at odds with much of contemporary social science. One way of obtaining a focus on the conflict is to indicate that the commitment of a critical social science violates the doctrine of ethical neutrality. Ethical neutrality holds that the social scientist ought to be a dispassionate observer of social reality who, in his or her role as a scientist, embraces no political or social ideals. The doctrine rests on the assumptions that the failure to be dispassionate is quite likely to interfere with the search for truth, and that a commitment to ethical ideals can never be rationally justified.

The first of these two assumptions is considered and rejected by Richard Miller in Chapter Four. Although Miller deals primarily with the problem of explanation, in the very first part of his paper he considers the "methodological dogma" that the social sciences are and should be value-free. Adopting the strategy that this dogma be treated as an empirical claim, Miller submits it to empirical scrutiny and concludes: first, that the adoption of an "objective" or "value-free" stance hardly ensures the discovery of truth and the advancement of science; and, second, that adoption of a "critical" or "partisan" stance can produce, and in fact has produced, just these results. In the social sciences, concludes Miller, partisanship can be scientifically useful.[16]

Miller's argument cannot be dismissed as irrelevant by drawing attention to the now familiar view of the methodologically sophisticated that value-neutrality is in practice, and perhaps even in principle, impossible to realize. For this view usually has in mind *unconscious* biases, whereas Miller is defending the *deliberate* adoption of a normative or partisan approach to social inquiry. His position can be compared to the unreflective attitude typical of social scientists who, when forced to defend their research interests, complacently reply that it is "interesting" (or worse yet, that it is fundable). Such attitudes seem in our view either naive or irresponsible—naive when they reflect ignorance of the uses to which social science information, opinion, and knowledge are put by those in a position to do so; or irresponsible if, aware of the connections between the products of social science and the quality of social life, the social scientist nevertheless disavows any responsibility for either.

If a value orientation to social inquiry can facilitate scientific progress and if, from an ethical point of view, a researcher's values should be deliberately embraced, then the case for a distinctively critical orientation being adopted by social scientists gains in viability. However, it is possible to concede some force to the attack on ethical neutrality and still maintain that the social sciences are endangered, not when values guide research, but when one particular value orientation comes to dominate an entire community of researchers. In this case, a "diversity of values" is openly prescribed on the explicit expectation that it would encourage the investigation of a diversity of problems from a diversity of perspectives—and on the implicit hope that it would cut off any attempt to convert social scientists to one particular value orientation or set of ethical commitments.[17]

Several of Miller's observations are relevant to the call for "value diversity," however, precisely because they raise scepticism about it. In practice, scientific communities tend to embrace a dominant value orientation, usually well entrenched because unconsciously held and thus difficult to challenge and change. Such dominant orientations or tacit perspectives tend to influence "expectations as to what projects are apt to produce definitive, scientifically useful results," to determine "what research techniques and bodies of data are elaborated and refined," and to establish the criteria used in distinguishing, among scholars and scholarship, the competent and important from the incompetent and trivial. As illustrations, Miller discusses the largely unconscious eth-

22

nocentricism and racism which dominated nineteenth-century anthropology, and the consignment to marginal status of Marxist scholarship within the contemporary Anglo-American social sciences.

Although Miller's observations are undoubtedly accurate, they leave open the hard questions. Which critical standards, what normative goals, should the social scientist embrace in order to guide research and practical criticism? And why should they be chosen? That is, how might specific critical values be rationally justified or defended as superior to values of competing approaches? As we indicated earlier, these questions have been taken up by Habermas in a potentially fruitful, and certainly challenging, way. Hence his work in this area receives the critical attention of Stephen K. White and J. Donald Moon in the last two chapters of this volume.[18]

One way of approaching Habermas's work on these problems is to recognize the value he places on communicative interaction. As Dickens explains in his overview essay, Habermas adopts the essentially hermeneutic/phenomenological view that it is in communicative interaction that social actors achieve an intersubjective understanding of themselves and of their world. In addition, communicative interaction is the means by which people establish mutually agreed-upon criteria for determining claims to truth and, in social and political life, normative claims and ideals. In Chapter Seven, Stephen White continues this discussion in an essay originally published elsewhere but revised for *Changing Social Science*. White begins by describing the distinction Habermas draws between ongoing, unreflective "communicative action" and critical, reflective "discourse." Ongoing communicative action is held to presuppose a background consensus on four kinds of "validity claims" conveyed in speech: "(1) the comprehensibility of the speech act; (2) the speaker's veracity; (3) the truth of the propositional component; and (4) the correctness or normative validity of the performative component" (p. 159).

The important point about the background consensus is that it can, indeed often does, break down or become "disturbed." When this occurs, any of the four validity claims may be scrutinized in order to reestablish their validity and secure the possibility of continuing communication. When the truth of the utterance or the validity of its normative component is involved—when, that is to say, either of these break down or begin to be questioned—the appropriate manner for testing and reestablishing validity is through discourse (truth in "theoretical discourses" and normative validity in "practical discourses"). The goal of discourse is to attain a new, rational consensus based on the force of rational argumentation.

The justification of practical norms thus rests on the possibility of achieving a rational consensus or, failing this, a fair compromise, through practical discourse. Yet for this possibility to be actual, there must be the opportunity for distinguishing a rational consensus from false, deceptive, or unreflective argument. For Habermas, making this distinction involves reference to an "ideal speech situation" (ISS) where, as White explains on p. 166, discourse is "freed both from constraints external to the structure of communication . . . and from constraints internal to the structure of communication, which thus cause systematic distortions of discourse." It is Habermas's contention that if an ISS could be realized within a political community it would enable the citizens to achieve a rational consensus and/or a fair compromise on practical norms—that is, on the normative goals and standards regulating political and social life.

The conditions which make an ISS possible could only be achieved in an ideal world. Consequently, they provide the social scientist with an orientation for research and accompanying standards for practical criticism and advocacy. For example, two conditions necessary for the realization of an ISS are that participants in it be able to discern and express their true interests and needs. In order for this to occur, the participants must be free from false consciousness (so that they can discern their true interests and needs) and free from fear (so that they can openly express their interests and needs). Social and psychological factors which promote and maintain false consciousness or inhibit open discussion ought therefore to become subjects of research and their eradication the basis for practical criticism and advocacy. In addition, the social scientist can hypothesize that, for any given community, certain norms would be chosen by its citizens were they to participate in an ISS. These hypothesized norms, as well as the conditions defining the ISS, are to be advocated and used to criticize existing values.

Why should the social scientist, or anyone else for that matter, be guided by the conditions of the ISS and why should he advocate the norms which, by hypothesis, emerge from it? The central purpose of White's essay is to explain and defend Habermas's response to this obviously crucial challenge.

Essentially what is claimed is that the ideal conditions of the ISS are in fact presupposed and anticipated in all forms of communication. When individuals engage in ongoing conversation and especially when they engage in serious dialogue or discourse, they "impute" the ISS. If they failed to make this imputation, no validity claims could be rationally established; if no validity claims were rationally established, communication would be impossible; if communication was impossible, social and cultural life would be impossible. As White explains, this argument provides one with good reason for adopting the ideals founded on the ISS, although it remains open to the criticism associated with the so-called naturalistic fallacy involved in deriving norms ("oughts") from conditions of social life ("is's"). We believe that White's response to this criticism is successful, but the reader is left to judge for himself or herself.

Should White's defense be thought to carry the day, J. Donald Moon points out that Habermas's position is open to still other objections. Moon develops two important arguments against Habermas's contention that realization of the ISS enables citizens to achieve a rational consensus and/or a fair compromise on normative goals and standards. The first argument reflects Moon's belief that there exists within modern communities incommensurate conceptions of human needs and interests based on a plurality of conflicting "models of man." And although he maintains that "we should always be able to give good reasons for adopting one model of man against another," Moon argues that Habermas fails to provide "any reason for supposing that a consensus on one particular model" would emerge in an ISS. To suppose that a consensus could emerge, he concludes, is to presuppose the dubious proposition that "there is only one conception of what it is to be a person that is adequate to our experience as human beings" (pp. 182, 183).

Moon's second argument arises out of a discussion concerning the ecological crisis. Pointing out that writers such as E. J. Schumacher present a basically reverential view of man's relationship to nature, Moon contends that the ISS presupposes what someone like Schumacher disputes: the desirability of using generalizable interests as the sole basis for establishing rational agreement on norms. Because the religious point of view conceives that "humanity and nature both serve purposes beyond themselves," it must reject any human-centered view that nature is to be used (or managed) in order to maximize the satisfaction of human interests. It is precisely such human-centered, instrumental conceptions, however, which are required by the claim that norms should be based on, and disputes resolved by, the appeal to generalizable interests. Thus, the appeal to this standard "prejudges a practical issue which is itself to be settled in the context of discourse." Compromise on this issue would also appear to be ruled out, since what is in dispute in this case is not different interests but conflicting "moral ideals and world-views" (pp. 186–187).

Moon's emphasis on conflicting conceptions of human interests and needs, and on the seemingly irreconcilable clashes generated by differing ideals and world-views, leads him to the conclusion that Habermas has failed to overcome the "pluralism of apparently ultimate value orientations." This argument implies, as Moon stresses, that the advocacy role of critical theory remains "problematic." Moon's critique could also imply the desirability of a liberal-pluralist vision of political life. The liberal-pluralist vision takes as its point of departure precisely the "pluralism of apparently ultimate value orientations" afflicting modern societies and seeks, not to eliminate the conflicts which this situation engenders, but to manage them. It does so by encouraging social tolerance and by guaranteeing to individuals certain basic rights, including the freedom to pursue their own life-styles within the broad bounds necessitated by civil order.

This extrapolation of Moon's argument underscores the fact that all conceptions of social science have political consequences, a theme first emphasized by Ball in the context of naturalist social sciences. But now this fact must be a cause for reflection also by those who would embrace a critical social science.

The Need for Reflexivity

Moon's criticisms, and his conclusion on p. 188 "that our hopes for a radical restructuring of political and social theory must be tempered [though not given up]," are both welcomed and expected in this volume. As we have tried to emphasize, a habit of critical self-awareness is crucial to the social sciences, however conceived. Hence a critical social science can hardly expect to be exempted from criticism. On the contrary, it must internalize and encourage critical self-reflection as it seeks to clarify and establish through argument its suppositions, limits, and possibilities. Of course, attempts to delineate the contours of a critical social science have been undertaken before, but primarily through its polemical comparison with noncritical approaches.[19] As a result, the impression can arise, and probably has arisen, that what makes an enterprise "critical" is its negative attitude toward competing approaches instead of its own self-critical perspective. Moreover the impression is only reinforced when the primary task of critical social theorists is identified as the attack on the conservative implications of mainstream social science and of other alternative approaches as well. If, however, critique is also undertaken outside of polemical contexts, the question is sharpened as to whether emancipation is the only goal of critique and whether radicalism is the sole exemplar of the critical attitude. Does critical inquiry have to be either negative in tone or revolutionary in spirit?

Many of the essays here in *Changing Social Science* put into question the widely held presumption of emancipatory critique, but the contributions of Ball and O'Neill are especially striking in this regard. They establish the case for widening the perspective toward critical inquiry by appealing to the political outlook of Arendt and to the sociological program of Schutz in ways that are clearly not revolutionary in spirit nor negative in tone. Ball and O'Neill do this without any desire to abandon critical self-awareness and inquiry, but instead with a view toward deepening and enlarging our understanding of their possibilities.

Ball's exercise in reflexivity draws, as we have explained, on "conceptual history." Applied to the history of political thought, conceptual history discloses for the critical thinker a "history of successive self-understandings of what it means to think and act politically." Conceptual history has a critical function with respect to modern political understanding insofar as it "discloses alternative self-understandings and in so doing exposes the time-bound character of our own." Ball identifies the truisms which capture the modern self-understanding of political action, but primarily to contrast them with the positive inspiration he finds in the Greek conception of political action as recovered and reconstructed by Arendt. Central to this conception is the idea that political action is synonymous with public speech spoken in a fraternal "tone of expostulation" among equals. This tone of speech between free citizens of the *polis* is contrasted to the coercive "tone of command" characteristic of speech between unequals and so sadly common in contemporary societies where private individuals are directed by hierarchically organized and distant governments (pp. 37–38).

Ball and Arendt use the resources of conceptual history to question the modern assumptions of political science, including its (and our) conception of politics. We learn, for example, that the introduction of economic considerations into the political arena was in the Greek view a source of confusion between the private and public realms. Because our quite different conception of politics is uncritically assumed, Ball's employment of this specimen of conceptual history makes us confront it directly. The act of historical recovery is at the same time a liberating discovery; we are presented with an opportunity to change present ways of thinking by calling to mind a past criticizable only insofar as it does *not* affect the present. Ball asks us to conserve—not negate—the Greek conception of politics so that we might criticize and challenge our sad and parochial views.

O'Neill's perspective is also helpful in elucidating what it means to be reflective and what the possibilities and limits of a critical social science might be. As explained earlier, O'Neill argues that social scientists ought to follow the lead suggested by the phenomenology of Schutz and should realize that their descriptions and explanations will only be successful to the extent that their typifications adequately reflect the typifications of phenomena by their subjects. In short, social scientists should submit to Schutz's "postulate of adequacy." As described by O'Neill, the postulate of adequacy is intended to insure, not exact correspondence, but *compatibility* between the concepts and explanations developed by social scientists and the constructs of everyday life. It does this by requiring social scientists to submit their concepts and explanations to the scrutiny of the social actors to whom these concepts and explanations refer. If the social actors cannot understand, or if they find dubious or erroneous, the social scientists' constructs, social scientists must rethink and revise their position.

O'Neill does not need to be told that the postulate of adequacy appears to give to "ordinary" men and women authority over the social sciences. Nor need he be told that it seems to limit social science to the representation of "received knowledge." For it is precisely such objections to an interpretive science of man—voiced by naturalists and critical theorists alike[20]—which O'Neill is at pains to defeat. What he demands is that social scientists reflect on these objections in a more critical spirit. To aid them, he offers a number of subtly crafted arguments, all of which are built around a central theme: the hubris of the social sciences in both their naturalistic and critical guises. The rejection of the postulate of adequacy, he argues, is a manifestation of this hubris; acceptance of the postulate would be a positive first step toward undermining it.

Thus, for example, O'Neill argues that adoption of the naturalist stance and rejection of the postulate isolates the researcher from social reality and encourages the very mistakes and errors he seeks to avoid. Taking as his paradigm "the observation of nature," the researcher "adopts a timeless and objective stance," and so becomes necessarily "immune to the reciprocity of viewpoint" which characterizes social interaction and informs common-sense knowledge (p. 60).

The naturalist eschews reciprocity on the assumption that ordinary men and women entertain simplistic versions of the world. Similarly, the critically inclined social scientist displays an attitude of doubt toward the routines of everyday convention in order to open up possibilities for "demystification" and the disclosure of new alternatives. O'Neill protests against this posture:

> It cannot be sufficiently stressed that *the commonsense world is not a reified and unreflexive praxis* . . . . It is self-critical and, above all, capable of dealing with the contradictions and paradoxes of social life that otherwise drive sociologists off into utopias, anachronisms, and nostalgias that make ordinary people suspicious of the intellectual's grasp of reality. (p. 68; emphasis in original)

O'Neill's aim is to defend the rationalities of everyday life against the inroads made by sociological experts of any stripe or persuasion. The postulate of adequacy respects and insures the right of men and women to check the claims to knowledge made by the social sciences. To deny this right is to deny the competence of men and women to understand and judge their *own* affairs. O'Neill insists, therefore, on a kinship between sociology and common sense which allows for the equal possibility of fraternal criticism by the latter of the former, as well as vice versa; indeed he suggests that it should be from this interaction that we ought to derive critical interests and standards.

O'Neill claims that his argument is conservationist in spirit and not blindly conservative. The point is an important one for deciding the nature and potential future direction of critical inquiry. For Ball's use of conceptual history is also intended to conserve a conception of politics threatened with extinction. The charge of blind conservatism can easily be fended off in this instance by noting Ball's intention of challenging and changing present ways of thinking by calling to mind past alternatives. The charge is more difficult to adjudicate with respect to O'Neill, who finds that the critical attitude can too easily become uncritical in looking at everyday conventions as rigid and reified. As a generalization such a claim about conventions cannot stand as completely warranted, but the opposite generalization is in equal need of substantiation.

In any case, Ball and O'Neill seriously undermine the assumption that critical inquiry has to be revolutionary in spirit and negative in tone. The judicious appeal to conceptual history and a proper appreciation for everyday custom and knowledge are not necessarily equivalent to settling into an inherent conservatism or falling prey to a Candidean optimism. If both Ball's and O'Neill's arguments were to be accepted, critical inquiry would have the option of being conservationist, reformist, or revolutionary in character. Moon's argument, as we have suggested, points in a similar direction. Consequently, the idea of a critical social science developed in *Changing Social Science* may well be construed by some as weakening critical awareness and/or critical inquiry beyond recovery or repair. We think, on the contrary, that it paves the way to a positive characterization of critical inquiry which, being genuinely reflexive, can truly change the way social science is conceived of and practiced.

CHAPTER TWO

The Ontological Presuppositions and Political Consequences of a Social Science*

Terence Ball

A new science of politics is needed for a New World.

—Tocqueville

Tocqueville's remark draws our attention to the idea—a philosophical commonplace after Kant—that some worlds are more amenable to scientific analysis and explanation than are others. What kind of science one can have depends, in some sense, upon the constitution of that science's object. Thus, for example, a Newtonian science of nature presupposes the law-like regularity of natural phenomena. In a universe ruled by a capricious God with a penchant for performing miracles, Newton's science would be utterly unthinkable. But what of the social-political world? Is it not composed of capricious creatures whose actions are often inexplicable, not to say unpredictable? Given such an "object," how—to paraphrase the question that Kant raised in connection with Newtonian physics—is a science of society possible? The answer most often given to this question is that human behavior in the aggregate, like natural phenomena, exhibits certain discoverable "regularities" and that these regularities can be expressed in laws or law-like generalizations. This is the answer supplied by the "naturalist" or "positivist" metatheory or philosophy of science.

The question that I should like to address here is: *What conception of politics and human action is presupposed, and reinforced, by this*

*I should like to thank Albert O. Hirschman, James Farr, Peter Sederberg, and the editors for their comments, criticisms, and encouragement. None should, of course, be held responsible for the uses to which I have put their good counsel.

naturalist model of scientific inquiry and explanation? In other words, what social arrangements and self-understandings make this model plausible and credible? Here I shall only be able to address several selected aspects of this question, and to suggest—briefly, and in an intentionally exaggerated and provocative way—several strategies for answering it. I shall begin by suggesting some crucial affinities between the still-dominant behavioral persuasion in political science and the naturalist or positivist model. This conception of science requires a peculiarly modern conception of politics. To see just how this is so, I shall, secondly, explicate the classical conception of politics, contrasting it with our modern view of politics as a self-interested activity. A positivistically conceived science of politics applies not to just any world, but to one in which political activity is understood in instrumental terms as the pursuit of interests of a broadly economic kind. My third move is to provide an historical account of the connection between self-interestedness and the new science of politics, by showing how and why some theorists came to believe that a world in which people pursued their own private "interests" was safer, quieter, more secure—and more *predictable*—than one in which they pursued other, more dangerous "passions." My fourth move is to suggest that this theory of rational self-interest was put into practice—i.e., given concrete institutional form—in the founding of the American Republic. Political science was made possible, as it were, by the advent of a "scientific" politics. We in the United States are apt to forget that we live in, are shaped by, and act in the first scientifically designed and engineered political arena. It is therefore perhaps not too suprising that our behavior in the aggregate exhibits certain law-like behavioral regularities and uniformities of the kind required by a positivistically conceived science of politics. Small wonder, too, that the American science of politics has been rather more successful in accounting for the political behavior of Americans—or at least those Americans who are rationally organized into interest groups and so on—than it has been in explaining the often apparently irrational, deviant, and anomalous behavior of other peoples in other times and places. My fifth move is to return whence I began, with Tocqueville's remark that a new science of politics is needed for a new world. I shall suggest that Tocqueville saw only too clearly what the rest of us have seen only belatedly: that a science of politics is not without its ontological presuppositions—nor its political price.

I. "Positivism" and "Behavioralism"

The connection between "positivism" and "behavioralism" was a hotly debated topic only a few years ago. The debate—or was it a quarrel?—was never satisfactorily concluded. One was left with the distinct impression that the protagonists had been talking past one another, or speaking different languages. Perhaps this is because "positivism" and "behavioralism," like most "isms," are not so much well-defined doctrines as they are matters of spirit and style. One of its most eminent proponents speaks of the "spirit" of positivism, another of its distinctive "standpoint" or "outlook."[1] In a similar vein, behavioralism in political science has been characterized by Dahl as a "mood;" by Easton as an "approach;" and by Eulau as a "persuasion."[2]

Still, neither "positivism" nor "behavioralism" is so vague and amorphous as to defy all attempts to adumbrate their respective characteristics. Easton, for example, lists eight "major tenets of the behavioral credo."[3] In a similar vein, von Wright has identified three main tenets of "positivism":

> One of the tenets of positivism is methodological *monism*, or the idea of the unity of scientific method amidst the diversity of subject matter of scientific investigation. A second tenet is the view that the exact natural sciences, in particular mathematical physics, set a methodological ideal or standard which measures the degree of development and perfection of all the other sciences, including the [social sciences]. A third tenet, finally, is a characteristic view of scientific explanation. Such explanation is, in a broad sense, "causal." It consists, more specifically, in the subsumption of individual cases under hypothetically assumed general laws of nature, including "human nature."[4]

Few modern political scientists would subscribe wholeheartedly and without reservation to all three tenets of "positivism" as outlined by von Wright. But if one focuses primarily upon the third tenet of positivism—its deductive-subsumptive or "covering law" theory of explanation—then virtually all who call themselves "behavioralists" might be accounted "positivists" as well. This, it seems to me, is the grain of truth in the antibehavioralists' contention that the modern behavioralist is a positivist manqué.[5]

Since the deductive-nomological or covering-law model of explanation will be familiar to most readers, it requires little discussion here. It is perhaps enough to say that the clearest statements of the model are to be found in the writings of Sir Karl Popper and Carl Hempel. Popper, for example, holds that, "To give a causal explanation of an event means to deduce a statement which describes it, using as premises of the deduction one or more *universal laws*, together with certain singular statements, the initial conditions."[6] Or, to borrow Hempel's terminology: In a causal explanation, the statement describing the event to be explained (the *explanandum*) must be exhibitable as a deduction from premises (the *explanans*) containing at least one law-like statement, along with singular statements describing certain relevant conditions.[7]

If all this seems familiar enough, that is probably because the covering-law model in one form or another has long been a standard feature of most textbook accounts of social-scientific explanation. Thus, for example, nearly a half-century ago, George Catlin wrote, "Politics is a science in the sense that it is a body of knowledge that admits of statement . . . in general laws." The possibility of such a science rests, he said, upon "two constants: the recurrence of like situations and the persistence of like human impulses—in brief, a human nature." Human nature reveals itself in the uniformity, repetition, and regularity of human behavior. We may therefore infer that human behavior conforms to certain discoverable behavioral "laws" and that these laws form the basis of a genuine science of politics:

> There can be no science of politics unless there are these political uniformities, these constants of behavior, which admit of formulation as laws. And [these laws are] as timeless as the laws of mechanics, holding for the human race wherever and whenever it is found. And men in so far as they obey [sic] these laws will act in as timeless a fashion as . . . atoms act in their chemical combinations according to formula. We are looking for this and nothing else.[8]

Nowadays the language of "metapolitics" is rather less bold and perhaps more precise than Catlin's; yet the ideas remain much the same. Indeed, with the advent of the behavioral movement came a more insistent call for political scientists to discover "laws," "regularities," or "uniformities" of behavior. David Truman found in behavioral political science "a renewed commitment . . . to the discovery and statement of behavioral uniformities."[9] In a similar vein David Easton lists the features that distinguish "behavioralism" in political science. Heading this list is: "*Regularities:* there are discoverable uniformities in political behavior. These can be expressed in generalizations . . . with explanatory and predictive value."[10]

34

Such restatements of the covering-law approach appear with almost law-like regularity in most contemporary discussions of social-scientific explanation. Almost any introductory textbook of the "scope and methods" variety will be found to contain simplified accounts of the model. It seems safe to say that, despite all the criticisms levelled against it by "antipositivists," "antibehavioralists," and/or "post-behavioralists" the covering-law model of explanation continues to enjoy widespread acceptance among behavioral political scientists.

If these regularities make possible a science of politics, positivistically conceived, what makes these regularities possible? One answer to this question we have encountered already, in the work of Catlin: Behavioral uniformities or regularities stem, he suggests, from a fixed *human nature*. This answer is at least as old as Hobbes.

But there is another school of thought that—to quote Ortega y Gasset—holds that, "Man has no nature; he has only his history."[11] This school—whose most prominent representative is Karl Marx— maintains that such "regularities" are apt to be artifacts of a mutable social order, and hence that such "laws" apply only to certain periods or epochs, and only for as long as they operate, in Marx's phrase, "behind men's backs."[12] There is, in other words, a sense in which behavioral "laws" hold true only as long as people *believe* them to be true (or rather, more precisely, *don't question* their truth); should they discover that things don't *have* to be that way, they have, within certain limits, the option of *changing* the relationships described by the law.[13] Hence laws purporting to explain human behavior—unlike those that permit us to explain and predict natural phenomena—presuppose a *normative consensus* among those subject to such "laws." By speaking of a "normative consensus" I do *not* mean that people voluntarily regulate their conduct in accordance with freely chosen and agreed-upon norms and that behavioral regularities are merely artifacts of self-regulated activity. Quite the contrary: the normative character of behavioral regularities must remain hidden from public view; behavior guided by changeable norms must be made to *appear* eminently "normal" or "natural"—and conduct that does not conform is adjudged aberrant, abnormal, or deviant, in short, "*un*natural."

The "naturalness" of certain modes of behavior—and the unnaturalness of others—is in any social system *institutionally constrained*. At one level this is of course obvious: deviant behavior is punished in one way or another, and "normalcy" is thereby reaffirmed. But at another level the institutional constraint is far from obvious: In any society certain options will appear not only unattractive, but very nearly *in-*

conceivable, not to say silly or irrational. Some matters are not, as it were, "up for discussion"; they are not on the agenda, precisely *because* they are viewed as normal and natural concomitants of human nature itself. As Kenneth Keniston puts it, "The myth of an age can be found in the issues it takes for granted—in the questions it never asks, in the assumptions so universally shared they remain tacit."[14] Thus when a proposition appears to be too utterly obvious and banal to be stated, that is a tell-tale sign that it belongs to the domain of the dominant, but unarticulated, myth of the age. Such myths are presupposed not only by our social life but by our social science.

At the risk of appearing to be both obvious and banal, let me submit for your consideration three propositions:

(1) People act out of a due regard for their own interests.

(2) To act rationally is to pursue one's interests through the most efficient means available.

(3) Politics is the pursuit of private interests through public channels.

I should be greatly surprised if these three truths were not met with a resounding yawn. Yet today's truisms may prove, when one takes a longer historical view, to be less than self-evidently true and obvious. As Keniston remarks, "It is often only in contrast with other societies, with other myths, that we become aware of our own."[15] It might be useful, then, to compare our everyday understanding of politics with the political self-understanding of an earlier age.

II. The Classical Conception of Politics

It is sometimes said that the "traditional" or "normative" political science of our classical forbears is defective in either of two ways. Either their pronouncements are "normative" assertions of "subjective" value or preference and are therefore untestable, not to say undisputable, matters of taste, or the few testable propositions proferred by our Greek ancestors are manifestly false. Consider, for instance, Aristotle's contention that man is by nature a political animal. Professor Dahl maintains that (contemporary) experience disproves this proposition and shows, contra Aristotle, that man is by nature and inclination a private animal, jealous of his own interests and distrustful of others.

One of the central facts of political life is that politics—local, state, national, international—lies for most people at the outer periphery of attention, interest, concern, and activity. At the focus of most men's lives are primary activities involving food, sex, love, family,

36

work, play, shelter, comfort, friendship, social esteem, and the like. Activities like these—not politics—are the primary concerns of most men and women. . . .

The sources of the myth about the primacy of politics in the lives of the citizens of a democratic order are ancient, manifold, and complex. The primacy of politics has roots in Greek thought and in the idealization of the city-state characteristic of the Greek philosophers. That initial bias has been reinforced by the human tendency to blur the boundaries between what *is* and what *ought* to be. . . . This ancient myth about the concern of citizens with the life of the democratic *polis* is false in the case of New Haven. Whether or not the myth was reality in Athens will probably never be known.[16]

Empirical evidence, so Dahl claims, suggests that, "Man is not instinctively a political animal."[17] Confronted with such a statement, one hardly knows whether to laugh or to cry. Clearly, Dahl has mistaken Aristotle's understanding of the phrase *zoōn politikon* and has read the text anachronistically, not only by reading it in English (which requires some caution) but by reading into it our contemporary liberal pluralist interest-group conception of "politics."[18]

The idea that present-day behavior can "disconfirm" or falsify propositions drawn from a theory like Aristotle's is, I think, grievously confused. It is perhaps enough to say here that the idea rests upon a highly problematic view of the relation of political theory to political fact, and fails to take into account three crucial considerations: (1) that the structure of many modern political institutions have been theoretically prescribed (and *alternative* structures theoretically *proscribed*); (2) that these institutions constrain political behavior by foreclosing alternative visions and possibilities; (3) that our self-understanding of what it means to think and act politically is "theory-laden" in the sense that the categories and concepts through which we think are theoretically prescribed and institutionally constrained.

The best—indeed I think the only—way in which we can break out of our conceptual prison is to think historically, i.e. to trace the history of concepts and categories which shape and indeed constitute our self-understanding. "Conceptual history" discloses alternative self-understandings and in so doing exposes the time-bound character of our own. The history of political thought, understood as conceptual history, is the history of successive self-understandings of what it means to think and act politically. To speak in the idiom of Lukàcs, we might say that the study of past ideas "de-reifies" the reified ideas of the present.

That is why a work like Hannah Arendt's *The Human Condition* is so valuable. Arendt de-reifies the present by recovering and reconstructing an older understanding of what it means to think and act politically. And in so doing she succeeds in exposing the political and ontological presuppositions of at least one positivistically conceived social science, viz. political science. After briefly outlining the pertinent parts of Arendt's argument, I shall suggest where it falls short and how it needs to be supplemented and enriched if we are to discover and disinter the presuppositions of a positivistically conceived political science.

Arendt distinguishes three types of human activity. *Labor* includes all the activities necessitated by man's animal existence. He must labor in order to live; that is, he must produce the means of his subsistence (food, etc.) and he must reproduce the species. Labor is characterized by its cyclical nature, its sameness, its repetitiveness, and its necessity. In his capacity as laborer, man produces in order to consume, and consumes in order to produce. The scene of such activity is the *oikos*, or household: "Labor" is preeminently an "economic" category. *Work* is the activity of fabricating durable things, of transforming and setting one's stamp upon material objects, not for purely utilitarian purposes but for enjoyment.[19] Arendt's third category—*action*—refers to activities undertaken for their own sake, not for the sake of something else; of activities involving words and deeds; of discourse that discloses the identities of the speakers.

"Action" thus corresponds to the Greek notion of *praxis*, and is distinguished from *techne*, i.e., the sort of technical or instrumental activity that Weber has characterized as *Zweckrational*. Arendt distinguishes between "action" and "behavior": Action is free and unpredictable in a way that behavior is not. For Arendt, as for the Greeks, *praxis* or action is preeminently political activity. It takes place, in other words, in the intimate and intense "public space" of the *polis*, in which men in their capacities not as private members of their respective households but as *citizens*, gather to argue, discuss, and debate. Politics or political action is synonymous with speech (*lexis*) of a certain kind—the unconstrained, uncoerced, fraternal "tone of expostulation" which Pericles took to be the proper mode of address between citizens, and which he distinguished from the coercive "tone of command" characteristic of speech between unequals.[20] De Jouvenel adverts to this older connection between speech and political action: "The elementary political process is the action of mind upon mind through speech."[21] And much the same idea is expressed by Habermas, with his notion of free and undistorted communication.[22]

According to the classical conception of politics, to introduce "economic"—i.e. household—considerations into the public sphere was to confuse two distinct spheres of activity and orders of existence—the public and the private realms, the realm of freedom and the realm of necessity; it is, in terms of the Greek self-understanding, to depoliticize the public sphere and to "publicize" the private or "economic" sphere, thereby destroying both.

Our modern interest-based conception of politics is the antithesis of the classical conception. We are apt to view politics as the continuation of economic activities; to view the public sphere as a marketplace of competing interests; to view citizens as buyers, sellers, and consumers in this competitive market; and to regard government as a "broker" in the center of this swirl of self-interested activity.

How did such a radical shift of perspectives come about? How did it happen that our own conception of politics diverged so completely from its ostensible sources? Any of a number of answers may be suggested. The first and most obvious is that politics in the classical sense was an activity confined to, and made possible by, the *polis*; with the demise of the *polis* came the demise of "politics." In the vast size and scale of nation and empire, the meaning of politics and citizenship changed. Politics came to be "power politics"; the fraternal tone of expostulation was replaced by the tone of command. "Politics" in a large and diverse nation or empire came to be "interest politics," since each group in the uneasy alliance had to receive its share or due if the "political association" was to survive.

A crucial conceptual change reflected—and reinforced—this shift of meaning and focus. Originally Aristotle had contrasted the *polis* with other forms of human association. It differs, for example, from the family, which is a society of unequals whose purpose is production and reproduction. *Polis* is contrasted with *oikos*. The *polis* also differs from contractually based associations entered into for purposes of self-protection or economic gain. The main concern of the *polis* is the moral development and well-being of its citizens, not their physical protection or economic welfare; otherwise it would be a "mere association," a *koinonia symmachia*. The Latin translation of this phrase, as found in Roman Law, is *societas*, meaning an "alliance" or "association" entered into for a specific purpose. Thus, for example, a robber band was a *societas*. With the demise of the *polis* Aristotle's distinction was lost.

Seneca felt no qualms about translating Aristotle's *zoōn politikon* into the Latin *animal socialis*, thereby not merely obliterating but actually *reversing* Aristotle's meaning. Thomas Aquinas later collapsed the distinction between the "political" and the "social" by substituting the latter for the former. As Arendt remarks, "More than any elaborate theory this unconscious substitution of the social for the political betrays the extent to which the original Greek understanding of politics had been lost."[23]

The demise of the *polis* and its distinctive conception of political activity coincided with the rise of "society" and its "social" conception of politics. By the seventeenth century the transformation was complete: one entered into "civil society" by means of a "social contract" for the purpose of protecting one's life and property. The "body politic" has as its sole raison d'être the preservation of the individual bodies composing it. As Hobbes puts it: "The final Cause, End, or Designe of men . . . in the introduction of that restraint upon themselves (in which we see them live in Commonwealths), is the foresight of their own perservation . . . ."[24] Or, as Locke says: "The great and *chief end* . . . of Men's uniting into Commonwealths and putting themselves under government, is the Preservation of their Property."[25] The classical conception of politics was as dead as the proverbial doornail.

III. Science and Self-Interest

The demise of the classical conception of politics and its replacement by the understanding of politics as a social and economic activity makes possible a positivistically conceived political science. Only when unpredictable political action was replaced by orderly and regular "behavior" could the social universe become the object of scientific scrutiny and interest. As Arendt explains:

> It is . . . the assumption that men behave and do not act with respect to each other, that lies at the root of the modern science of economics, whose birth coincided with the rise of society and which, together with its chief technical tool, statistics, became the social science par excellence. Economics—until the modern age a not too important part of ethics and politics . . . —could achieve a scientific character only when men had become social beings and unanimously followed certain patterns of behavior, so that those who did not keep the rules could be considered to be asocial or abnormal.[26]

A positivistically conceived science of *action* would be as inconceivable as a Newtonian science of a universe in which God intervened in miraculous and unpredictable ways. Action, according to Arendt, is "miraculous" in that it breaks the bonds of the ordinary and expected, thus beginning something new and unpredictable; and our modern science of behavior can thrive only in the absence of such "miracles." If such a science is to be valid, "action" must be ignored, outlawed, or eclipsed. And this, she suggests, is an easy feat in a society as large as ours:

> The laws of statistics are valid only where large numbers or long periods are involved, and acts or events can statistically appear only as deviations or fluctuations. The justification of statistics is that deeds and events are rare occurrences in everyday life and in history. Yet the meaningfulness of everyday relationships is disclosed not in everyday life but in rare deeds, just as the significance of a historical period shows itself only in the few events that illuminate it.[27]

In statistical terms, the entire "population" of the Greek *polis* scarcely even constituted an acceptable "sample." The political activities of its citizens, therefore, could not be subjected to any sort of valid or reliable statistical analysis. To cite a self-evident but politically significant truism: The law of large numbers requires large numbers. As Arendt notes:

> The application of the law of large numbers and long periods to politics or history signifies nothing less than the willful obliteration of their very subject matter [viz., action], and it is a hopeless enterprise to search for meaning in politics or significance in history when everything that is not everyday behavior or automatic trends has been ruled out as immaterial.
>
> However, since the laws of statistics are perfectly valid where we deal with large numbers, it is obvious that every increase in population means an increased validity and a marked decrease of 'deviation'. Politically, this means that the larger the population in any given body politic, the more likely it will be the social rather than the political that constitutes the public realm. The Greeks, whose city-state was the most individualistic and least comfortable body politic known to us, were quite aware of the fact that the *polis*, with its emphasis on action and speech, could survive only if the number of citizens remained restricted. Large numbers of

41

people, crowded together, develop an almost irresistible inclination toward despotism, be this the despotism of a person or of majority rule; and although statistics, that is, the mathematical treatment of reality, was unknown prior to the modern age, the social phenomena which make such treatment possible—great numbers, accounting for conformism . . . and automatism in human affairs—were precisely those traits which, in Greek self-understanding, distinguished the Persian civilization from their own.[28]

These social phenomena also serve to distinguish our modern society—and our conception of politics—from that of our Greek forbears. These same social phenomena, moreover, constitute the precondition of a social science, positivistically conceived. "The unfortunate truth about behaviorism and the validity of its 'laws'," Arendt continues, "is that the more people there are, the more likely they are to behave and the less likely they are to tolerate nonbehavior [*vide* Tocqueville and J.S. Mill]. Statistically, this will be shown in the leveling out of fluctuation." The meaning of this development is not, however, expressible in statistical terms:

> In reality, deeds will have less and less chance to stem the tide of behavior, and events will more and more lose their significance, that is, their capacity to illuminate historical time. Statistical uniformity is by no means a harmless scientific ideal; it is the no longer secret political ideal of a society which, entirely submerged in the routine of everyday living, is at peace with the scientific outlook inherent in its very existence.[29]

Scientifically speaking, the larger and more populous the society the "better" it is. As I shall suggest in a moment, at least one modern society was "scientifically" designed for just this purpose.

Arendt mentions, but does not account for, another feature of a society amenable to scientific analysis: the interest-governed behavior of its members. She simply assumes, I think, that "society" just *is* the sort of human association whose members pursue their own individual interests; thus there is something like a conceptual connection between the form of the association and the kinds of activities carried on within it. If this is indeed her view, it requires qualification. We cannot, I think, simply assert without argument that in a certain (kind of) society some kinds of activity are *necessary* while others are *impossible* or *inconceivable, tout court*. What we *can* say is that in a certain kind of society some kinds of activities are more likely than others to be considered intelligible, rational, correct, and commendable, and that, in consequence, more people will be favorably disposed to these activities than to those deemed unintelligible, silly, pointless, irrational, or incorrect.

In the kind of society variously termed "civil," "capitalist," or "bourgeois," pursuing one's own economic interest is generally considered to be not merely intelligible, but rational, prudent, correct, even commendable. This assessment of self-interested activity both aided and was aided by the emergence of capitalism. But whence came this ethic of self-interest and, with it, the modern understanding of politics that contrasts so sharply with the classical view? The vulgar-Marxist answer is that any ethic or self-interpretation—any "ideology,"in short—is a "superstructural" by-product of changes in the economic "base," and is therefore uninteresting in its own right. (This, I hasten to add, is *not* Marx's own view.)

A more interesting, and I think satisfactory, answer is to be found in the history of successive self-interpretations, rationales, and justifications out of which the ethic of self-interest emerged. This story is reconstructed with great verve and insight by Albert Hirschman in *The Passions and the Interests.* Briefly, Hirschman argues that the way was smoothed for the triumph of capitalism by means of an *ethical* argument. Greatly simplified, the argument goes as follows. The "passions" of men—lust for power, sexual lust, avarice, and so on—are violent and strong to a frightening degree, and the capacity of religious mores and institutions to check them is weak and ineffectual, and growing weaker. The answer that was eventually arrived at—articulated most fully by Montesquieu, Sir James Steuart, and Hume—Hirschman calls "the theory of countervailing passions." The theory held that one particularly "calm" passion—avarice—can serve as a brake or check upon the other, more violent passions. The pursuit of one's own interest ought therefore to be not merely permitted but encouraged. The greater the number of people pursuing private gain, the smaller the number of those sating their other passions. More than that, an interest-governed world is vastly more *predictable* and *constant* than a world rocked to and fro by the violent pursuit of the passions. Pursuing the public interest is no less dangerous than pursuing one's private passions. A society of virtuous and public-spirited citizens—the classical Greek ideal—was as dangerous as a society of licentious and passionate vagabonds. As Steuart put it:

43

Were miracles wrought every day, the laws of nature would no longer be laws; and were everyone to act for the public, and neglect himself, the statesman would be bewildered . . . . Were a people to become quite disinterested there would be no possibility of governing them. Everyone might consider the interest of his country in a different light, and many might join in the ruin of it, by endeavoring to promote its advantages [rather than their own].[30]

"Interest" operated at two levels: Within each individual, the more violent passions would be checked; and between individuals, interest would check interest. And since "interest"—understood as avarice or "the love of gain"—was the most persistent, constant, and uniform of the passions, it was always at the ready to check the other, more irregular and episodic passions. Moreover, the persistence, constancy, and uniformity of "interest" made an interest-governed world *predictable*. A world in which people pursued their own interests—unlike one in which they pursued their own "passions" *or* the "public interest"—was at last a fit object of scientific scrutiny. It would exhibit the behavioral "regularities" and "uniformities" so prized by our modern methodologically self-conscious behavorial scientists. The social world would at last be made safe for science.

If, however, there is to be a new science of *politics* for this new world, the number of decision centers must be multiplied; ideally, the number of decision centers would approach the total number of people in a given society. The form of government best suited to the new science of politics would, in other words, be not only a *popular* but a large and *populous* one.

IV. Inventing America

Garry Wills speaks, rightly enough, of the "invention" of America. The United States was indeed the first scientifically designed and made-to-order polity.[31] Its designers met in Philadelphia in 1787, and three of their number collaborated in writing a stunning and singularly successful defense of the new design. *The Federalist Papers* can be read as the fullest and most elaborate statement of the *political* relevance of the theory of countervailing passions. The American system of government was the first to constitutionally sanction—indeed to sanctify— the pursuit of private interests. If in such a society great things might not be achieved, great evils would at least be prevented. Its "policy of supplying by opposite and rival interests, the defect of better motives,

44

might," says Madison, "be traced through the whole system of human affairs. . . ."[32] The irony of Madison's position is of course that such "system" as there is in "human affairs", is largely due to the interest-governed behavior of individual human beings.

The focus here is indeed upon "behavior" in Arendt's sense. The large and populous American Republic is to be the antithesis of the small and intimate *polis*. In the *Federalist*, Hamilton looks back with feelings of "horror and disgust" at the "petty republics of Greece" and "the distractions with which they were continually agitated." The new American Republic, by contrast, is designed in accordance with the latest scientific principles—principles unknown to the ancients, and only recently discovered: "The science of politics, . . . like most other sciences, has received great improvement. The efficacy of various principles is now well understood, which were either not known at all, or imperfectly known to the ancients."[33] This New Science is above all the science of self-interest: "The safest reliance of every government is on men's interests. This is a principle of human nature, on which all political speculation, to be just, must be founded."[34] If this insight is not a new one, its institutional implications are nevertheless quite novel. Among the "wholly new discoveries" Hamilton includes the system of representation and of checks and balances. But perhaps the most important single principle underlying the new Constitution, backed by the new science of politics, is "the ENLARGEMENT of the ORBIT within which such systems are to revolve. . . ."[35] As Madison declares, passions are diminished in a large republic, especially one in which interests are multiplied and "ambition is made to counteract ambition."[36] Nothing is more dangerous to a republic, Hamilton adds, than "a contracted territory." In a small commonwealth there is, as it were, no spatial check upon the passions; such great force, compressed into so small and intimate a space, must produce periodic explosions. This is reason enough, Hamilton suggests, for not taking the course—advocated by some in 1787, and later by Jefferson with his "ward system"—of subdividing the Republic into *polis*-like commonwealths. Hamilton's hackles are raised by the prospect of "splitting ourselves into an infinity of little, jealous, clashing, tumultuous commonwealths, the wretched nurseries of unceasing discord and the miserable objects of universal pity or contempt."[37]

The new science of politics, then, was, first, a science of self-interest, and, second, a science of *space*. It sought solutions for moral and political problems. This spatial motif, so pervasive in *The Federalist Papers*, was not the exclusive property of Hamilton and Madison. Five years before the Constitutional Convention, Crevecoeur celebrated the open spaces of America. Almost as if anticipating the "spatial" argument of Hamilton and Madison, Crevecoeur wrote: "Zeal in Europe is confined; here it evaporates in the great distance it has to travel; there it is a grain of powder enclosed; here it burns away in the open air and consumes without effect."[38]

The idea that sheer size could prevent enmity by precluding intimacy was invariably expressed in "scientific" terms. Society was viewed as a closed space in which people were contained. The larger the container, the lower the pressure; the lower the pressure, the cooler the contents. This was nothing less than Boyle's law, applied to politics. Such imagery was commonplace in the late eighteenth and the nineteenth centuries. Frederick Jackson Turner likened the open spaces of America to a "safety valve," and fretted about what might happen when this valve was closed with the closing of the frontier. One could of course cite many other examples of this outlook. Here it is perhaps enough to say, rather dogmatically, that the American consciousness has been a *spatial* rather than an *historical* one. As Richard Hofstadter once remarked, "Time is the basic dimension of history, but the basic dimension of the American imagination is space."[39] This spatial sensibility is not, however, due solely to geography; it is part and parcel of a theoretically mediated interpretation of the political meaning and significance of space.

Unlike our Puritan forbears—who emphasized the necessity and importance of a "contracted territory"—the authors of *The Federalist Papers* stressed the need for a fragmented and dispersed citizenry. Only in such a setting, they argued, could interest check interest and ambition counter ambition. Sheer size and numbers will contribute to political stability. A large and populous polity ensures economies of scale unknown in a contracted commonwealth. In the Tenth *Federalist* Madison makes what we might call the economy-of-scale argument:

> The smaller the society, the fewer probably will be the distinct parties and interests composing it; the fewer the distinct parties and interests, the more frequently will a majority be found of the same party; and the smaller the number of individuals composing a majority, and the smaller the compass within which they are placed, the more easily will they concert and execute their plans of oppression. Extend the sphere and you take in a greater variety of parties and interests; you make it less probable that a majority of the whole will have a common motive to invade the rights of

other citizens; or if such a common motive exists, it will be more difficult for all who feel it to discover their own strength and to act in unison with each other.[40]

And later, in the Fifty-first *Federalist*, Madison waxes ecstatic over the prospect that, "In the federal republic of the United States . . . the society itself will be broken into . . many parts, interests and classes of citizens. . . ."[41] This proliferation of decision centers renders majority tyranny unlikely, even as it makes possible a science of politics. The latter development is, on reflection, not wholly surprising. For what is better suited to be an object of political science, than a scientifically designed polity?

Could this perhaps be what Tocqueville meant when he said that "a new science of politics is needed for a new world"?[42] Is there, in other words, something like a symbiotic relationship between the new science and the politics of the New World? The peculiarity of America—which John Stuart Mill, following Tocqueville, called "this great existing fact"[43]—resides in the "theoretical" character of the observed "facts." In a phrase: Theory determined constitution, and constitution institutionally constrained behavior. Or, to put it differently, we might say that the theory that was institutionalized through the constitution— namely the theory of countervailing passions—"constituted" its "object," viz., the self-interested behavior of the citizenry. Not only did the theory behind the Constitution "constitute" its object (the pun is intended); it also *legitimated* it, and in so doing rendered alternative visions and theories suspect, if not subversive.[44]

Because no one, before or since, has appreciated so well as Tocqueville the close, even symbiotic, connection between new theories and new worlds, I shall conclude by enlarging and elaborating on this crucial but heretofore unnoticed theme in Tocqueville's work.

V. Tocqueville on the Promises and Perils of a Scientific Politics

Arendt argues that the *political* realm of "action" has been replaced by the *social* realm of "behavior," and that while there could be no science of *action*—because of its revelatory and novel character—there can be a science of *behavior*. One finds a startlingly similar argument in the twentieth chapter of Part I of the second volume of Tocqueville's *Democracy in America*. The lackluster title of this chapter—"Some Characteristics Peculiar to Historians in Democratic Ages"—might mis-

47

lead the unwary reader into dismissing it as a decorative and inconsequential piece of French fluff. Nothing could be farther from the truth; it is a truly remarkable chapter in a remarkable book.

This chapter occupies a peculiarly revealing place in Tocqueville's magnum opus. It is paired with the immediately preceding chapter on "Some Observations on the Theater Among Democratic Peoples," and both are sandwiched between chapters on "bombast" and "eloquence" in the speech of the Americans. The juxtaposition is more telling still when we recall that speech, in the classical conception of politics, was the preeminently political medium—the medium of discourse and debate, persuasion and argument. Tocqueville's discussion of the theater is, I think, meant to recall the classical connection between politics and the theater, between "action" and "drama". After all, our own word "drama" comes from the Greek verb *dran*, "to act."[45] Play-acting is an imitation of acting, i.e., of publicly revealing oneself through speech and deed. This connection is not entirely lost even today, for we too speak of political "actors," playing "roles" on the political "stage," and the like. At any rate Tocqueville is quite explicit in drawing parallels between "acting" on the stage and "action." "The drama more than any other form of literature, is bound by many close links to the state of society."[46]

The theatrical parallel is reiterated in Tocqueville's following chapter on "historians in democratic centuries." "Historians of aristocratic ages, looking at the world's *theater*, first see a few leading *actors* in control of the whole *play*. These great personages who hold the front of the *stage* strike their attention and hold it fixed."[47] Historians in aristocratic ages focus, in other words, upon those who "act" in novel, noteworthy, or extraordinary ways; their subject is action in Arendt's sense of the term. Historians in democratic ages, Tocqueville writes, "show contrary tendencies": Their attention is fixed, not upon individual men but upon movements, tendencies, and processes characteristic of men in the aggregate—that is, upon "behavior" in Arendt's sense. If we substitute "social (or political) scientists" for Tocqueville's "historians of democratic ages," we can see our own modern "scientific" presuppositions and pretensions clearly anticipated and mirrored. We are, Tocqueville remarks, likely to explain even "the smallest particular events" in terms of "general causes." In criticizing this "social-scientific" perspective Tocqueville is uncharacteristically caustic:

Monsieur de LaFayette says . . . that an exaggerated belief in general causes is wonderfully consoling for mediocre public men. I would add that it is the same for mediocre historians. It always provides them with a few mighty reasons to extricate them from the most difficult part of their task, and while indulging their incapacity or laziness, gives them a reputation for profundity.[48]

Still, there are reasons, quite apart from laziness, which serve to explain this recourse to "general causes"—reasons to be found in the political structure of the American republic itself:

> When all the citizens are independent of one another, and each is weak, no one individual can be found to be exercising very great or . . . lasting influence over the masses. At first sight individuals appear to have no influence at all over them, and society would seem to progress on its own by the free and spontaneous action of all its members.[49]

Whereas "the historian of an aristocratic age has simply to analyze the particular action of one man or a few men amid the general mass of events," the historian of the democratic age is confronted with a different—and vastly more difficult—problem: How to identify and explain the interactive effects of many individual actions.

Invoking the idiom of the late-nineteenth-century neo-Kantians, we might say that Tocqueville subscribes neither to the ideographic-interpretivist view that only individual actions matter nor to the nomothetic-positivist view that only general processes, trends, and tendencies constitute the object of social-scientific inquiry:

> For my part, I think that in all ages some of the happenings in this world are due to very general causes and others depend on very particular influences. These two kinds of causes are always in operation; only their proportion varies. *General causes explain more, and particular influences less, in democratic than in aristocratic ages* . . . [T]herefore historians who describe the happenings in democratic societies are right in attaching much importance to general causes and in spending most of their time discovering them.[50]

In "democratic" ages "action" is largely replaced by "behavior." That Tocqueville subscribes to something like Arendt's distinction (not surprising, since both take this from the classics) can be seen in his speaking of "actions" with reference to individuals, and "happenings" and "events" when referring to the aggregate behavior of groups:

> Historians who live in democratic ages are not only prone to attribute each *happening* to a great cause but also are led to link facts together to make a system . . . [S]eeing the *actors* less and

the *events* more, [they] can easily string facts together in a methodical order.[51]

This "systemic" inclination—so characteristic of the social sciences—is, as Tocqueville rightly remarks, a distinctly modern development:

Ancient literature, rich in fine historical writing, has not left us one great historical system, whereas even the poorest of modern literatures is swarming with them. Apparently classical historians made too little use of general theories, whereas our own are always on the verge of using them too much.[52]

But Tocqueville's concerns are not exclusively, or even mainly, methodological. They are, first and foremost, *political*. For "those who write in democratic ages"—social scientists, in other words—"have another tendency that is even more dangerous":

Once the trace of the influence of individuals . . . has been lost, we are often left with the sight of the world moving without anyone moving it. As it becomes extremely difficult to discern and analyze the reasons which, acting separately on the will of each citizen, concur in the end to produce movement in the whole mass, one is tempted to believe that this movement is not voluntary and that societies unconsciously obey some superior dominating force.

Even supposing that it is on earth that we must find the general law controlling the particular wills of all individuals, that does not serve to preserve human freedom. A cause so vast that it bends them all together in the same direction, may easily seem irresistible. Seeing that one does yield to it, one is very near believing that one cannot stand up to it.

"Classical historians," Tocqueville adds, "taught how to command; those of our own time teach next to nothing but how to obey." This modern "doctrine of fatality" impairs vision, inhibits action, and encourages conformity; it "forg[es] a tight, enormous chain which girds and binds the human race."[53] Changing the metaphor only slightly one could, without much change of meaning, substitute Weber's "iron cage" for Tocqueville's "tight, enormous chain." The spirit of both is captured in Arendt's observation:

The trouble with modern theories of behaviorism is not that they are wrong but that they could become true, that they are actually the best possible conceptualization of certain obvious trends in modern society. It is quite conceivable that the modern age—which began with such an unprecedented and promising outburst of human activity—may end in the deadliest, most sterile passivity history has ever known.[54]

The "polar night of icy darkness and hardness" that Weber saw as the inevitable accompaniment of a modern rationalized and routinized society[55] does not merely require social-scientific explanation. There is a sense, I have tried to suggest, in which a routinized and regularized life-world is itself a *requirement* for a positivistically conceived science of society. And that is why, I should like to suggest rather cryptically by way of conclusion, a critique of the concepts and categories of a positivistically conceived social science is necessarily a critique of the covertly manipulative precepts and practices of the society in which we now live, and of the instrumentally rational world-view which serves to legitimize it.

CHAPTER THREE
Mutual Knowledge
John O'Neill

I. The Linguistic Turn in the Social Sciences

Human societies are self-interpreting institutions. Historically this hermeneutical work has fallen to priests, philosophers, and artists who were gradually usurped by scientists, lawyers, economists, and sociologists. This, of course, is not an undisputed shift, although we generally accommodate to it by allowing scientists their say-so with respect to nature, while clinging to our own right to an opinion on religion, politics, business, and the arts. In these areas, too, there are advocates for the dominance of scientific discourse, who seek to persuade us that laymen can at best chatter upon the nature of society. Those who favor the analogy between nature and society as the dumb material of science are therefore inconvenienced by the seemingly inextricable relation between ordinary language and social reality. Indeed, they are likely to consider those who stress the constitutively spoken nature of human society to be idealists, romantically tied to convention and conservatism. In practice, the scientistic ambitions of sociology are well entrenched in Western societies, politicians having persuaded laymen and themselves that the complexities of modern living can only be settled through a trustful delegation of analysis and initiative to the technical sciences. But today there is a civic tendency to question the bureaucratic processing of everyday life. To keep pace, professional voices have risen to question the scientistic model of constructivist sociology as an expropriation of an ordinary civic competence with the sensible conduct of human affairs. To keep on top of these developments, even self-styled critical sociologists find themselves having to straddle the double claims of scientific and commonsense accounts of social life. In this way, they hope to preserve professional face by chastising their colleagues while also instructing them in new methods of holding on to what they may have lost forever.

Something like this provides the background to Anthony Giddens' persistent, if not repetitive, attempts[1] to refurbish the grounds of the mutuality of commonsense and sociological knowledge[2], or what he calls the "double hermeneutic" of the social sciences. It is necessary to examine Giddens' argument, because it betrays a fundamental ambivalence towards commonsense knowledge even where he, as a sociologist, has tried to bring about a rapprochement between the moral claims of lay and expert knowledge. Giddens thereby misses a serious communicative issue in the power relations of political democracies. Since he draws heavily upon what we may call *the linguistic turn in the social sciences*, we should recall the basic propositions on which Giddens constructs his argument:

(1) (a) Social science must treat action as rationalized conduct ordered reflexively by human agents;
(b) It must grasp the significance of language for the practical accomplishment of rational and reflexive action.
(2) (a) The recognition of the linguistic accomplishment of the reflexivity of human conduct ought also to be introduced into the conduct of sociological research and method;
(b) Social science theories are not simply neutral "meaning frames" but moral interventions in the life of the society they propose to clarify.[3]

In themselves these prescriptions are hardly news and, in fact, are recognized in the daily practice of sociological research that is quite ignorant of the tradition of European social theory—or at best happy to leave it on the mantelpiece, along with the bric-á-brac of early science. Nothing, then, is to be gained from elaborating upon these mnemonic devices as they stand.

It is therefore in another way that we must be concerned with the *constitutively spoken (sprachlich) subject matter of sociology.* The purely methodological issue is that the social sciences, while aspiring to the practice of the natural sciences in their operations of definition and generalization, lack an analogously dumb material of reference. That is to say, while the natural sciences benefit from the indifference of natural and physical processes to scientific formulation, the social sciences are not similarly privileged in their encounters with persons and institutions. This is not simply the complaint, revelled in by British critics of the jargon of the social sciences, that the latter have yet to reach that stage of scientific maturity where their language cannot be found to be a thin disguise for commonsense expressions. While this is often the case, and might be taken to defend us against the pretensions of the social sciences, it is not an argument we wish to use. Our purpose is not to enter a plea for the preservation of sociology but to confront the *political ambivalence in its critical practice*, let alone in its scientific versions. As I understand it, the seriousness of the political issues to which we are led by the communicative reflexivity of commonsense knowledge of social structure derives from the concern it holds for the public in Western democracies. Here it is the voice of the social science experts and technicians in the service of the Party, whether right or left, which threatens to erode civic competence and political responsibility.

II. Commonsense Sociability as Communicative Competence

What has evolved from the phenomenological and neo-Wittgensteinian critique of positivism is a shift from compliance theories of knowledge and social reality to a competence model of the pretheoretical and sentimental foundations of everyday social life.[4] To the extent that this existential or phenomenological shift in the validation of commonsense structures of knowledge and values that turn upon native linguistic competences represents a "radical" break with scientistic sociology, Giddens needs to endorse it. But because he suspects Idealism in the linguistic turn, he introduces some further propositions for a constructivist critical sociology whose central concepts of structure, power, and change might render commonsense knowledge more rational.[5]

We need first to set out what is attractive in the sociology of everyday life, and then we shall see how Giddens manages his ambivalence with regard to *the critical problem of the radical relativization of scientific and everyday accounts of persons and society.* Although Schutz himself seems not to have had any political ambitions for interpretative sociology, I believe that it is not difficult to provide one for the *critical turn in phenomenological sociology.*[6] Here I am at odds with Giddens. I shall argue that commonsense knowledge and values do not depend upon scientific reconstruction for the exercise of critical reflection. It is a prejudice of science and philosophy to think of common sense as a poor version of reason. On the contrary, the practice of science is enriched and would be quite impossible without its ties to the practices of commonsense reasoning. Moreover, the strict subordination of commonsense knowledge to the social sciences would constitute a political practice so far envisaged only in philosophical and science-fiction utopias. Indeed, it is a mark of the latter that they abjure common sense. The essential distinction between the natural and social sciences, which makes the standard of rationality fostered by the social sciences intrinsically a problem of the *politics of knowledge*, is that human relationships, customs, and institutions are not merely "orders" produced by scientific reconstruction. The human order is initially a *pretheoretical institution*, resting on the unarticulated "commonsense" knowledge of others as "kindred" with whom we experience dependable needs and wants, expressed in the "relevances" of time, place, and the human body. The nature of this order cannot be settled through a dogmatic rationalism that subordinates commonsense knowledge of individual and social life to the standards of realism and objectivism. The latter are maxims of scientific conduct but not obviously normative for all social praxis. Indeed, a fundamental task of the sociology of knowledge must be its reflexive concern with the grounds of *communication* between everyday commonsense reason and scientific rationality. Such a concern would contribute to the possibility of a democratic society in the modern world by defending the fundamental grounds of social life as the *inalienable competence of individuals* exhibited in their everyday lives together.

It is quite unthinkable that society could ever be a construct of sociological reasoning alone.[7] In Marxist terms and, I believe, Schutzian (implicit in his preference for such metaphors as "the stock of knowledge"), commonsense knowledge of social structure supplies an enormous *surplus value of meaning and value* without which analytic social reasoning would itself be entirely unworkable. Thus the primacy of the everyday world as a self-interpreted structure of practical knowledge and values is fundamental to the investigative procedures of interpretative sociology. It is the foundation of the universality of experience that eludes both a transcendental ego, and the convenants of an empirical ego locked in the pursuit of self-interest.

Schutz, Simmel, and George Herbert Mead all agree that the social world is the product of an essentially human capacity for adopting the attitude of the *generalized other* towards oneself (Mead), and thereby building up a structure of *typifications* and *relevances* (Schutz) whereby we are able to interact without solipsistic anxieties as to the ordinary and dependable course of our interaction with our fellows:

> In abstract thought the individual takes the attitude of the generalized other toward himself, without reference to its expression in any particular other individuals; and in concrete thought he

takes that attitude insofar as it is expressed in the attitudes towards his behaviour of those other individuals with whom he is involved in the given social situation or act. But only by taking the attitude of the generalized other toward himself, in one or other of these ways, can he think at all; for only thus can thinking—or the internalized conversation of gestures which constitutes thinking— occur. And only through the taking by individuals of the attitude or attitudes of the generalized other toward themselves is the existence of a universe of discourse, as that system of common or social meanings which thinking presupposes as its context, rendered possible.[8]

Like Mead, Simmel rejects any notion of the construction of a common social world as the product of scientific abstraction and synthesis: the unity of society needs no observer. It is directly realized by its own elements because these elements are themselves conscious and synthesizing units. Nor does Simmel see the synthesis of social life as the direct focus of individual action, but as the by-product of innumerable specific relations governed by "the feeling and knowledge of determining others and being determined by them." This is not to say that the sociologist for his own specific purposes may not elaborate an "additional" synthesis. But the problem here is that the synthesis of external observation which takes as its paradigm the observation of nature is not analogous to human unity, which is grounded in understanding, love, or common work. The social synthesis is the work of individuals for whom others have the same reality as themselves and are not reducible simply to the contents of individual consciousness, but function to orient language, thought, and conduct toward the social world. We *think* the other but at the same time we are so *affected* by him that sociation is better regarded as a "knowing" than a "cognizing," says Simmel. But neither is sociation simply an empathic projection of psychological similarities:

> We see the other not simply as an individual but as a colleague or comrade or fellow party member—in short, as a cohabitant of the same specific world. And this inevitable, quite automatic assumption is one of the means by which one's personality and reality assume, in the imagination of the other, the quality and form required by sociability.[9]

Schutz has examined in detail the range of typifications, from face-to-face to increasingly anonymous situations, removed in time as well

57

as space, that provide the framework of the ordinary person's social repertoire of relevances, interests, and values. These he can pursue in common with others, without any radical break in what can be taken as matter of course and what needs particular reflection because of contradictions, deceits, and puzzles. In short, the social world is not, as constructivist analysts wish to make out, an intrinsic puzzle that requires scientific mediation and reconstruction in order to make rational sense.

As Peter Winch has argued, it is only permissible for social scientists to make culture strange in order to reveal the massive trust and unchallenged sense that members invest in it.[10] And indeed the deep sense of the *incongruity procedures* of Goffman and Garfinkel is to show that the sense of social possibility, and its techniques of face and impression management, is false to the unarticulated structure of our *everyday trust and social competence* with one another.[11] In contrast with manipulative and expert knowledge, our mundane experience of the self and its social situation is given to us through the same set of typifications and motives that are the convenience of anyone. It is only by some incongruity of experience, some outrage or manipulation, that I discover that my self is not synonymous with selves in general, or that what I take to be the perceivedly normal and typical features of my situation are not in fact shared by or available to anyone like me. Thus it is the starting assumption of every social relationship that each of us knows with whom he is interacting. This involves the typification of each partner's actions, motives, and situation. What is required is that each person be able to observe the rules of *self-respect* and *considerateness* that sustain the ritual of social interaction:

> A person's performance of face-work, extended by his tacit agreement to help others perform theirs, represents his willingness to abide by the ground rules of social interaction. Here is the hallmark of his socialization as an interactant. If he and the others were not socialized in this way, interaction in most societies and most situations would be a much more hazardous thing for feelings and faces. The person would find it impractical to be oriented to symbolically conveyed appraisals of social worth, or to be possessed of feelings—that is, it would be impractical for him to be a ritually delicate object.[12]

It is not necessary that the typifications of respect and consideration be accessible in a perfectly *reciprocal* way in order to sustain social interaction. Person and action typifications are *corrigible* through experience and interaction. But what is not true, is that we withhold our trust in others until we have *absolutely* certain grounds for it. Socially speaking, seduction precedes both deduction and induction as the basis of our experience with others. Thus, in the ordinary course of life we take others at face value, and expect to be sustained in the face that we ourselves project. In these exchanges, the primary focus of social interaction is the expressive communication between self and other. We must then regard language, gesture, task, motive, and situation as primary resources for social bonding, and as the *precontractual basis* for all other convenants, even those in which we deceive one another.

Interpretative sociology, therefore, treats the natural attitude of daily life as *generative maxims of conduct* whereby social agents derive their ordinary sense of competence from the practices of their surrounding institutions as a claim to moral membership in those institutions. In other words, the way social agents have of deciding the sensible status of their own actions or of events in their lives is to refer to the particulars of these events as the *occasioned evidence* of their grasp of the institutions of language, work, family, or school. In turn, these institutions furnish the *indexical grounds* of their actions and talk, whose sense therefore is never *wholly* at stake in members' questions, answers, descriptions, and the like. The maxims of commonsense social interaction and communication permit ordinary persons to locate themselves and others in meaningful schemes of action. Their sense is generalized due to a common ability to locate the *occasional*[13] or *indexical*[14] properties of talk and behavior as an essentially unthematic accomplishment:

> In exactly the way that persons are members to organized affairs, they are engaged in serious and practical work of detecting, demonstrating, persuading through displays in the ordinary occasions of their interactions the appearances of consistent, coherent, clear, chosen, planful arrangements. In exactly the ways in which a setting is organized, it consists of methods whereby its members are provided with accounts of the setting as countable, storyable, proverbial, comparable, picturable, representable—i.e., *accountable events.*[15]

Although it would lead us too far afield to pursue in detail, I believe it should be pointed out that these basic ethical features of commonsense social and communicative competence are precisely the grounds presupposed by Habermas's ideal speech community.[16] The critical task of this community would be seriously limited if it could not depend upon the vital competences of the everyday life-world:

Such communication must therefore necessarily be rooted in social interests and in the value-orientations of a given social life-world. In both directions the feedback-monitored communication process is grounded in what Dewey called "value beliefs." That is, it is based on a *historically determined preunderstanding*, governed by social norms, of what is practically necessary in a concrete situation. This preunderstanding is a consciousness that can only be *enlightened hermeneutically*, through articulation in the discourse of citizens in the community.[17]

III. The Mutuality of Commonsense and Scientific Rationality

The commonsense attitude of everyday life is not just a given. It is something that is evinced in social conduct as part of an agent's grasp of how things are, as his ability to handle his social surroundings, relevant others, and his own "face". The attitude of everyday life is thus not simply a cognitive attitude, but also an expressive or *ethical competence*, which Garfinkel refers to under the concept of *trust*, that is, "a person's compliance with the expectancies of the attitude of *daily life as a morality*."[18] Given that everyday action reveals an intrinsically ethical competence, we cannot submit it to the ironies of scientific reconstruction without altering the moral universe that is the field of social investigation. Thus it is necessary to come to understand the social scientist's conduct as itself a *form of life*,[19] governed by its own maxims for the conduct of rational inquiry. We cannot impose these standards upon lay members, as though the latter were otherwise incapable of meaningful action. Schutz formulates the structures of scientific interest and relevance as dependent upon maxims of conduct that require a radical break with the everyday life-world. The scientist suspends the spatiotemporal relevances motivated by his own presence in the world. He adopts a timeless and objective stance, in which space-time coordinates function solely to state the conditions for repeating an experiment. Because the scientist has no "here" within the world, and is immune to the reciprocity of viewpoint, with its horizons of intimacy and generality, he is obliged to construct a *model actor*, to whom he imputes a *rational consciousness* interacting with others destined similarly to act like any rational man:

The homunculus is invested with a system of relevances originating in the scientific problem of his constructor and not in the particular biographically determined situation of an actor within the world.

It is the scientist who defines what is to his puppet a Here and a There, what is within his reach, what is to him a We and a You or a They. The scientist determines the stock of knowledge his model has supposedly at hand. This stock of knowledge is not socially derived and, unless especially designed to be so, without reference to social approval. The relevance system pertinent to the scientific problem under scrutiny alone determines its intrinsic structure, namely, the elements "about" which the homunculus is supposed to have knowledge, those of which he has a mere knowledge of acquaintance, and those others he just takes for granted. With this is determined what is supposed to be familiar and what anonymous to him and on what level the typification of the experiences of the world imputed to him takes place.[20]

Schutz, however, is not content simply to cordon off lay practices of social theorizing from interference by the practice of scientific sociology. Rather, he insists that inasmuch as social scientists have no other subject matter than the self-interpreting practices of lay social interaction, they are obliged in their own accounts of social behavior to meet the requirement of *the postulate of adequacy*:

Each term used in a scientific system referring to human action must be so constructed that a human act performed within the life-world by an individual actor in the way indicated by the typical construction would be reasonable and understandable for the actor himself, as well as for his fellow-men. This postulate is of extreme importance for the methodology of social science. What makes it possible for a social science to refer at all to events in the life-world is the fact that the interpretation of any human act by the social scientist might be the same as that by the actor or by his partner.[21]

Giddens finds it difficult to accept the Schutzian postulate of adequacy. Taken along with the generally static conception of the stock of knowledge—although this is unfair to Schutz, as we shall see—the postulate of adequacy seems to limit sociology to the representation of received knowledge, which hardly seems useful to its critical purpose.[22] Because it focuses attention upon action as meaning rather than action as praxis, i.e., the practical realization of interests, it fails to give sufficient attention to *the problem of power* in social life. Moreover, these two issues are interrelated, inasmuch as the operation of power and the conflicts that arise over it are issues of differential interpretation of the "same" idea system. Since the postulate of adequacy restricts the formation of technical concepts to the level of lay comprehension, it would hinder the development of a critical social science as the necessary instrument of social and political change. Giddens therefore seeks to reformulate the adequacy postulate in a more progressive version:

> The conceptual schemes of the social sciences therefore express a *double hermeneutic*, relating both to entering and grasping the frames of meaning involved in the production of social life by lay actors, and reconstructing these within new frames of meaning involved in technical conceptual schemes.[23]

The double hermeneutic of the social sciences may be given a progressive rather than conservative turn, Giddens argues, provided we take the actor's first order meanings to rest upon a shared symbolic framework which provides for the *communicative intent* of his actions to be given a conventional sense. Human interaction is successfully coordinated because all subjective meaning is logically and sociologically dependent upon a shared but inarticulable background of *mutual knowledge*. How this differs so far from Schutz's or even Winch's position is hard to see, even supposing we accept the insistence upon the passivity of commonsense knowledge. It is with two further claims that Giddens believes his position to be quite distinct:

> The production of interaction has three fundamental elements: its constitution as "meaningful"; its constitution as a moral order; and its constitution as the operation of relations of power.[24]

In speaking of the *moral order of interaction*, Giddens argues that it is necessary to distinguish the *enabling* and the *constraining* features of norms and not to emphasize one aspect at the expense of the other. Interaction as a moral order involves a system of rights and duties which can be negotiated by actors, since its enforcement is dependent upon sanctions that do not fall upon them in the same way that the sun destroyed the wings of Daedalus. Thus it is clear that anyone breaking the law enters into a complex series of negotiations whereby the nature of the sanctions to be applied is determined with respect to the rights of both the plaintiff and the defendant. Furthermore, it is mistaken to assume that actors internalize the moral order without reservations. Social norms may be observed cynically, they may be exploited, subverted, or reformed. Indeed, as I have shown elsewhere,[25] we may expect these responses. Because the reflexive elaboration of the normative system of values, knowledge, science, law, and art is tied to the institutions of power, authority may be challenged by anyone decoding the official definition of reality, order, meaning, and value. Despite Giddens, an important element in the radical protest of the sixties, at least, was furnished by the subversive practices of interpretative sociology.

But rather than forget these efforts, we must face part of their lesson in what we may call *the paradox of social reform*. It is that we need to lean upon institutions in order to change them. Therefore, to some extent they must always be open to change, even when we find fault with them. What this means, as the New Left discovered, is that we cannot gain a leverage upon institutions by standing entirely outside of them. It is necessary, therefore, to avoid the absolute antithesis of good and evil attributed respectively to the conservative and radical positions, since this only forces a confrontation which narrows the available space for negotiation.[26] Worst of all, as in acts of terrorism, it may weaken the very fabric of society. In other words, then, even when we differ, we are obliged not to destroy the fundamental background assumptions of our society. Admittedly, this may involve moving to very general principles of agreement, but it may be preferable to the violence of civil war and terrorism.

The paradox of social reform, then, involves the avoidance of a reified version of social institutions which cuts off their members from morally intelligent dialogue about the values, directions, and capacities of these same institutions. The political arts involved here may be compared to the art whereby as speakers we turn language, which as an institution always precedes us, into a personal articulation of meaning and expression through which we realize ourselves. Although he protests against the analogy, Giddens has no better way than to appeal to the relation between language and speech in order to correct what he perceives as the failure of interpretative sociology to take account of the influence of large institutions of society. This is because he, too, needs some way to express a nonreified approach to the relations between structures and agency whereby he can account for the coexistence of order and change:

> Interaction is constituted by and in the conduct of subjects; *structuration*, as the reproduction of practices, refers abstractly to the dynamic process whereby structures come into being. By the *duality of structure* I mean that social structures are both constituted *by* human agency, and yet at the same time are the very *medium* of this constitution. In sorting out the threads of how this happens

we can again profit initially by considering the case of language. Language exists as a "structure," syntactical and semantic, only insofar as there are some kinds of traceable consistencies in what people say, in the speech acts which they perform. From this aspect, to refer to rules and syntax, for example, is to refer to the reproduction of "like elements"; on the other hand, such rules also *generate* the totality of speech acts which is the spoken language. It is this dual aspect of structure, as both inferred from observations of human doings, and yet also operating as a medium whereby those doings are made possible, that has to be grasped through the notions of structuration and reproduction.[27]

It is therefore curious that Giddens should want to locate the reification of institutions solely in the life-world of lay actors. His critique of interpretative sociology as an idealist hindrance to critical social analysis seems to rest upon nothing else than this scientistic prejudice towards commonsense language. He believes that lay language alone refers to social institutions in a reified mode. It thereby fails to distinguish institutions as necessary *objectifications* of social interaction with their untoward consequences as *estranged, thing-like* obstacles to human purposes.[28] Yet he also notices that common sense is not impervious to expert knowledge and, thus, in his own words:

> This therefore raises the crucial questions: *In what sense are the "stocks of knowledge,"* which actors employ to constitute or to make happen that very society which is the object of analysis, *corrigible in the light of sociological research and theory?*"[29]

With this question Giddens turns full circle to reconsider the implications of the postulate of adequacy and the double hermeneutic of the social sciences. He rests his case on the claim that every competent social actor is himself a social theorist engaged in the ordinary course of his affairs in rational and instrumental appraisals of his affairs. This is normal practice in Western societies, which are also characterized by the practice of social science: hence the two, after all, do have a certain affinity.

IV. The Radicalization of the Postulate of Adequacy

Giddens worries that Schutz's postulate of adequacy may lead sociology into the backwoods. Admittedly, Schutz's clarification of the postulate is minimal. But it surely is not intended to unstick sociology or economics, for which Schutz had an obvious admiration. What he had in mind is that all human sciences are just that—human achievements that in the most radical sense can never be totally alienated from ordinary human intelligibility and competence. Now, Schutz knew that none of us participates equally in the production and consumption of human knowledge, goods, and services. Indeed, in this regard he laid the foundations for a fundamental sociology of the social distribution of knowledge which would be the missing link in externalist, Marxist approaches to this problem.[30] Giddens is concerned with only one small linkage in this chain, whereas Schutz's canvas is very broad. For our purposes, it will be enough to draw upon his remarks upon the epistemological status of the well-informed citizen.[31] What Schutz has in mind is not just an attitude or a social type but a dimension of knowledge that in any individual may coexist with several others, which he differentiates as follows:

(1) *the expert*: The expert's knowledge is restricted to a limited field, but therein it is clear and distinct. His opinions are based upon warranted assertions; his judgments are not mere guesswork or loose suppositions;

(2) *the man on the street:* The man on the street has a working knowledge of many fields which are not necessarily coherent with one another. . . . This knowledge in all its vagueness is still *sufficiently* precise for the practical purpose at hand;

(3) *the well-informed citizen*: On the one hand, he neither is, nor aims at being, possessed of expert knowledge; on the other, he does not acquiesce in the fundamental vagueness of a mere recipe knowledge or in the irrationality of his unclarified passions and sentiments. To be well informed means to him to arrive at *reasonably founded* opinions in fields which as he knows are at least mediately of concern to him, although not bearing upon his purpose at hand.

Each of us may be a composite of these attitudes. In a complex society, depending upon achieved levels of education and access to publications and media, it is more likely that even the expert will be relatively ignorant of others' expertise. Hence we have the option of living with imposition of others' knowledge that each of us accepts as a common man, or else we must strive to achieve some sort of educated understanding of matters outside our strict competence because of their general bearing upon our community. As I understand Schutz, he considered the attitude of the well-informed citizen to involve a special duty, if the political life of modern democracies is not to be handed over to technical experts. The duties of the well-informed citizen are:

(1) to consider himself perfectly qualified to decide who is a competent expert, and

(2) to make up his mind after having listened to opposing expert opinions.

Giddens never considers that the professionalization of the social sciences in the service of the administrative state maximizes the bureaucratic ethos and undermines the civic competence that Schutz and many others consider vital to democratic life. Incidentally, Schutz sharply distinguished the debased politics of public opinion from a democracy built upon the well-informed citizen. The latter is not just a romantic or populist construct of interpretative sociology. To become well-informed required that the citizen recognize his own laziness and prejudices. The same is true of the expert whose professionalized expertise renders him just as vulnerable as the man on the street with respect to specialities outside his own. Schutz states:

> A certain tendency to misinterpret democracy as a political institution in which the opinion of the uninformed man on the street must predominate increases the danger. It is the duty and the privilege, therefore, of the well-informed citizen in a democratic society to make his private opinion prevail over the public opinion of the man on the street.[32]

What the postulate of adequacy may be seen to require is *the institutionalization of the translatability and thereby accountability of expert knowledge* in order to raise the level of the well-informed citizen. Several institutions are potentially relevant: the schools and universities, the press, radio and television, trade unions, and political parties. In short, the postulate of adequacy implies the need to create a pedagogy that will subordinate expert knowledge to the needs of political democracy. Habermas has described the basic issues here,[33] although Giddens' account ignores this concern of critical theory; and O'Neill has described the complementary colonial context of such a pedagogy, emphasizing that the issue of *relative illiteracy* can be generalized to urban, industrial problems.[34]

What the postulate of adequacy reminds us of is that what "we" sociologists call society is in fact a plurality of worlds, each with its own lively structures of practical reasoning and belief. Thus, as everyone knows, we do not easily move from one little world to another in anything but a superficial way, as much dependent upon the tolerance of our hosts as on the superiority we attribute to ourselves as visitors and observers. This is true not only of travel, but vis-à-vis any trade, craft, or profession whose practices are not known to us firsthand. Inasmuch as social scientists are professionally devoted to crossing such frontiers, they need to remember that in broadening their minds they may well know less about everything. In fact, if we compare the practices of so-called comparative sociology with those that obtain in classical studies, very few sociologists have anything like the skills required to master local histories, languages, philosophies, art, and literature that are the basis of the monumental studies in these fields. Part of the professional sociological uneasiness with ethnomethodological studies, in my own opinion, derives from their commitment to the study of the orderliness of absolutely local phenomena, that is to say, with the fine arts whereby institutions come to have for their members a here-and-now objectivity that is for them "the world." This humbles sociological ambition. Moreover, I think it challenges the deepest prejudice of all constructivist sociology, whether critical, Marxist, or whatever.

What Schutz, Garfinkel, and Marx all rejected is the prejudice that the everyday world is meaningless unless categorized by the social scientist. What underlies this prejudice is the expropriation of the Kantian discovery that nature is a subjective construction. Positively, the Kantian discovery vis-à-vis society, which is a *moral phenomenon* and not a natural phenomenon, is that the social world is an intersubjective construction, a kingdom of ends that each wishes for all. It is curious that sociologists should indulge in ironies upon the poverty of commonsense knowledge and values when their own practices are unthinkable without such a background. In short, then, *we need to relativize science and common sense*, to allow for the positivity of common sense and to avoid the negativity of science in relation to it, thereby checking the pretension of science to absolute knowlege. Science waits no more than common sense upon logic for the construction of what is to be known in a manner external to the multiplicity of practices whereby we come to treat things as real, unreal, true, false, efficient, consistent, and the like. Sociologists are quite mistaken in imagining that natural scientists apply to their own practices of discovery standards of rationality that are wholly external to the standard of *normal practice* prevailing in the community of science.[35] Moreover, as Schutz shows, we can account for how persons accommodate or deviate from the standards of their community of belief and action through the use of the notion of normal practice as a *regulatory concept* that is implicit in the very claim to membership in any epistemic community.[36] The postulate of adequacy reminds the sociologist that it is abortive to seek a standard of rationality that is external either to the community of belief and action under study, or to his own practices as a member of a scientific community.

Indeed, there is a considerable irony in the sociologist's self-exemption from the standards of commonsense knowledge and action, when, in fact, his own marginality may render him the least able to understand them, let alone see through them. Moreover, only a moment's reflection is required to recall the variety of opinion and belief within the sociological community as to the worth of its own enterprise. It cannot be sufficiently stressed that *the commonsense world is not a reified and unreflexive praxis.* It is full of art and humor, it is explored in literature, art, song, film, and comic strips. Commonsense knowledge is far from being a poor version of science. It is self-critical and, above all, capable of dealing with the contradictions and paradoxes of social life that otherwise drive sociologists off into utopias, anachronisms, and nostalgias that make ordinary people suspicious of the intellectual's grasp of reality. We ought to reject the social science stereotype of the rigidity of custom, habit, and instinct in human affairs. It involves a false contrast between traditional and modern societies, as well as an arrogant moral posture. As Michael Oakeshott has very well observed:

> Custom is always adaptable and susceptible to the *nuance* of the situation. This may appear a paradoxical assertion; custom, we have been taught, is blind. It is, however, an insidious piece of misobservation; custom is not blind; it is only "blind as a bat." And anyone who has studied a tradition of customary behaviour (or a tradition of any other sort) knows that both rigidity and instability are foreign to its character. And secondly, this form of the moral life is capable of change as well as of local variation. Indeed, no traditional way of behaviour, no traditional skill, ever remains fixed; its history is one of continuous change.[37]

The liveliness and self-organizing nature of practical reason with respect to the contexts and local relevances of everyday life, is the fundamental ground of all sociological reflection and the touchstone of its praxis. This is not a rule of blind conservatism. It is rather a *conservationist argument*, one essential to the defense of the rationalities of everyday living against the inroads of scientistic sociology and its expert interventions that so often presume upon their privileged sense of the orders of living. The postulate of adequacy is therefore a basic proposition in what I have called *wild sociology*,[38] which ought to be understood as a great insistence upon *the kinship between sociology and common sense.*

Commonsense knowledge has been the butt of philosophy and science from the very beginning. It is only when philosophy and science reach the absurd heights of rationalism, scholasticism, and crippling asceticism that the voice of commonsense everyday knowledge gets a hearing. Then we look around for the suppressed resources of that other side of our moral tradition that has always been at grips with the dominance of scientism in philosophy, art, literature, and politics. In this tradition, as Gouldner suggests, the concept of everyday life has been an instrument as well as itself an object of struggle.[39] Throughout the ages, everyday life has been the source of resistance to the extraordinary, the mystifying, and the destructive heroism of the elites of religion, war, and commerce. The virtues of the everyday life are antiheroic, unseen, and enduring. Gouldner likens everyday life to the kind of life Western societies have imposed upon women, and I have compared it to the family of man. In either case, everyday life does not simply lead us away from politics, as Giddens and others fear.

Rather, then, everyday life points up the nature of the realm of politics and history as a realm of crisis, of constant departures from ordinary life which is at the same time leaned upon for these very departures, sending its sons to war and its food to the towns, and suffering destruction or neglect in return. The sociologist who neglects the claims of everyday life promotes the realm of crisis. Forgetful of his own attachment to everyday life, he then speaks of "discovering" social reality. This way of talking, however, merely overlooks the massive fact of the *already known* everyday world. In viewing the very same considerations as those summarized in the postulate of adequacy, Gouldner joins his earlier conception of the reflexive sociologist to the task of defending everyday life from the critical neglect of the commonplace by social scientists.

The alternative to this attention to the commonplace is to treat men as things, which is to ally sociology with the forces that already seek to dominate them or to bring about their compliant subjugation. Much of the "scientificity" of the study of man is already in the paid service of this project of political control. Moreover, it is this ambition to subjugate men that makes it necessary for scientistic sociology to express so much concern with the construction of external accounting systems for discovering patterns or order and deviance in its subject populations. This is, admittedly, the hard work of normal sociology. It is, however, not welcome to the people. For as Gouldner argues, at best the findings of such sociology will seem "obvious" or "ordinary" to them. In this, however, they reject not only the narcissism of the sociologist but also his pretended omnipotence, his claim to have reached the bottom of lives and institutions from the outside and without the pains of ordinary existence. Is there any other way? This question will always divide sociologists, for it lies at the heart of the Western embrace of domination and its increasingly ambivalent response to its own success. In the meantime, the defense of everyday life, of commonsense knowledge and values constitutes the radical task of interpretative sociology. It requires that sociologists be prepared to set aside their narcissism in order to work as the underlaborers in the world of everyday life with which in all other respects they retain kinship.

PART TWO
Method and Explanation

CHAPTER FOUR
Fact and Method in the Social Sciences
Richard W. Miller

At one and the same time, we think about methodology in the social sciences in two different ways. These ways of thinking conflict, and that conflict has crippled the social sciences.

On the one hand, we think of methodology as consisting of principles describing what a social scientist should do in pursuing his or her explanations. This first way of thinking about methodology is unavoidable. If there are no general principles describing what research and explanation should be like, there is no methodology.

The second way of thinking about methodology almost always accompanies the first, though it is usually unannounced. In the first and unavoidable view, methodology consists of principles regulating empirical social-scientific research. In the second view, avoidable but nearly universal, methodology consists of social-scientific principles requiring no research. We limit ourselves to statements about social reality that require no controversial empirical commitments. We only rely on principles of logic and the analysis of such concepts as "adequate explanation," "fact," and "value," together, perhaps, with thoroughly obvious factual considerations and armchair reflections giving rise to intuitions of the truth. The methodological, here, is the a priori.

The unavoidable conception of the goals of methodology conflicts with the pervasive conception of the basis for methodology. The questions defining the subject matter of methodology cannot be answered a priori. In the contrary view, which I shall be defending, methodology does not stand above social science, unalterable by it, like the law of the excluded middle. It includes principles governing science that might be changed in light of changes in science, like principles of telescopic observation in astronomy.

My argument will be a survey of some leading issues in the methodology of the social sciences. First, I shall consider the status of value freedom and of methodological individualism. Despite the assumptions to the contrary shared by both their partisans and their opponents, these doctrines, I shall argue, are empirical theses. They depend on controversial theories concerning the impact of social circumstances on individual psychology (including, in the case of value freedom, the social scientist's own psychology). Certain extremely plausible aspects of Marxist social theory, usually neglected in these debates, suggest nontraditional outcomes for these traditional methodological disputes.

Finally, I will discuss the two related questions: "What makes a hypothesis, if true, an adequate explanation?", and "What makes it rational to accept an explanation, in light of available data?" In the covering-law model of Hempel, Popper, and other positivists, the capacity of a true hypothesis to explain a phenomenon is just a matter of its logical relations to that phenomenon. Similarly, at least in standard and central cases, an explanation is confirmed by a body of data because of its logical relations to that data. I shall argue that this division of labor between logic and empirical theory needs to be shifted. In typical cases, adequacy and confirmation depend on empirical principles not part of the hypothesis itself or included in the data. While I shall usually contrast this new approach to the logic of explanation with the positivist model, I shall also discuss the great distance between this approach and critical theory. Here, much more than elsewhere, critical theory resembles its positivist rival, basing explanation on a repertoire of a priori principles, and accepting the positivist analysis of explanation in the natural sciences.

Value Freedom

That the social sciences should be value free is the closest thing to a methodological dogma in Anglo-American social science. It has a sacred text of sorts, Weber's methodological writings. Like many dogmas, it is often misunderstood by orthodox believers and heretics alike.

Value freedom, for Weber, includes two claims, which he constantly mixes together. On the one hand, evaluations are excluded from the content of explanations. A valid explanation of a social phenomenon never makes a value judgment.[1] A social scientist respecting this rule cannot, for example, explain the downfall of the Stuarts, in Whig fashion, as due to Stuart injustice. Note, however, that nothing in this antimoralizing principle precludes describing people's evaluations in an explanation so long as one does not endorse or disapprove them. The downfall of Stuart autocracy may well have been due to the widespread *belief* in its injustice.

Along with this constraint on the content of explanations, value freedom calls for a constraint on the context in which social-scientific explanations are pursued. Once he or she has chosen what explanatory questions to answer, the social scientist should, so far as possible, try to forget his or her extrascientific commitments in pursuing the answer.[2] The timing of nonpartisanship is crucial, here. Weber is well aware that the choice of a question guides subsequent research, that it is rational to choose more important questions over less important ones, and that judgments of importance depend on moral and political judgments.[3] Once the choice of questions has been made, however, the researcher should try to pursue the answers dispassionately, or, more precisely, warmed only by the passion for the truth as such.

Value freedom has always had its critics. But both critics and defenders have accepted common, a priorist rules of debate. They assume that value freedom, if true, depends on logical distinctions and mere common sense; if false, it depends on logical confusions or *obvious* distortions of reality.

Weber bases the exclusion of evaluation from the content of social-scientific explanation mainly on an alleged characteristic of all scientific propositions. A scientific proposition, if valid, must be demonstrable, in principle, to everyone possessing all relevant data. Value judgments, Weber claims, are not universally demonstrable, as scientific propositions should be.[4]

Depending on how demonstrability is understood, either the denial of this characteristic to all value judgments is wrong empirically, or undeniably scientific propositions cannot meet the test of demonstrability any better than some value judgments. When he speaks of demonstrability to all, Weber seems to have in mind demonstrability to all actual rational people. His examples always refer to actual cultural and political differences.[5] With typical ethnocentricity (and its political equivalent), he denies that there is hope of establishing socially significant value judgments for everyone, "even" a Chinese or a revolutionary socialist.[6]

In fact, there seem to be a number of value judgments that any actual rational person could be brought to accept, if he or she knew all relevant facts. There is no evidence of any moral framework in which chattel slavery or the Nazis' Final Solution is less than evil, when all the facts are in. Indeed, even Nazis and slaveholders speaking among themselves had to rely on false statements of fact concerning Jews and enslaved peoples to justify their actions. A justification based on the real facts, "German Jews typically have a slightly different culture from non-Jews; though a small minority, they are a somewhat disproportionate one in banking and the arts; therefore they should be killed," is as blatant a non sequitur as any blunder in scientific inference.

Perhaps, though, Weber meant to require that a scientific proposition be demonstrable (if true) not just to all actual but to all possible rational beings. In this conception, the bare possibility of an ultimate Nazi for whom the death of Jews is an intrinsic good, standing in need of no justification, makes the condemnation of the Final Solution relevantly nondemonstrable.

Perhaps no value judgment can pass this test. If not, neither can the most important explanatory hypotheses in the social sciences. In the realm of bare possibility, there exists an ultimate anti-Weberian for whom it is fundamental truth, requiring no justification, that businessmen do not let religious beliefs interfere with their business practices. Weber's own social-scientific thesis about Calvinism and the rise of capitalism could not be demonstrated to this possible being. Surely, his resistance should not deprive Weber's thesis of scientific status. Perhaps the ultimate anti-Weberian is irrational, because he does not see that this separation of religion from business requires justification. There are no grounds, however, for denying rationality to him, but not to the ultimate Nazi, who does not recognize that killing people with a certain family background requires justification.

Weber offers some other arguments for value freedom, along similar lines. I have argued elsewhere[7] that they fail for similar reasons. They depend either on a far-fetched estimate of the actual diversity among the moral outlooks of rational people, or on a standard of scientific status so high that even the most interesting and important social-scientific propositions cannot meet it.

Weber's denial that value judgments are subject to scientific argument has harmed not just the official methodology, but the practice of the social sciences. If stated at all, the value judgments that guide an investigator are usually treated as stipulations, not requiring the theoretical or empirical justification that equally basic social-scientific claims would need. Yet, often, the questioning of these evaluative assumptions is the most obvious, urgent, and coherent means of developing alternatives to the explanatory hypothesis which the investigator supports.

Consider, for example, the discussion of United States foreign policy after World War II in Theodore Lowi's *The End of Liberalism*. The failures of United States foreign policy after the Second World War are traced to the dispersal of leadership among a variety of cabinet and subcabinet departments and government agencies, allied in turn with diverse interest groups. Central to Lowi's argument is the claim that crises, which dictate temporary unification of leadership, "tend to bring out the very best in Americans," in contrast to the normal dispersal of leadership. This claim is only supported through a brief list of "postwar examples of exemplary behavior in crisis": "Greek-Turkish aid and the Truman Doctrine, the Berlin Airlift, the response to the Korean invasion, the Dienbienphu crisis of 1954, the Arab-Israeli intervention of 1956, and 1962 Cuban missile crisis, the 1967 and 1973 Arab-Israeli Wars." Lowi acknowledges in a footnote that here, as elsewhere, he makes value judgments, based, essentially, on the belief that effective United States action in foreign affairs has reflected "vital," "legitimate," and "rational" interests.[8]

Lowi's acknowledgment of his value judgments is typical of that combination of forthrightness and theoretical sophistication that have made his writings so influential. But here, as usual, labelling judgments as evaluative serves as a license for avoiding crucial arguments. What about responses to crises missing from the list: interventions in Guatemala, Lebanon, Iran, and the Dominican Republic, the response to the uprising in South Vietnam of 1956, or the response to the demonstrations which brought down the Shah in 1978? Did these crises produce initiatives reflecting a legitimate, vital and rational interest involving the people of the United States as a whole? Even among the crises on Lowi's list, is it obvious that vital and legitimate interests were rationally served by suppressing a popular uprising in Greece, by providing massive material aid for the French empire in Indochina, or by bringing the world to the brink of war over the missiles in Cuba?

Of course, an investigator must choose which issues to discuss in detail, and has a right to brief pronouncements on questions outside the chosen subject matter. But in fact it is the evaluative challenge to the legitimacy of United States foreign policy, both in crisis and in between, that has been the impetus for arguments in support of the main alternative to Lowi's own thesis: Failure and drift in United States foreign policy have reflected a fundamental opposition between the interests dominating foreign policy, on the one hand, and, on the other, the interests and fundamental moral convictions of most people in the United States and most people in the world.

77

Later, I shall argue that testing a hypothesis is always a matter of comparing it with relevant rivals. In this perspective, exiling evaluative disputes over foreign policy beyond the realm of detailed and substantive argument is a main cause of Lowi's inadequate testing of his book's hypothesis.

In practice, Weber assumes that the exclusion of evaluation from the content of explanations entails nonpartisanship in the pursuit of explanations, as well. Certainly he offers no independent argument for the latter aspect of value freedom. But the inference does not work. Even if true explanations do not evaluate, there may be contexts in which a researcher is most apt to arrive at true explanations when committed to certain value judgments. In general, the absence of certain kinds of propositions from the content of explanations does not dictate their absence from maxims governing the pursuit of such explanations. Valid astronomical hypotheses do not refer to drunkenness or sobriety. We do not explain an eclipse as due to the moon's being drunk. But it is a sound maxim only to make astronomical observations while sober.

Arguments to the effect that the social sciences should be value-laden are, typically, just as nonempirical as Weber's that they should be value-free. Often, partisans of values oversimplify Weber's thesis, then knock down their straw man with truisms. In particular, Weber's acknowledgement of the importance of values in choosing questions is widely ignored.[9] Another common strategy is to attack Weber's fact–value distinction, arguing that value judgments may be factual statements as well.[10] This is a necessary preliminary to introducing value judgments into the realm of social-scientific explanations. But it is hardly sufficient. Statements about the stars are factual, too. But few social scientists are so astrological as to suppose that they should figure in social-scientific explanations.

The question of whether the social sciences should be value-free is an empirical question. I shall try to show this by sketching a particular empirical case for a nontraditional resolution of the question of value freedom. The case depends on claims about the social basis of social thought characteristic of Marxist social theory, but shared by many non-Marxists as well. It supports the conclusion that certain kinds of partisanship are sometimes the best scientific policy, even though the best explanations do not evaluate. While I do not have space to establish the relevant empirical claims, I shall try to make them relevant and plausible. That is enough to show that value freedom is an empirical issue, and to indicate what it is like to approach methodological issues in an empirical spirit.

In their prejudices and hunches, self-ignorance and self-criticism, enthusiasms and hesitations, scientists are influenced by social forces outside of science. In the social sciences, these social forces may have an important influence on typical expectations as to what projects are apt to produce definitive, scientifically useful results. They may determine what research techniques and bodies of data are elaborated and refined. They may determine, in important ways, who becomes a famous and influential figure. When these social forces create strong pressure away from the truth, the counterpressure of certain partisan commitments to change the status quo may be more scientifically productive than neutrality.

Consider the situation of an anthropologist in the 1880's. According to the reigning ideology, the cultures of nonliterate nonwhite peoples are perhaps subhuman, at best crude simplifications of European culture. Indeed, this ideology is even embedded in grammar. In European languages in the 1880's, there is no plural for "culture," a word reserved for the traditions stemming from the ancient Greeks. As a result, research techniques and professional rewards in the investigation of nonwhite nonliterate peoples center on geography and physical anthropology, above all the intensive measurement of skulls to determine how low such peoples stand on the ladder of evolution.[11]

Along with more important costs, this ideology was the main barrier to scientific progress in anthropology. There, progress depended on the insight that nonliterate societies are held together by social and symbolic structures of great complexity. The anthropologists such as Boas who made this discovery did so through projects that were widely regarded as doomed to failure, that employed few established research tools, that challenged the views of respected figures in the profession, sometimes people of undeniable competence. Having embarked on the investigation of the social systems and mythologies of nonliterate nonwhites, these pioneers were under great pressure to give up prematurely or to come up with the wrong answers.

How are such truth-distorting pressures best resisted? One strategy is the Weberian one. The anthropologist should passionately commit himself to pursuing the truth, and should otherwise forget all moral and political commitments, whether racist or antiracist. But perhaps this vaccine would be too weak to prevent the disease I have described. If slander against someone is pervasive enough, you may have to like him and hate his enemies, if you are not to succumb to it. Perhaps, typically and over the long run, an anthropologist of the 1880's could not clearly see the complexity and ingenuity of nonliterate nonwhites if he did not sympathize with them, feel outrage at the contempt in which they were held, or hate their oppression by the colonial system. More precisely, the probable scientific gains of keeping alive one's attachment to antiracist value judgments in doing reseach might outweigh the associated risks of wishful thinking and sentimentality. If so, then an injunction to cultivate antiracist sentiments in the course of research would be better methodology than the injunction to be neutral.

There is evidence from the history of anthropology that the partisan maxim would be scientifically superior. The pioneers of modern anthropology were typically sustained by antiracist commitments during their years of fieldwork and bitter controversy. Boas, for example, always regarded the survival in his childhood home of "the ideals of the Revolution of 1848" as a crucial influence on his scientific activity.[12]

The scientific usefulness of egalitarian commitments is not only plausible for the *eighteen*-eighties. In the present-day United States, the one-fifth of one percent of the spending units who own two-thirds of the individually held corporate stock have disproportionate influence on the media, the foundations, and government, and therefore have important influences in turn on large scale projects, research tools, and the roads to fame in the social sciences. These extrascientific forces strongly support a consensus that present-day hierarchies cannot be changed and have many hidden benefits. As a result, in the real-life social setting of social science no political scientist is forced to defend the view that the United States working class (referred to by some euphemism) is deeply conservative. No economist is forced to defend the view that racism and unemployment are against the interests of corporations. In these and other cases, consensus reigns in spite of compelling contrary evidence.[13] Scientists operating outside the consensus are usually consigned to marginal status in a "left-wing" fringe. Perhaps a commitment to the truth is a sufficient defense against social pressures to conform. More likely, a lively commitment to social change is an important scientific good in the 1980's, as it was in the 1880's.

This argument for partisanship does not imply in the least that explanations of social phenomena should ever themselves include evaluations. There is evidence from the history of social science that the best explanations do not evaluate. Evaluative explanation is most promising where large social changes are explained as due to moral defects of the old arrangements. However, at least since the time of Harrington

80

and Hobbes, the most productive framework for explaining social change has appealed to the interests, resources, social relations, and cultural traditions of social groups, described in nonevaluative terms.

A social scientist operating in this framework need not be totally Weberian. He need not deny that an evaluation may yield a *true* explanation. But he will, at a minimum, regard such explanations as more vague and less fruitful than those that are yielded by the study of interests, resources, and cultural traditions. Thus, histories of slavery in the United States emphasizing the shifting resources and interests of plantation owners, slaves, farmers, industrialists, and merchants do not contradict the appeal to the injustice of slavery as a source of its overthrow. Typically, they provide at least some evidence supporting it. But the study of the political economy of the westward expansion of slavery has yielded more explanations, and more precise ones, of the history of its overthrow than the study of slavery's immorality, as such. This contrast is typical of the study of change, from English constitutional history to current debates over the Nazi seizure of power.

I have barely sketched some elements of a case for commitment to fighting inequality in the course of social research combined with the exclusion of evaluations from the explanations produced. All sorts of factual questions might be raised. That is my point, for present purposes. Value freedom is an empirical issue, not a refuge from the factual debates that dominate political controversy.

Methodological Individualism

The debate over methodological individualism raises very different issues from the value freedom controversy. But, here too, a dispute that should be empirical is traditionally based instead on conceptual analysis and the assertion of truisms.

By methodological individualism, I mean whatever methodologically useful doctrine is asserted in the vague claim that social explanations should be ultimately reducible to explanations in terms of people's beliefs, dispositions, and situations. Karl Popper, his student J.W.N. Watkins, and George Homans argue explicitly for this claim.[14] It is a working doctrine of most economists, political scientists, and political historians in North America and Britian. Neoclassical economists, and most Keynesians as well, assume that economic phenomena must be explained as due to the psychology of rational buyers and sellers. Historians and political scientists express their working commitment to individualism in protests against the mysteriousness of hypotheses in which someone's political behavior has sources of which he is not aware. "The Marxist assessment of fascism," writes one historian, "stands on metaphysical or at least transhistorical grounds and as such ordinary historical analysis can scarcely challenge it. The imputation of a class basis to diverse groups which themselves were usually supra-class in conscious ('subjective') orientation [is a hypothesis] which one must . . . either accept on faith or reject out of hand as unrealistic."[15] Two political theorists, as it happens leading critics of the pluralist establishment, ask, "Suppose there appears to be universal acquiescence in the status quo. Is it possible, in such circumstances, to determine whether the consensus is genuine or instead has been enforced by nondecision-making [i.e., the restriction of opportunities for political controversy]? The answer must be negative. Analysis of this problem is beyond the reach of the political analyst and perhaps can only be fruitfully analyzed by a philosopher."[16]

Methodological individualism is an extemely influential idea. Yet the debate over it has been dreary, in a way that is typical of methodological disputes. Partisans of individualism usually claim that it amounts to some truism, that, say, social change is the result of what people do, or that we could reverse any social process if we had appropriate beliefs and resources and the will to do so.[17] But these truistic claims are so obvious that no social theorist, not even the most holistic, not Durkheim or Marx or even Hegel, has ever violated them.

On the other side, opponents of individualism argue to the opposite effect in much the same style. They associate methodological individualism with some totally implausible doctrine, then show it is wrong. For example, it is easy to show that the vocabulary of social science cannot be defined entirely using basic terms which could refer to isolated individuals. "Bank check" cannot be so defined, much less "the state".[18]

In fact, there is an interesting doctrine which is sometimes advanced by explicit partisans of methodological individualism, and which is an important influence on the practice of much economics, history, and political science. It is the sort of methodological individualism which is worth debating. According to this thesis, large-scale social phenomena, those affecting the characteristics of enduring institutions, should be explained as due to people's reasons for acting as they do together with the resources available to them. More precisely, those explanations should refer either solely to those reasons and resources or in addition only to processes and causal connections which can be explained in turn as due to participants' reasons and resources.

This thesis cannot be dismissed a priori. It is the framework of Weber's encyclopedic *Economy and Society*, where sociology is restricted to the explanation of social phenomena in terms of the subjective meanings that participants attach to their behavior. At the same time, it is not obviously right. In particular, it is wrong if objective interests which guide a person's behavior, even though they are not his reasons for acting as he does, play a crucial social role.

The power of objective interests to guide someone's actions when they are not his reasons for so acting is a common enough phenomenon in everyday life. A friend of mine has a brother who is a nuclear engineer. He says his brother believes that nuclear plants are quite safe. In my friend's view, the reason why his brother believes this is that he wants to see his profession as socially useful. He thinks his brother has overwhelming evidence that the plants are not safe, and "should know better." At the same time, my friend is very far from saying that an interest in serene professional pride is his brother's *reason* for asserting the safety of nuclear plants. The technical considerations to which his brother appeals really *are* his reasons.

The question of methodological individualism has now become thoroughly empirical: Does a sort of mechanism that could, a priori, play a crucial role in large-scale social processes actually do so? Once again, aspects of Marxist social theory suggest a different answer from the one that dominates Anglo-American social science. In particular, the theory of ideology is crucial here. According to that theory, beliefs and behaviors of great social significance are molded by class interests in ways of which the bearers of those interests are often not aware. If this thesis is true in significant cases, then methodological individualism is wrong.

The truth, in important cases, of the theory of ideology is surely worthy of empirical investigation. Consider the spread of the so-called "positive good" doctrine of slavery in the antebellum South. Around 1820, Southern plantation owners rather suddenly stopped portraying slavery as a temporarily necessary evil, which should be allowed to die out. They began to defend it as a positive good, above all for the benefits it brought to the slaves. There is no basis for supposing the typical plantation owner lied when he or she extolled the civilizing influence of slavery. But it is not plausible that this sudden shift in opinion was actually due to an influx of evidence of the civilizing influence of slavery. A more likely candidate is the cotton gin. The gin turned slavery from an archaic relic to the basis of a thriving industry for cotton planters in the Deep South, and for the Old South slave breeders who supplied them with victims. This was not the slaveowners' reason for believing in the doctrine of "positive good." Yet, quite plausibly, it is the reason why they had this belief.

This example can stand for many others. No one can read the political and social debates under Cromwell's Commonwealth and doubt the sincerity of the religious reasoning of all sides. But historians from Hobbes to Hume to Marx to Macpherson have noticed what different conclusions were often derived from virtually identical religious premises, and have explained the divergent tendencies on the basis of rival objective interests. Closer to our time, Eisenhower, Kennedy, and Johnson may not have been lying when they based United States involvement in Indochina on the defense of freedom. But the Pentagon Papers suggest that the reason for their behavior was, primarily, an interest in continued American domination over the so-called "underdeveloped countries."

Empirical claims about how people behave are the right basis for judging methodological individualism. That thesis is neither a truism nor a confusion. It is either an empirically valid means of simplifying the range of hypotheses which social scientists must consider, or, based on empirical falsehoods, a factually inappropriate device for excluding explanations which may well be the best.

The Logic of Explanation

When is a set of propositions an adequate explanation of why a social phenomenon occurred? Obviously, an adequate explanation ought to provide true descriptions of prior conditions. Almost as obviously, this requirement is not enough. That the Kaiser sneezed before World War I broke out is hardly an explanation of the outbreak of the First World War. The argument as to what further qualifications make a set of true propositions a valid explanation is the most enduring, the most fundamental, and perhaps the fiercest dispute in the philosophy of the social sciences.

In this century, the center of the dispute has been an analysis of explanation developed by positivist philosophers out of Hume's discussion of causality. In rough outline, this analysis makes explanation, whether in the social sciences or the natural sciences, a matter of subsumption under general laws. A valid explanation of an event must describe general characteristics of the situations leading up to the event and appeal to general empirical laws dictating that when such characteristics are realized, an event of that kind always (or almost always) follows. Carl Hempel, in particular, has elaborated this so-called "covering-law model" in great detail, and defended it with unparalleled resourcefulness.[19]

Except in the writing of history, the covering-law model dominates the practice of the social sciences. The pioneers of modern non-Marxist sociology, anthropology, and economics—Weber and Durkheim, Radcliffe-Brown and Malinowski, Menger, Jevons, and Walras—all regarded subsumption under general laws as the essence of scientific explanation, and took the discovery of such laws to be the means for making the social sciences truly scientific. Commitment to the covering-law model has a powerful influence on the direction of social research. For example, when social anthropologists discovered that their fieldwork yielded few interesting general laws involving such relatively concrete characteristics as "grandfather," they did not abandon the pursuit of general laws. Many responded by seeking such general relationships among more abstract structural characteristics, such as "binary opposition." Many economists elaborate the internal logic of some general model, serenely accepting that their work makes no appreciable contribution to explaining specific episodes of inflation, unemployment, or of internal trade. The intellectual justification is, basically, that the elaboration of general models is the most promising route to the discovery of general laws, in turn an essential aspect of explanations.

Most opponents of the covering-law model work in a tradition, going at least as far back as Dilthey, that emphasizes the existence of autonomous methods in history that are radically different from those in the natural sciences. The covering-law model is regarded as an accurate analysis of natural science explanation. The crucial positivist mistake is said to be its extension of the model to the realm of social explanation. Thus for Habermas the covering-law model does describe the goal of natural science inquiry, a pursuit of general laws through experiments, guided by an interest in instrumental control over the environment. But it fails to validate the insights yielded by other sources of knowledge more important for social explanation: hermeneutic understanding, that is, the capacity to interpret the words, acts, and symbols of others in the interest of mutual understanding, and self-reflection, that is, the ability to achieve the moral knowledge and self-awareness of a responsible person through self-analysis.[20]

Despite the furious controversy between positivists and those working in Dilthey's and Habermas's hermeneutic tradition, both sides share two important common assumptions. In each framework, once we know that a set of propositions is true we can tell whether they constitute an adequate explanation without committing ourselves to further, controversial claims about social reality, based on empirical research. In the covering-law model, we need only analyze the logical relations between the hypothesis and the statement of what is to be explained. In the hermeneutic approach, we mull the hypothesis over in appropriate ways, to determine whether it satisfies relevant human faculties. Also, in both approaches, the covering-law model is accepted as an accurate analysis of natural science explanation.

These common assumptions are wrong, and disastrously wrong. They bar the way to a more accurate understanding of what counts as a valid explanation and of how explanations should be chosen in the real world of social and of natural science.

In arguing against the positivist approach and (in passing) the hermeneutic one, and in constructing an alternative model, my methods will be less empirical and my goals more modest than my earlier ones. I will be using a priori arguments to reveal the inadequacy of a priori logics of explanation. By analyzing judgments as to the circumstances in which true propositions should serve as explanations, I will try to show that such judgments depend on empirical principles. I will describe the functions that those principles fulfill. But I will not make the necessarily empirical arguments as to what those principles should be.

This modesty is dictated by the diversity of the empirical principles that give true hypotheses explanatory status. According to the alternative model I will sketch, there is no framework of empirical principles determining what counts as an explanation in all social sciences. Rather, there are particular frameworks for particular fields. Each specific framework is, in turn, highly complex, with components serving many functions. Whether a true hypothesis explains, or whether a hypothesis should be accepted as explaining, in light of given data, is determined by facts specific, say, to the study of power structures or investment decisions. My present arguments are a preliminary to an indefinite series of partial discussions, which will look more like debates over pluralist versus elite theories in political science or over Keynesian versus neoclassical versus Marxist theories in economics than disputes over the covering-law model as such.

My illustrations should be understood in light of these limitations. Often, though not always, I will be describing possible facts which would dictate the choice of a more Marxist over a less Marxist explanation. In contrast to the discussions of value freedom and methodological individualism, these illustrations are not meant to argue in favor of relatively Marxist explanatory principles. They are simply meant to show the relevance of questions of fact to questions of explanatory adequacy, in ways not recognized by either the positivist or hermeneutic traditions.

Beyond the Covering-Law Model

Valid departures from the covering-law model always turn out to be of two general kinds. The Dilthey-Habermas tradition to the contrary, these departures occur in both the social and the natural sciences. The adequacy of these explanations to explain phenomena without covering laws suggests a new theory of explanation.

In one enormous class of valid departures from the covering-law model, the true generalizations, to which one might point as establishing the explanatory role of the particular facts in question, are not empirical laws, but tautologies, truths as nonempirical as, "All bachelors are single." Suppose we discover Robert E. Lee's secret diary and read the entry for that famous morning at Appomatox: "Today, I heard that Sherman has reached Savannah, cutting the Confederacy in two. I despair of our cause. I have therefore sent a message of surrender to Grant." Surely, we are now in a position to explain Lee's surrender as due to his despair over Sherman's reaching Savannah. But to what true empirical law can we appeal as the generalization linking despair and surrender, here? Surely not, "When a general despairs of success, he surrenders." Even among Confederate generals, others, such as Thomas Hunt Morgan, well aware that their cause was lost, fought on for weeks after Appomatox. Other potential covering laws are, similarly, either false or not known to be true.[21] This should not be surprising. We do not even have a sketch of a general theory of despair with laws describing conditions in which surrender must occur.

A true generalization, showing how facts established by Lee's diary explain his surrender, might take this form: "If a general despairs of success, and if the despair is intense enough to produce surrender, given the kind and degree of stubbornness, pride, and other countervailing factors, then he surrenders." However, this generalization is not an empirical truth. "Lee despaired, his despair was intense enough to produce surrender, countervailing factors were not of a kind or degree to prevent surrender, and he did not surrender" is as absurd, a priori, as "Lee was a husband and a bachelor." What is empirical and has explanatory force is not the generalization about despair but the particular fact that Lee's despair was intense enough to produce surrender, under the circumstances.

In the explanation of human behavior, the generalization revealing the connection between cause and effect is, very often, a tautology. This is almost always so when we explain someone's actions as due to his having information that gave him good reason to act in that way. We may, for example, be guided by the tautology: "If a person who is acting rationally sees that a course of action is the best means, on balance, of satisfying his or her total interests, he or she chooses that course of action."

The central role of such tautologies in explanations of human behavior might suggest that only these explanations depart from the covering-law model by relying solely on nonempirical generalizations. Nothing could be further from the facts of natural science explanation.

After a standard examination of a sore throat, a physician takes a throat culture, and discovers a streptococcal infection. She now has a warrant for explaining the inflammation as due to the infection. But present knowledge of immunology is so primitive that she cannot even sketch a general empirical law describing conditions in which streptococci always or almost always produce inflammation. Of the typical causes of sore throats, only one, an infection, has been found. The indication that this particular infection was strong enough under the circumstances at hand to produce a sore throat is simply the sore throat itself. The generalization connecting cause and effect is a tautology: "If a bacterial infection is virulent enough to produce inflammation, given the state of the tissue infected and the rest of the body (e.g., the immunological system), then it will."

The other departures from the covering-law model are of a different kind. In these cases, we point to an empirical principle as giving the particular facts their explanatory role. But that principle is not general in the way the covering-law model requires. It is restricted to a certain time or place or person referred to by name, not marked off by general characteristics. Suppose a historian seeks to explain why a counter-revolutionary uprising with popular support occurred in the Vendée region of France, in 1793. No other such uprising occurred elsewhere. The historian finds only one relevant difference. The clergy of the rural Vendée had a unique monopoly over access to the outside world. As the Parisian government became increasingly anticlerical, the Vendean clergy mobilized the peasantry in support of the royalists. That is why a royalist uprising occurred.

This explanation might be acceptable even though we are very far from being given a general description of conditions under which a counter-revolutionary uprising must in general occur. If sufficiently philosophical, the historian might link cause and effect by appealing to some tautology. But another tactic is also acceptable. He might assert that in late eighteenth-century France, clerical monopoly of access to the outside world was sufficient to produce peasant conformity to the clergy's political interests. For all he knows, the same connection does not exist in other societies, in which peasant attitudes, relations between town and country, or other social facts are relevantly different. Sketching a general description of the difference between societies obeying this law of clerical power and those that don't is not a job he needs to perform to explain the Vendée rebellion. If in tenth-century Japan the clergy dominated peasant access to the outside world, but could not get peasants to conform to their political interests, this is not a fact he needs to explain away before he can ask us to accept his explanation of the Vendée uprising.

Many natural sciences depart from generality in the same way. Geologists explain mountain formation on the earth. They do not expect Martian mountain formation to obey the same laws. Indeed, they now have good evidence that it does not. Perhaps there are or might be other planets on which the buckling of continental plates which creates mountains here, creates ravines or great sheets of debris. At present, geologists cannot describe the general conditions under which the buckling of continental plates is bound to create mountains. Still, data from the Earth justify their claims that this process, occurring under earthly circumstances, explains the formation of earthly mountains.

That the above departures from the covering-law model are valid has considerable negative importance. Going a step further, and understanding why the imagined explainers are justified in their explanatory claims, provides the raw materials for a positive alternative theory of explanation.

In explaining Lee's surrender as due to his despair over Sherman's success, our historian relied on a diary entry and on the fact that Lee did surrender. To reach his explanatory conclusion, he employed ideas concerning the evaluation of autobiographical statements. For example, he must have been committed to some such principle as this: An intelligent general's private description of his motives for a deed actually performed is likely to be accurate, unless there is a strong motive for self-deception specific to the case at hand. This statement might be called an auxiliary hypothesis. It is a hypothesis in that it is not a statement of particular observed facts. It is auxiliary in that it is not part of the proposed explanation itself, any more than principles governing the use of telescopes are partial explanations of why the planets move in ellipses.

The use of auxiliary hypotheses is not just characteristic of particular departures from the covering-law model. It blocks an important general argument used to support the model. The assertion that an event does not merely precede another but, in addition, explains it, is often said to be unverifiable except by the testing of an implicit covering law. That is plausible so long as we view verification as the direct confrontation of a proposed explanation and a body of data. How could the explanatory connection be tested, then, except by seeking a counterinstance to the covering law of the explanation among the facts in the data? In reality, however, there are many other actors in the drama of explanation-testing, part of neither the proposed explanation nor the data by which it is confronted. They may make acceptance or rejection rational without supporting or overturning a law-like part of the explanation. Thus, though general itself, the principle for interpreting autobiographical claims supports explanations of surrenders without affirming any general law of surrendering. The role of auxiliary hypotheses changes the whole logic of explanation-testing. An adequate theory of such testing must describe these functions at the outset, not treat them as mere elaborations of the central theme, the direct confrontation of explanatory hypothesis and data.

The explanation of the Vendée uprising illustrates a related point. The division of labor between the logical and the empirical in the analysis of explanatory adequacy needs to be shifted. Judgments which might seem to depend on logical relations turn out to require commitments concerning empirical facts.

Consider a general argument often used in support of the covering-law model. A rational explainer (the argument states) must either sketch a covering law or abandon his explanation when he considers the counterexamples from other situations that might refute his explanation of the phenomenon at hand. Either our French historian abandons his explanation in light of the existence of societies in which clerical dominance of access to the outside world does not produce political dominance. Or he explains those cases away by describing relevant general properties distinguishing those societies from France in 1793. In the latter case, he has arrived at a general law of political dominance of the covering-law type.

This argument depends on the principle that anything with the logical form of a counterexample is a genuine counterexample. If someone explains the presence of G in a certain case as due to the presence of

F, he must explain away every case of *F* without *G*, or abandon his initial explanation. In fact, whether a formal counterexample is a real one depends on whether the respective situations are so similar that the same cause is likely to have similar effects in both. And that is an empirical question.

There is no reason to suppose that ninth-century Japan and eighteenth-century France are so similar that if clerical news-monopoly produces political domination in one society it will in the other. The French historian need not explain away the purported counterexample from ninth-century Japan. On the other hand, a counterexample from seventeenth-century England cannot simply be ignored. Here, the societies are quite similar, and are passing through similar revolutionary transformations. If High Church clergymen dominated access to the outside world in rural counties under the Commonwealth, and could not instigate counterrevolutionary activity, the explanation of the Vendée really is challenged. In general, the theory of explanation must allow such abstract questions as, "Does this count as a counterexample?" to be resolved, in part, by reliance on empirical claims.

The Causal Definition of Explanation

A theory of explanation that does justice to the expanded role of the empirical and to the many qualitatively different roles of empirical hypotheses will be more complex than the covering-law model. It is best seen as consisting of two different theories, an analysis of what a true hypothesis has to do in order to be an adequate explanation, and a description of general rules for deciding when a hypothesis is doing this job.

The proposed definition of adequate explanation employs causal notions, not notions of regularity or of accessibility to a hermeneutic faculty. The definition is: An adequate explanation is a true description of underlying causal factors sufficient to bring about the phenomenon in question.

By a causal factor I mean something necessary under the circumstances for the occurrence of the phenemenon in question. If Lee's surrender would not have occurred if he had not despaired over the news from Savannah, then that despair was a causal factor.

The most difficult and most promising task in the definition of explanatory adequacy is the analysis of the relevant sort of causal sufficiency. When have we described factors sufficient to bring about the phenomenon in question? The factors must be sufficient to bring it about in the circumstances at hand. But to require merely that is to require too little. In the circumstances at hand, a wave of selling in the Stock Market in 1929 produced the Great Depression. But no economic historian supposes that the Great Depression is explained by that wave of selling. The task of explaining why the Great Depression occurred largely consists of describing the circumstances in which a stockmarket crash would trigger a general economic collapse. On the other hand, to require a description of all the causally relevant factors, factors that taken together would produce the phenomenon in question no matter what the further circumstances, is to require too much. This demand would reimpose the covering-law model.

There seems to be no general rule valid a priori for distinguishing causal factors that need to be described from those which can be consigned to an undescribed background of "circumstances at hand." Rather, particular rules of causal sufficiency are part of specific theoretical frameworks, subject to empirical debate.

The history of natural science is a story of shifts from one rule of causal sufficiency to another. For example, in Aristotelian physics, there are two patterns of adequate explanation of motion. In one, the scientist derives the motion of an object from the inherent tendencies of its component elements. In the other, he or she attributes to episodes of interference any deviations from this guidance by inherent tendencies. In the latter case of deviation from the course of nature, the derivation of precise trajectories is unnecessary, indeed impossible. That this obstacle, say, produced that deviation from the course of nature in the case at hand is an adequate explanation. In the seventeenth century, a new physics arises in which an adequate explanation must describe the pushes, pulls, and impacts of matter on matter producing the trajectory in question, no matter what the circumstances. Aristotelian laxity in explaining departures from the course of nature is regarded as an admission of defeat.[22]

Sometimes, however, greater laxity is the way of progress. In many Greek and Renaissance theories of disease, disease is an imbalance among bodily fluids. An explanation of symptoms describes the increase or diminution of fluids, including all relevant circumstances, i.e., all relevant changes in ratios of fluids. In these theories, causal factors must be described which are bound to produce the symptoms in all circumstances. Later, in the germ theory of the late nineteenth century, many symptoms are ascribed to the invasion of microorganisms. Obviously, appropriate circumstances are required for infection to produce disease. A description of those circumstances is not required. In this period, scientific progress typically requires willingness to break off the task of explanation when the infectious agent has been identified.

In the social sciences, rules of adequacy are also a part of theoretical frameworks. For example, many political historians operate in a framework in which adequate explanations may simply describe actions of political leaders sufficient to bring about the event to be explained in the circumstances at hand. Thus, the downfall of the French Bourbons can be attributed to the blunders of individual kings and ministers. But other historians employ frameworks which require, in addition, the description of the social conditions which gave individual actions their power to produce large-scale effects. For them, an explanation of the downfall of the Bourbons as due to a series of mistakes is inadequate, since it does not describe the social conditions which made those blunders lethal for a whole system.

Different rules of adequacy govern the same subject matter at different times or among different explainers. But all are not equally valid. A valid rule must single out as crucial a causal factor that really does exist, as Aristotelian inherent tendencies do not. Moreover, a rule is invalid if practice guided by it is an inferior source of further discoveries. Thus, historians who tend to confine themselves to decisions of kings and ministers argue that the investigation of the social conditions giving those decisions their effects has mostly produced falsehoods and trivialities while directing attention away from important unresolved questions about the actions of the famous. If they are right, their narratives are adequate explanations of large-scale social events.

An explanation must describe causal factors sufficient to bring about the phenomenon in question under the circumstances at hand. In doing so, it must describe at least as many causal factors as required by a relevant *empirically valid* rule of adequacy. Thus, the adequacy of a true explanatory description is not determined by logic alone, but by empirical considerations.

The task of explanation has a further aspect. A description of causal factors sufficient to bring about a phenomenon is not an explanation if those causal factors lack sufficient depth. In the definition of explanation, I indicated the importance of depth by requiring that *underlying* causal factors be described.

A causal description may fail to explain through shallowness of two kinds. The factor described may be too shallow in that, had it not occurred, something else would have occurred, filling the same causal role, in a process producing the same effect. Thus, Hindenburg's invitation to Hitler to become Chancellor is sometimes portrayed as a senile blunder, involving a stupid underestimate of Hitler's political ability. Suppose this was the case. Certainly, in the actual course of events, the offer of the Chancellorship was a crucial stage in the Nazi seizure of power. Still, it may be, as some historians have argued, that the political needs and powers of German big business and of the military would have led to state power for the Nazis, even if Hindenburg had been brighter. The same destination would have been reached by a different route. In that case, Hindenburg's mistake does not explain why the Nazis came to power. Rather, the needs and powers of big business and the military are the underlying cause.

The other sort of depth depends on a kind of causal priority. Often, there are causal relations among the causal factors producing a phenomenon. Some cause others. If so, the ones that are caused may be too shallow to be explanatory. Among explanations of the Nazi seizure of power that appeal to broad social forces, some explain the Nazi regime as a revolt of the middle classes, a product of the radical rightward drift of German middle class opinion during the Great Depression. This was the initial explanation offered by the leaders of the German Social Democratic Party. Others, left-wing Social Democrats such as Neumann and Communists such as Plame Dutt, argued that the rightward turn of middle-class opinion was a result of the ideological political power of German big business, a power that resulted in the Nazi seizure of power in the conditions of the Great Depression. Both sides in this furious debate (which still continues) accept that the more Marxist explanation is not just a supplement to the "revolt of the middle classes" explanation, but a rival. If the revolt of the middle classes was just one of the means by which big business domination of Germany produced a fascist response to German economic crisis, then the Nazi seizure of power cannot be explained as due to the rightward turn of the middle class.

There is an attractive picture of explanation according to which the explainer tries to piece together an unbroken causal chain between one event and another. The requirements of depth make it clear that this picture is too simple. Whether a description of a causal chain explains depends on the location of the chain in the whole network of causal relations. To put it another way, an explanatory claim is intrinsically comparative. It does not merely describe how a phenomenon was produced. It denies that any other casual process is deeper in the two relevant ways.

94

How to Choose an Explanation

If this is, in rough outline, what an explanation must do, how should we choose an explanation in light of the evidence available to us? The complexity of the causal definition of explanatory adequacy makes it unlikely that the associated theory of explanation-testing will be as simple as the traditional ones. Radically different sorts of phenomena can function as causal factors. The realm of causal sufficiency changes from subject matter to subject matter. Considerations of depth introduce complex comparative presuppositions into the simplest explanatory claims. Still, even in the brief space remaining, I can sketch some of the main features of a theory of explanation-testing, features sharp enough to provide some guidance for social scientists.

In positivist models, explanation testing is the confrontation of a hypothesis with a body of observed facts, a confrontation whose outcome depends on logical relations between the two sides. This conception is excessively narrow along two dimensions. Explanation-testing almost always has an array of rival hypotheses as its object. More specifically, it is almost always a comparison of an alleged explanation with its current rivals. Moreover, the background against which this comparison is performed does not just consist of the supremely general realm of logic and the highly specific realm of particular observed facts, the data. A whole spectrum of intermediate kinds of knowledge is relevant.

The testing of a hypothesis typically consists of comparing it with its current rivals to see if it is superior. Thus, a scientist may accumulate all sorts of observations implied by a hypothesis without in any way confirming it. For those observations may be implied as well by a rival hypothesis. Robert Dahl's book, *Who Governs?*, is an attempt to show that independently functioning politicians, maneuvering among a wide variety of social forces, determine the direction of political change. He points to many facts entailed by this hypothesis, mainly the political triumphs of Mayor Richard C. Lee of New Haven. As it happens, these innovations and maneuvers are of the sort one would expect on most of the ruling-elite theories of political power, the rivals in the background. On these theories, one would expect a mayor to fare at least as well as local economic notables when issues are discussed in official forums. A major goal of bourgeois or power-elite dominance is supposed to be the exclusion of social decisions worth fighting about from official forums. For example, funding decisions within the bourgeoisie are supposed to provide a powerful constraint on governmental discussions. For these and related reasons, the rich data of *Who Governs?* do not confirm Dahl's hypothesis, because they are not an adequate basis for comparison.

Popper's theory of confirmation, an important variant of positivism, does account for the possible irrelevance of even a vast body of positive instances. On this view, testing is the pursuit of negative instances, observations incompatible with the hypothesis. Confirmation is the unsuccessful though strenuous pursuit of such observations. However, this theory neglects the important role of comparison in falsification. It is perfectly normal and rational for someone to remain committed to a hypothesis that conflicts with observations, i.e., is logically incompatible with some observation when the latter is combined with relevant beliefs about auxiliary hypotheses and factual circumstances. Every important explanatory hypothesis generates some anomalies of this sort. Anomalies only disconfirm when the anomaly is best explained as due to the falsehood of the hypothesis. Typically, that argument is made by showing that a rival hypothesis better explains the data. In the natural sciences, for example, a numerical result which is precisely that predicted by a hypothesis being tested is an uncommon fluke, mostly of interest for the suspicions it arouses. Deviations are interesting when they are crucial evidence for a rival hypothesis, like the small deviations from Newtonian values of the orbit of Mercury, which became of fundamental importance when they become a way of comparing Newtonian and relativist physics.

Rival hypotheses are compared against a background of beliefs occupying the whole spectrum stretching from the utterly general and a priori principles of logic to the most concrete and empirical observational beliefs. Most of these background beliefs are empirical. Most are concerned with an indefinite number of situations other than the immediate object of investigation, and are held on account of diverse evidence drawn from those other situations. Unlike hermeneutic principles, they are not valid a priori. Yet they are not, typically, either covering laws or descriptions of initial conditions. The practicing scientist ignores these empirical principles at great peril. For example, in pursuing disagreements with others, he or she may simply miss the point at issue, unless he or she is aware that propositions all along the spectrum may be at stake.

Here are the main kinds of background beliefs intermediate between particular facts and a priori principles that play a crucial role in the choice of explanations. Auxiliary principles guiding the interpretation of different kinds of data are usually crucial. They include, for example, the principle for interpreting generals' autobiographical testimony that was sketched before, and principles for interpreting images in telescopes or microscopes. They also include principles of empathy like the ones given prominence in the hermeneutic tradition.

The spectrum of relevant knowledge also includes theories, laws, and vague generalities concerning the behavior of the kind of situation in question. Some may function as covering laws. But other functions are at least as important for explanation choice. For example, principles asserting that certain situations are sufficiently similar such that similar causes are likely to have similar effects do function, as we have seen, as certificates of authenticity for counterexamples. An apparent counterexample drawn from outside the case at hand must be certified as genuine by such a principle.

Generalizations may also serve as measures of depth, telling us whether a causal description is deep enough to serve as an explanation. For example, many social scientists are committed to the vague principle that ruling classes are willing to resort to war to resolve basic but uncertain questions of dominance. They are led by this principle to deny that the aggressive temperaments of Kaiser Wilhelm, Lord Grey, and Clemenceau explain the outbreak of World War I. The particular facts about these leaders need not be in dispute. Rather a general principle is at work, implying, in light of other generally accepted facts, that less rambunctious leaders would have adopted essentially the same policies, or would have been replaced.

Finally, generalizations may function as criteria of causal likelihood, telling us when it is plausible to consider that something operates as a causal factor. Such a generalization may assert that a certain kind of phenomenon is likely to have one of a limited number of causes. For example, it might tell us that a disastrous decision by a usually competent general is likely to be the result of inadequate information, pressure of time, a rigid adherence to inappropriate tactics, or an inappropriate attitude toward risk. If we discover that just one of these causal factors is present, we are justified in supposing that it explains the disaster even if we do not go on to investigate such further possibilities as psychotic break or an unbearable toothache. Of course, such principles always presuppose that there is no special evidence already available, specific to the case at hand, that a nonstandard causal factor was operating.

Another sort of criterion of causal likelihood tells us that a certain kind of causal factor is usually the most important influence on a certain kind of behavior. Thus, in Keynesian economics, investment decisions in manufacturing are typically dominated by expectations concerning effective demand for consumers. This principle does not rule out a monetarist explanation of a slump as due to tight credit for business ventures. After all, the unusual does sometimes happen. The typically secondary may be primary, at times. But the general principle does put the monetarist explanation at a disadvantage, in competition with an explanation appealing to declining demand. Unless it is further elaborated, the monetarist explanation creates an explanatory loose end: Why were businessmen so sensitive to credit restrictions in this particular case?

Against this motley background of generalizations, the scientist chooses among rival hypotheses. The question he or she poses is, "Does reality behave as one would expect on the basis of one of these hypotheses, more so than its rivals?" The answer is regulated by background generalizations in two ways. Whether a particular observed fact among the data is more to be expected on the basis of one hypothesis than on the basis of another depends on whether it is more likely when the hypotheses are joined with the background generalizations. One would not expect Lee's diary entry to correspond to the proposed explanation of his surrender if one believed that generals' diaries are typically instruments of self-deception. In the second place, the general facts described by the background principles are themselves part of the reality with which hypotheses are compared. Such comparison occurs, for example, when "depth measures" are applied. The explanation of World War I as due to Kaiser Wilhelm's aggressive temperament might be rejected, not because it conflicts with particular observed facts about the situation in 1914, but because the identification of the Kaiser's temperament as the underlying cause conflicts with such facts together with the general fact that a ruling class, whatever the temperament of its leaders, resolves uncertain issues of dominance by violent means.

Empirical generalizations are enormously important in this theory of explanation choice. So are likelihoods, in that a hypothesis is chosen if the actual course of reality is one that would be more likely on the basis of this hypothesis than on any current rival. Is the alternative theory, then, old positivist doctrine set to a new tune?

Three differences are especially striking. For one thing, there is no suggestion in the present theory that an acceptable explanation must show why the event to be explained was certain or almost certain to occur. Often the favored hypothesis will make that event *more* likely than it would be if rival hypotheses were accepted. (Often, but not always. There is no such implication, for example, when the choice is made on the basis of the depth of the chosen explanation.) But even when this is so, we need have no basis for supposing that the event in question was likely, in absolute terms, to occur. The facts may fit the historian's hypothesis about the Vendée uprising better than any rival hypothesis. Still, he need not have brought to bear background knowledge of a law to the effect that in late eighteenth-century France clerical monopoly of access to the outside world almost always produced dominance. Rather, by comparing rival hypotheses, he argues that political dominance resulted in this particular case. He is not offering us a crystal ball through which he could have predicted the occurrence of an uprising in the Vendée even if the episode had been erased from the historical record.

In the second place, the generalizations in the background typically do not function as covering laws. Indeed, they need not, in any way, be part of the preferred hypothesis. For example, the principle that generals' diaries are usually accurate does not describe a causal factor bringing about surrenders. Finally, there may be indispensable generalizations in the background that are restricted in scope to particular periods and places, mentioned by name, say, "late eighteenth-century France" or "post-Renaissance European countries overthrowing absolutist monarchies." Thus, although generalizations are enormously important in the present model, they may be generalizations of different kinds, functioning in different ways, and achieving different goals from the positivists' covering laws.

In effect, this discussion of explanation-testing has been limited to an ideal case in which background beliefs are uncontroversial bits of knowledge. But what about the real world? How should rival explanations be compared when background beliefs are themselves controversial or in doubt? A grasp of the logical functions of background principles makes it possible to lay down some rules for a rational response to this enduring problem in the social sciences. I will sketch a few of the most general maxims.

One pair of maxims might be called the principles of explanatory risk. One face of this Janus figure looks to the risks of commitment to background principles, the other to the risks of noncommitment. On the one hand, the choice of an explanation does not have a stronger justification than the weakest background principle necessary for that choice. Greater respect for this principle would improve the practice of the social sciences, forcing social scientists to describe their most dubious background principles. For example, an economist following this maxim would not frustrate our desire to know what we have to believe to accept his explanation of inflation. On the other hand, many social scientists need to be more vividly aware of the perils of noncommitment. A choice may depend on the absence from the explainer's framework of a principle to which others are committed. If so, the certainty of that choice is no greater than the certainty that the others are wrong. For example, social scientists sometimes believe that they play it safe when they dispense with theories identifying social forces and their inevitable results. But agnosticism has its risks, here. If the omitted theories are right in relevant respects, the agnostics' explanations may from their superficiality fail to explain.

One further maxim is a principle of fair play. In the real world of social science, an explainer is frequently confronted with hypotheses that are only plausible in frameworks other than his own. In this situation, he does not make a valid argument against those alternatives, if his argument depends on unsupported premises which are invalid in the alien frameworks. Dahl's argument that a coalition centered on the mayor, rather than dominance by an economic elite, shaped New Haven urban renewal, is invalid if it assumes measures of influence which conflict with the framework principles that generate the hypothesis of a ruling economic elite. Who among us has not sinned in this way? The path of righteousness, here, is to identify the crucial framework differences, and to conduct the argument over these differences using facts and principles acceptable in both frameworks.

This description of a logic of explanation has been sketchy and tentative. Whatever the problems of detail, if the underlying theory is basically right, traditional expectations are thoroughly wrong. The logic of explanation is traditionally expected to be a useful tool for excluding proposals as pseudoexplanations, unworthy of empirical research. In fact, the principles enabling us to judge whether a set of true propositions really explains are themselves empirical. Rather than helping scientists avoid empirical controversy, the logic of explanation should show them how their explanations depend on a variety of controversial empirical principles, usually resting on evidence far afield from the immediate object of explanation.

Conclusion

I will end with a historical speculation. I have defended a series of methodological principles which are not implausible, when stated, and which are often followed in practice by social scientists. Yet in the United States and Great Britain, explicit discussions of methodology almost always deny or ignore the scientific uses of partisanship, the role of nonsubjective interests, or the possibility of empirical but non-relativist standards of explanatory adequacy. That is a puzzle.

The answer may lie in the common effect of these denials. They make Marxism methodologically suspicious. Marxism is a result of partisan inquiries, emphasizes the role of objective interests, claims objective validity for explanations which are neither covered by general laws nor validated by empathy. A social history of methodology would show, I think, that methodological discussion has largely been used in universities as a way of excluding Marxist and other subversive theories without engaging in empirical controversy. (A kind of technological determinism can render Marxism itself nonsubversive, but that is another story, about other countries.) Methodology, I would suggest, has been significantly shaped by a tendency to avoid certain factual controversies. No wonder that the irrelevance of facts has become an underlying principle of methodology itself.

CHAPTER FIVE
General Laws and
Explaining Human Behavior
Brian Fay

I

In this paper I argue for three major theses that are often thought to be antithetical to one another. The three theses are: first, that explanations of human behavior in terms of its reasons (beliefs, desires, motives, goals) rest upon general laws because such explanations are causal in nature; second, that it is extremely unlikely that these general laws are statable in the intentionalist vocabulary of the social sciences; and third, that the social sciences must be genuinely theoretical if they are to be at all viable.

My purpose in this is, in the first instance, to present a model of the role general laws and what I shall call causal generalizations have in the explanation of human behavior. But there is a second, larger purpose as well, namely, to outline a picture of social-scientific theory. Briefly stated, I hope to show that, although general laws properly so called will not emerge from the social sciences, a certain sort of genuinely theoretical science of human behavior is still possible. The "sort" I have in mind is what is sometimes called Critical Theory. The paper is ultimately concerned to show, therefore, that a proper understanding of the nature and basis of the causal explanations of human behavior leads to a critical metatheoretic conception of social-scientific theory.

II

There is a widespread belief among certain (mostly post-Wittgensteinian) philosophers in what I shall call the "singularity thesis of human action."[1] According to this thesis, reason-explanations can account for human action without invoking or presupposing any general law; in the words of Hart and Honore, this thesis consists of the claim that, "The statement that a given person acted for a given reason does not require for its defense generalizations asserting connections between types of events."[2] This thesis, if it were true, would have profound consequences for any science of action, for it would mean that the explanations in this science would be particularistic, and it would mean that such a science could not be genuinely theoretical.[3] Instead, the social sciences involved in explaining action would be confined to elaborating the character of the particular reasoning process that results in the performance of certain historically located events: They would be backward looking, ad hoc, and ideographic.

I wish to begin by examining what I take to be the two most compelling arguments for this belief, and to show why I think they are mistaken. These two arguments might be called the "logical-connection argument" and the "essential-nature argument." My aim in doing this is to demonstrate, in an indirect manner, that reason-explanations do rest on general laws.

One major support for the singularity thesis is the claim that the connection between that which explains an action and the action itself is a logical one, and that therefore this connection is both intuitively clear and qualitatively different from the relationship which exists between events which figure in causal explanations.

Thus, William Dray maintains that reason-explanations invoke principles of action (as opposed to empirical laws) to explain human behavior, and that the relationship between principles and their outcomes is not essentially one of a recurring pattern, but is rather one in which the outcome (in this case the action) is intrinsically (logically, conceptually) connected with the principle itself. Reasons give the grounds for which the action is a consequent, and, since the relationship between ground and consequent is logical rather than empirical, he argues that reason-explanations do not require general statements linking a kind of reason with a kind of action.[4]

To take a concrete case. Alasdair MacIntyre, in his well-known (though now self-repudiated) article, "A Mistake about Causality in Social Science,"[5] analyzed Max Weber's explanation of the rise of capitalist behavior in terms of certain theological beliefs of Protestants. He concluded that, just because the connection between these beliefs and actions is a conceptual one, Weber's tactic of supporting his thesis by embedding it in large-scale historical generalizations was irrelevant; as MacIntyre wrote:

The use of Mill's methods is entirely out of place; we do not need to juggle with causal alternatives. India and China do not strengthen and could not have weakened his case about Europe. For it is not a question of whether there is a purely contingent relationship between isolable phenomena. And so constant conjunction is neither here or there.[6]

Now, in this argument I wish to support Weber against MacIntyre, for I want to maintain that explanations of particular kinds of action in terms of particular sorts of reasons do in fact rest on at least implicit general laws.

The crucial mistake in the logical-connection argument lies in its account of the way reason-explanations account for an action. According to it, explaining an action involves specifying the reasons that rationalize it, i.e., that show it to be the appropriate thing for the agent to have done, given his situation. However, this account is inadequate because it does not distinguish between those beliefs and desires that are a reason for the behavior but that did not cause it to happen ("a" reason for doing it) from those which in fact were responsible for its occurrence ("the" reason for doing it).

The distinction that is relevant here is between acting *and* having a reason and acting *because* of that reason. In the former case an agent may have a reason for his behavior, and it may therefore have been a rational and justifiable thing to have done. But unless the having of this reason was the cause of the agent's acting as he did, the reason does not explain the act, i.e., it does not show that the act occurred because the agent had the specified reason.

Broadly speaking, reason-explanations succeed in explaining when they show that it was because the agent thought that the act was the appropriate way to achieve his ends that he acted as he did. In other words, it isn't the reason that explains the act, but rather the agent's *having* this reason, and this having caused him to act in the way he did, that explains it. In another article, I have described this by saying that we explain the behavior in question in discovering the agent's practical reasoning processes that brought it about.[7]

If explaining an act by means of a reason-explanation is knowing the reasoning process which caused it, then I think it can be demonstrated that such explanations implicitly rest on general laws. Such a demonstration is a simple matter if one adopts a broadly Humean construal of causality. It is much more complex if one subscribes to a broadly realist construal of causal explanation. I will discuss each of these in turn.

On a broadly Humean construal of causality, a claim that x causes y involves the claim, among others, that x is regularly related to y. Thus, to employ Mill's account of the regularity thesis, to say that x causes y is to say that x is a sufficient condition of y's occurring, and/or that it is a necessary condition as well. But relations of necessary and sufficient conditionship obviously rest on general laws. For any claim that x causes y in the sense that x is a necessary and/or sufficient condition of y involves the assumption that whenever x occurs y will occur, ceteris paribus (otherwise x cannot be a sufficient condition of y), or that whenever x does not occur y will not occur, ceteris paribus (otherwise x cannot be a necessary condition of y), or both.

Given a realist construal, the matter is somewhat different.[8] According to the realist, providing a causal explanation of the form "x causes y" is to relate x and y by means of an actual mechanism which, in suitable conditions captured by "x," generates the observed outcomes described as "y." (The realist doesn't intend anything specifically mechanical by the term "mechanism." Thus, a practical reasoning process could itself be such a mechanism. Indeed, my account of reason-explanations as causal in form is broadly realist in that, on my reading, the reasons of the actor are connected to his behavior by means of real psychological reasoning processes.) In the realist view, causal explanations may start with an observed regularity between x and y, but this regularity is only evidence that a causal relationship actually exists. Only when the underlying mechanism that has certain natural powers is discovered can a genuine causal explanation be said to have been given. It follows from this, according to the realist, that causal explanations do not therefore rest on general laws.

But does this follow? I think not.[9] The reason why is that the realist's account of causal explanation surreptitiously smuggles Humean regularities back in on another level. The realist invokes a basic mechanism as a way of explaining why a particular sort of event will occur in certain circumstances. This mechanism is meant to have a particular nature such that, subject to conditions of an appropriate kind, it will perform in a specific manner. But all of this presupposes that there is a regular operation of the mechanism, that under certain circumstances the mechanism will act in a predictable manner. If this were not the case, then invoking the mechanism would not be genuinely explanatory, because then one would need to know why the mechanism worked as it did to produce the effect y in the case at hand. It is only because the notion of a causal mechanism carries with it the backing of a general law that such a mechanism can be a relevant part of a causal explanation.

To this the realist has an answer. He will claim that knowledge of the underlying mechanism does not consist of general laws that supposedly govern its operation; rather, such knowledge consists of knowing the "nature" or "essence" of the mechanism in question, and this includes knowing the powers that it has. This response is thus a variant of the second major argument which supports the singularity thesis, namely the essential-nature argument.

I will turn almost immediately to the essential-nature argument, but before I do so I want to point out that no matter how one interprets either the Humean or the realist construal of causal explanation, both accounts agree as to the relevance of generalizations in the assessment of causal explanations. In the case of the Humean, this is so because causal explanations just are generalizations of a certain sort. In the case of the realist, this is so because generalizations indicate that deeper causal mechanisms are at work. Thus, insofar as reason-explanations are a type of causal explanation, generalizations linking particular beliefs and desires with particular actions will be relevant in determining the worth of the explanation at hand. This is directly contrary to the singularity thesis.

Thus, to return to the example of Weber, it may well be the case that even though the matrix of beliefs, desires, values, and so on associated with Calvinism is an initially appealing explanation because it rationalizes capitalist behavior, and because it invokes elements in the experience and thought of a group of people that appear to be crucial motivational factors in their lives, it is indeed false. For it may well be the case either that many of the particular Protestants who did possess the relevant beliefs and desires nevertheless did not in fact act in the way that Weber thought they did, and/or that many people acted in a capitalist manner who were not in fact Protestants. If this turned out to be so, then Weber would have had to reject his interpretation as the explanation of capitalist behavior because he would now be in possession of evidence which indicated that "a" reason for the puzzling behavior was not, upon empirical investigation, "the" reason why people behaved as they did.[10]

So far I have argued that reason-explanations are causal in nature, and that on at least one construal (the Humean) of causal explanation this means that reason-explanations rest on general laws. I have also argued that another construal of causal explanation (the realist), though apparently not nomological, actually is so at a deeper level. Insofar as these arguments are right, the singularity thesis cannot be correct. However, I did allow that the realist could salvage his case by invoking the essential-nature argument, and I said earlier that this argument was itself one of the most important supports of the singularity thesis. I must, therefore, consider this argument.

The essential-nature argument amounts to the claim that good explanations are those which ultimately rest on an account of the nature of the basic entities involved. Knowing that the essence of an entity is to act in a certain manner means that the operation of this entity does not require further explanation in terms of some general law under which one could subsume its fundamental dispositions. Thus, to turn to the case of a practical reasoning process, the essential-nature argument says that, because it is part of the very nature of such a process to result in an action, the relationship between coming to have a reason and the action which this event explains is immediately apprehensible without recourse to any generalizations. We don't need to see the occurrence of these two events as instances of some generally recurring pattern in order for the occurrence of one to explain the occurrence of the other once we know what a practical reasoning process is. Thus, for example, when one is told that a person crossed the street because he inferred from his belief that this was the only way to buy cigarettes, and from his desire to have a smoke now, that he ought to cross the street, this explanation appears satisfying in itself: One doesn't need any further information to the effect that the person was of type x, and type x people engaged in type y reasoning act in z type way, because one can understand the relationship between the reasoning process and the act immediately.

Now it *is* a fact that in explaining an action we grasp a connection between a singular *explanans* and a singular *explanandum* such that we do not feel the need to subsume them under some general statement. But this is not because reason-explanations are not causal in form (as the logical-connection argument would have it), nor because the causal powers of the mechanism involved in producing the act involve some sort of "natural necessity" that does not admit or require further explanation in terms of a general law (as the realist would have it). *The reason is that reasoning processes are partially defined in functional terms.* One doesn't feel the need for general laws when explaining act z by the agent's desire for y and his belief that his doing z is the best means for achieving y, any more than we feel the need for a general law when we explain why a person feels relaxed by the fact that he ingested a tranquilizer. In neither case do we feel the further need for a general statement which supports the particular causal explanation, because the disposition to produce certain sorts of outcomes is built right into the concept "desire" and "practical reasoning process" just as it is built into the concept "tranquilizer." In both sorts of cases, discovering that the cause of an event is another event or object which is identified as one which characteristically produces events of the first type is (psychologically) satisfying in itself as an explanation.

Indeed, it is because reasoning processes (and poisons and tranquilizers) are entities specified at least partially in functional terms that scientists are generally interested in those cases in which they *don't* operate, i.e., when their causal force is defeated by external circumstances. In these cases, what is sought is some law which states that when a particular set of (necessary) conditions is not present, then the expected causal force of the entity will be inoperative. In other words, with functionally defined causes the general laws which are usually sought are those which explain their *breakdown* rather than their operation, just because in "normal" circumstances the entity's being of a certain kind is a sufficient condition for the occurrence of a certain event.

But it certainly does not follow from this that in the normal cases in which the appropriate effect is forthcoming the relationship between the explanans event and the explanandum event does not presuppose a general law to the effect that under normal circumstances these kinds of events are related in a specified way. On the contrary, as I argued above when I showed that the realist smuggles Humean regularities into his account of causality, it presupposes just this sort of statement. For to characterize entities functionally is partly to characterize them in terms of the general causal outcomes that they will produce.

Moreover, it is a deep mistake to think with the realists that explanations in terms of "basic nature" and "causal power" are as deep as science can go. For one of the ways that science progresses is specifying in more detailed and sharply defined terms under just what circumstances these sorts of events are related. Furthermore, in this process of articulating the general laws which govern the relations between functionally defined entities and certain events, it is quite often the case—contrary to Charles Taylor's thesis of asymmetrical explanation[11]—that the scientist will try to (causally) explain just why it is that a certain entity ordinarily produces the effects that it does.

Thus, while a relaxed condition is a natural and in some sense privileged outcome of a person's taking a tranquilizer—in Taylor's words, there is a certain "bent or pressure of events towards a certain consummation," an outcome which "does not come about by 'accident' but is somehow part of its 'essential nature'"[12]—the neurophysiologist will certainly try to explain why this is the case by investigating the neurochemical processes through which the tranquilizer causes this result. And in the same way, a psychologist may well try to explain why it is that people of a certain sort who engage in particular reasoning processes will ordinarily or "naturally" behave in a certain manner, by referring, for example, to their schedules of reinforcement or to the development of their mental capacities. The reason for this *further* level of explanation is not only the commonplace one that science seeks to include phenomena in a wider and wider range explainable by a smaller and smaller number of principles, but as well the more pertinent one that explanations in terms of functionally characterized entities tend toward the vacuous (á la the explanation of Molière's opium in terms of its dormitive powers).

Thus, though it is often the case that we feel satisfied with an explanation of an action which specifies the particular desires and beliefs which brought it about, and that we feel it is unnecessary to invoke a general law in virtue of which the particulars of our explanation would be seen to be instances of a generally recurring pattern, these psychological facts should not blind us to the logic of the situation. For these psychological facts are rooted in the peculiar feature of our characterizations of the mental events which cause actions, namely, that they are partially functional characterizations; and functionally characterized events are so characterizable just because we believe that they regularly produce certain outcomes, and thus that some general law involving their description is in the offing. This is why singular explanations which invoke functionally characterized events do not seem to require subsumption—the general law is implicitly brought into the situation in the very meaning of the description of the particular causal event. Moreover, it should not be forgotten that although we often do not seek to elaborate these general laws, social scientists must try to discover the larger causal patterns in virtue of which these conditions hold.[13]

If what I have argued so far is correct, then two conclusions can be drawn. The first is that reason-explanations account for actions by seeing them as the causal outcome of certain mental events, namely, practical reasoning processes. The second is that because they are causal and because causal explanations are essentially nomological, reason-explanations necessarily rest on general laws, at least implicitly.

However, there is a glaring fact regarding the explanations of action that seems to conflict sharply with my whole analysis of the nomological foundation of reason-explanations. The fact is that we *do* presently have reason-explanations for all sorts of actions, but we do *not* have available to us any general laws properly so called which link the having of certain reasons with the performing of certain actions—indeed, we are far more certain of singular causal connections than we are of any putative law governing the cases in which we assert their existence. (Thus, for example, Weber's causal generalizations are not general laws.[14]) This fact lends credence to the singularity thesis, and it seems to undermine the nomological thesis that I am supporting.

However, the drawing of such a conclusion because of this fact would be a result of a deep misunderstanding of the nature of the nomological thesis.[15] For this thesis does not consist of the claim that for every particular causal explanation there is ready at hand a general law under which it can be subsumed; indeed, the thesis does *not* entail even that it be known what form the relevant general law would take if it were statable. All that the nomological thesis asserts is that there is *a* general law under which the events invoked in a causal explanation fall.

There are three important ways in which it can be seen that this is so. In the first place, there are many cases in which the claim that "*x* causes *y*," or even that "*x*'s cause *y*'s" is true, and yet the general laws under which such claims are subsumed involve no use of *x* and *y* at all. In such cases the events which we initially described as *x* and *y* are redescribed by means of *a* and *b*, and only then are they linkable by means of a general law. It is quite consistent with the nomological thesis that the general law which figures in a causal explanation be formulated in terms quite unlike those used to assert a particular causal connection or even a particular type of causal connection.

Indeed, it is normally the case that scientists have had to redescribe events which they believed (correctly) to be causally related in order to be able to formulate the general laws which govern them. Thus, for example, it was necessary to redescribe the event type originally described as "the production of warmth" as "the increase in molecular motion" in order to generate the causal laws governing heat.

In this discussion, an extremely important, if a relatively obvious, point to remember is that phenomena as such are never explained, *but only phenomena as described in some way.* And it is also important to remember that there may be any number of different descriptions of the same phenomenon. By keeping in mind these two considerations, one can easily see how events that are described in one set of terms, and related to one another by means of these terms, may well be redescribed in conceptually quite dissimilar terms from those employed in the original description, and, as a result, only then be able to be seen as part of a generally recurring pattern of events.

Of course, in order for this to happen there must be a specific kind of relationship between the terms describing the events in question. In the first place, there must either be an equivalence in their extension, or at least the extension of the first term must be a subset of the extension of the second, redescribing term. In the second place, the redescribing terms must figure in a more comprehensive theoretical scheme that allows one to understand why the event as initially described could have the causal power ascribed to it, and that gives one the capability of articulating more general and more precise formulations of the causal relationships involved.

I should mention in passing that the sorts of considerations I have been discussing are particularly apt in the context of the philosophy of social science, since there seems to be a widespread belief among a number of its practitioners from quite divergent perspectives in what I call "the doctrine of superficial generalization." This doctrine holds that if one claims one event is the cause of another event, one is thereby claiming that the law upon which this explanation rests will consist of the very same terms as used in the particular descriptions of these singular events. Hart and Honore appear to be holders of this doctrine when they write: "To make such a singular causal statement is therefore to claim that the events which it relates are instances of such a universal connection between types of events."[16] And an instance of this doctrine can be found in Hempel's famous article, "The Function of General Laws in History"; there, in trying to demonstrate that the explanation of particular historical events requires a covering law, he writes:

> Now the assertion that a set of events . . . have caused the event to be explained, amounts to the statement that, according to certain general laws, a set of events *of the kinds mentioned* is regularly accompanied by an event (of the kind for which an explanation is sought).

And then he says by way of example:

> Consider, for example, the statement that the Dust Bowl farmers migrated to California "because" continual drought and sandstorms made their existence increasingly precarious, and because California

112

seemed to them to offer so much better living conditions. *This explanation rests on some such universal hypothesis as that populations will tend to migrate to regions which offer better living conditions.*[17]

Here the law which Hempel adduces is simply a more general version of the singular explanatory statement itself.[18]

This doctrine has often been responsible for objections to the nomological thesis on the grounds that social scientists are quite often willing to accept a singular explanatory statement which asserts a causal relationship between two events, and yet to deny the truth of any putative law or causal generalization formulated by using the same terms found in the singular explanation.[19] Thus, no matter how Hempel formulates his "universal hypothesis," it seems extremely implausible that we would be willing to accept it, even though his particular causal explanation seems evidently to be true. And this wedge between the particular and the general is supposed to demonstrate that the nomological thesis is false.

But it shows no such thing. For this sort of objection is rooted in the mistaken assumption that the nomological thesis consists of the claim that the laws which a particular explanation instantiates will be formulated in the same sorts of terms as those to be found in the descriptions of the particular case. In fact, however, the nomological thesis only asserts that there must be a covering law in order for a singular causal statement to be true; and it is quite in keeping with this that the actual laws that do cover these instances will be formulated in terms other than those found in the particular explanation.

The second important way in which it can be seen that a holder of the nomological thesis is not committed to the truth of any available general law, even though he is willing to assert the truth of some singular causal explanations, is to see that it is perfectly consistent with this thesis that there not be available a law under which a true particular causal statement is subsumable. For, as I have already had occasion to mention, all that the thesis maintains is that there is a law; but it does not follow from this that this law be currently known. Thus, for example, it is perfectly consistent for someone to claim that smoking causes lung cancer (under certain circumstances), to believe that such a claim rests on a general law which links together the two events now described as "smoking" and "the development of lung cancer," and yet to admit that as of this moment no such law exists. Indeed, it is probably the case that a majority of those causal ascriptions which both ordinary people and natural scientists currently make are not supported by fully adequate general laws. And thus it is no argument against the relevance of the nomological thesis for human behavior that although we are willing to believe a whole array of causal statements linking motives, beliefs, desires, and values with actions, we cannot provide a genuine general law under which they are subsumable.

Of course (as the example of smoking clearly shows), it does not follow from this that generalized statements and a whole range of empirical evidence are not therefore relevant to our making singular causal ascriptions. On the contrary, in order to provide an adequate causal explanation, we must have good evidence for believing that full-fledged causal laws which cover the relevant events actually exist. I will take this up again in Section IV; at this point I just wish to forestall a possible misinterpretation to the effect that, since the nomological thesis apparently does not require that there actually exists a formulated general law for every (true) causal explanation, it allows us to dispense with the need for generalizations of any sort.

The third important way in which it can be seen that the nomological thesis is consistent with the glaring fact that we presently do have reason-type causal explanations (some of which are undoubtedly true), but that we do not have available to us any general laws properly so called, is really only a product of the first two ways. This is that it is certainly possible for someone to be a proponent of the nomological thesis and at the same time believe that the general laws under which his singular causal explanations are subsumable will not be formulated in the same terms as those found in the causal explanations he presently gives.

Thus, for example, a historian may assert that soil erosion and the decline of agricultural production in a particular area are causally related, and he may assert this even though he also believes that it is impossible to formulate the laws which link these events by using such a gross term as "soil erosion." In fact, he may even believe that the event which he now describes as soil erosion will have to be redescribed in terms of a radically different sort before the appropriate law could be forthcoming—for example, it may be that he will have to introduce quite determinate physical concepts drawn from chemistry, such as the relative amounts of nitrogen, etc.

To borrow a distinction from Davidson,[20] the generalizations we have may be either *homonomic* or *heteronomic*. Homonomic generalizations are those whose positive instances give us reason to believe that the form and vocabulary of the finished law will be of the same type as the generalizations themselves; heteronomic generalizations are those which lead us to believe that the precise law at work can only be stated by switching to a different vocabulary altogether. Thus, in terms of our example of soil erosion, this causal explanation involves a heteronomic generalization.

The important point about heteronomic generalizations is that they allow for the possibility of one's developing a whole range of causal stories without at the same time committing oneself to the belief that the general laws which underlie these stories will be formulated in the same terms that one is currently employing. We need not wait on the actual development of the relevant scientific theories before offering causal explanations of the events around us. And we may offer these explanations even though we might well expect that ultimately the laws which govern the phenomena involved will be expressed in a radically different terminology from what we currently employ.

With this understanding of the nomological thesis—and particularly the possibility of heteronomic generalizations—I wish to turn to the social sciences that explain human behavior, with an eye toward understanding the nature of the causal explanations which they can and do offer. In particular, I want to examine whether it isn't the case that the causal generalizations found in these social sciences aren't heteronomic. For if this is the case, it will point to a deep difference between the sciences of intentional action and the sciences of nature.

III

In this section I hope to demonstrate that there is a good reason to believe that the laws which underlie the causal processes of mental events that bring about actions will not be forthcoming at the level of discourse that social scientists use to describe and explain actions, namely, intentional discourse. I want to show that the generalizations they employ possess features which make them unusable in highly deterministic theories, and which make them incapable of being indefinitely refined so that they might become so usable; that is, that they are heteronomic generalizations. In the social sciences there are genuine causal explanations rooted in genuine causal generalizations about how certain kinds of people think and act in certain sorts of circumstances; but these generalizations are *not* genuine laws, nor is it at all probable that they ever will be purified into general laws properly so called.

In order to see why this is the case it is crucial to understand that the identity of intentional objects and events described as such is partially a function of the propositional attitudes which they embody. Another way of putting this is that intentional objects are what they are partially in virtue of their content, i.e., in virtue of the ideas they instantiate. Thus, for example, an arm extended from the window of a turning car is an act of signalling partly because of the beliefs and desires which it expresses. This means that the very identity of human actions, institutions, and psychological states is partially determined by the conceptual distinctions on which they rest. We might call these conceptual distinctions the "constitutive meanings" of an intentional object.

As an example of this from social science, take the nature of the political realm. What politics is in a given social setting (i.e., what the nature and function of government is; what political power is; what political relationships consist of; and so on) depends to a large extent upon the ideas which the actors themselves hold, at least implicitly. Thus, the nature of political behavior can be a profoundly different thing depending on whether one is referring to the political activity in an African tribe, or the ancient *polis*, or Elizabethan England, or twentieth-century America; and the reason for this is that the political realm in each of these societies is rooted in fundamentally different constitutive meanings. This is, of course, a fact well recognized by social scientists; and a book like Samuel Beer's *Modern British Politics* is an exceptionally good one in showing how the periods in the political life of modern Britain are in some sense discontinuous partially because each of them has been structured around different sets of beliefs about the nature of the political.

The situation is similar for the mental phenomena which figure in the explanations of social behavior. Mental states and events are representational states and, as such, are what they are by virtue of what they are about, i.e., their contents. Thus, one belief is distinguished from another by specifying the content of each belief—the belief that it is cold outside is distinguished from the belief that it is warm outside by indicating *what* a person is committed to by virtue of having either of these beliefs. And the same is true for desires, motives, perceptions, and the like.

Now, an extremely important fact is that the self-understandings which constitute social and psychological objects and events are inherently historical because they are subject to the constant change resulting from the various conceptual innovations which a group's members introduce and come to accept.[21] These conceptual innovations assume a bewildering number of types and forms, and they may arise from any number of sources both internal and external to a given social group. (Of course it is true that rates of conceptual change may vary widely, that there are some kinds of societies which are more resistant to such changes than others, and that there are even some that institutionalize means by which such changes can be prevented. But *all* societies, even the most closed and isolated, are subject to the developments of thought occasioned by changes in what must be done to survive and prosper, by the shifting of relationships within the social whole, by contact with foreign groups, and by the widespread tendency of humans to ask further and further questions about their world.)

Thus, to return to our example of the political realm, starting in the seventeenth century in Western Europe, people gradually came to understand themselves and others as the possessors of individual rights. Now, this new self-understanding marks the occurrence of a real conceptual innovation that not only changed the way people—both theorists and laymen alike—talked *about* their political relationships and institutions, it also altered the very nature *of* these relationships and institutions as well. For example, governments had limits placed on their activity which they never had before, and they had duties to perform—such as defending the civil liberties of their citizens—that were essentially new. Such changes are themselves only moments in a continually evolving historical process in which the ideas that form the social space of people's lives alter and shift and combine in novel ways.

In fact, the kinds of historical changes that I am discussing are not merely accidental ones in human life (in the way in which a change in the average height of humans is accidental). For human beings are self-educable creatures capable of transforming the social and natural settings in which they live, and themselves in the process. That is, it is one of the distinguishing features of humans that they reflect on their experience and, within a certain range, alter the forms of this experience as a result of this reflection. Human life is essentially historical, not because changes in how it is lived have occurred, but because parts of these changes have been authored by the participants themselves in this historical process. I shall return to this point at the end of the paper, for it will serve as the foundation of my remarks on the critical theoretical character of social science.

The crucial point in all of this for my purposes lies in the pragmatic epistemic unpredictability of these sorts of conceptual innovations.[22] In a very well-known argument, Maurice Cranston has shown that it is logically impossible for anyone to make predictions about the occurrence of conceptual innovations,[23] and though this is *not* the argument I wish to make here (for reasons which will become clear in a moment), a brief examination of it will be useful in order to bring out what would be involved in making predictions about the future course of human beliefs.

Stated simply, Cranston's argument is that in order to predict an invention (whether conceptual or mechanical is immaterial) one would already have to be in possession of it; but if this is the case, then one couldn't be said to predict its novel appearance at some time in the future. The example he employs is the corkscrew, which he supposes to have been invented in 1650. In order to be able to predict at 1650 - n that in 1650 the corkscrew would be invented, the predictor would have to know at 1650 - n what a corkscrew is; but if this were the case, then he himself would be the inventor of this gadget, not the poor fellow in 1650. Trying to predict the discovery of an invention puts the predictor in the self-contradictory position of predicting at time $t - n$ the invention at t of a device that he himself had known of at $t - n$!

The same situation would exist in the case of a predictor trying to forecast in 1890 that Albert Einstein would originate the Special Theory of Relativity in 1905. For in order to be able to do so, the predictor would have to know at least roughly the contents of the Special Theory, and this means that Einstein could not have been the discoverer of the theory. Once again, the predictor would be in the logical bind of predicting the creation in the future of something already in existence.

However, while this argument makes a clever logical point, it really is of limited interest. For there is nothing in the argument which makes it a logical impossibility for someone to predict that at a future date a particular object will be fashioned or a particular theory will be formulated. All that Cranston's argument rules out is the possibility of predicting the discovery of a *novel* or *original* theory or invention; it is against the possibility of predicting an event described as the *first* of its kind that his argument is telling. Even if a predictor knew the Special Theory of Relativity in 1890, for all of Cranston's argument there would be nothing contradictory in his predicting that Einstein would produce such a theory in 1905.

Nevertheless, the main thrust of this argument is useful because it demonstrates what would be involved in predicting the future course of human thought. For what the argument does reveal is that in order to accomplish such a task one would have to be able oneself to make all the creative leaps that will recur later at some specified time. In order to have predicted in 1850 that the General Theory of Employment, Interest and Money would be proposed by Keynes in 1935, a scientist would have already had to have formulated the rough outlines of the theory himself.

And while there is nothing about such an event which would make it a priori impossible, from a pragmatic point of view such a Herculean effort is extremely unlikely. This is especially so for innovations which themselves depend on a whole range of other innovations, or for innovations which involve fundamental alterations in the basic theories and principles which underlie the broad mass of our knowledge. To predict in 1600 the emergence of Marx's social theory would require that the predictor be in possession of concepts which themselves depended on developments in philosophy ("dialectic," "alienation"), economics ("capital," "commodity"), sociology ("civil society," "bureaucracy"), and a whole range of other areas of thought, and so it would be necessary for him to elaborate these conceptual distinctions and intellectual strategies in order to predict for any distance into the future a social theory of the complexity of Marx's.

Moreover, the unlikeliness of such a situation is not based solely on the limits of the human mind; there is another reason such a situation is almost unthinkable. It is that, as Popper has forcefully pointed out,[24] successful prediction is only possible when one is dealing with a closed system, that is, with a system which is protected from external influences that would tend to upset the regular interaction of members in the system. All scientific predictions take the form, "if C, then E, in situation X, ceteris paribus; but C in situation X, ceteris paribus; therefore E;" and they are applicable to real situations only when the ceteris paribus clause has been satisfied, which is to say, when no untoward event occurs to upset the relationship between C and E.

But the collection of individuals who comprise a given social group (say, all atomic physicists, or all the members of the Ndembu tribe) is a most unlikely candidate to be a closed system. The possible influences on the minds of people are practically innumerable, and the amount and intensity of interaction between such collections so great, that the idea that a human group might be isolated enough so that a scientific prediction about its conceptual developments might be forthcoming sounds like a mad millenarian dream.

The difficulties involved in predicting conceptual developments are enormous; indeed, from a practical standpoint, it may be taken as a given that such predictions are so unlikely as to be almost certainly not realizable. And this means that even if it were the case that the course of human thought is law governed in some fully deterministic way there is a *pragmatic* epistemic unpredictability about the development of human thought.

Moreover, it should be clear from what I said about the constitutive role that concepts play in human actions and institutions that this unpredictability is not confined to the history of human *thought*; human actions and institutions are also unpredictable insofar as they change as a result of people's coming to think of themselves, each other, and the natural world in novel ways. Thus, as the lessons of Keynesian theory came to be appreciated first by the leaders of government and industry, and then in an attenuated form by the populace at large, new demands on the government were made and were seen to be justifiable, and a whole new class of laws, regulations, institutions, and practices emerged. As a result, the very nature of the relationship between the government and its citizens changed.

The conclusion to be drawn from all of this is that the objects of social science are open-ended in a practically unpredictable way. Social institutions and practices, as well as the beliefs and desires of the members of particular social groups, are continually in a state of flux and evolution which will always appear to be indeterminate to those who wish to study them. To understand what this actually means, it might be useful to draw an analogy suggested by Alasdair MacIntyre[25] to some imagined geologist's attempting to study rocks which changed their shapes, sizes, colors, and chemical compositions in a manner which (even though lawful) always eluded his predictive capacity. Retrospectively he would be able to understand why it was that a class of rocks assumed the form that it did; but prospectively he would be unable to know what form it will take: The objects of his research would be constantly changing in surprising ways. Now, this imagined situation of the geologist is like the real situation of the social scientist interested in explaining intentional behavior, just because all such behavior is what it is by virtue of its place in a social community, and because the life history of social communities is constantly changing in unpredictable ways.

What does all of this have to do with the heteronomic character of the generalizations in a science of action? Just this. In order to frame general laws properly so called, it is necessary that one use concepts which refer to objects which are in some sort of steady state, or which change in some regular way which is apprehensible. The reason for this is that general laws are universal well-confirmed empirical hypotheses which state that under situations X, if *a* then *b*, ceteris paribus; but if there is no way of describing an object or event so that it can be seen to be part of a regularly recurring sequence of events, then there is no way that one can know whether one's hypotheses are either universal or well-confirmed enough in order to be accorded the title of "general law."

It is as if the objects in the world will not stay still enough, or evolve in a predictable enough fashion, so that one can pick them out as part of a genuine natural pattern. To return to the example of the geologist and his rocks, if the objects to which his terms "rocks of type *a*" and "rocks of type *b*" refer are forever shifting in unpredictable ways, there is no way that the geologist could frame a general law using the concepts "rocks of type *a*" and "rocks of type *b*"; this is because there would simply be no way to know whether the purported general law which resulted by using such concepts held or not, and, if it did, over what range of phenomena. In other words, the basic problem about general laws in the social sciences of action is one of confirmation: In order to have general laws one must be able to predict outcomes as the result of the presence of a certain factor; but it is extremely unlikely that such predictions of social and psychological phenomena will occur, just because the concepts which partially make these phenomena what they are are subject to unpredictable change, and so the phenomena themselves are unlikely to be enough like the original to provide confirmatory instances.

Take, for example, the hypothetical case of a social scientist in 1800 who is trying to frame a general law about the political life of tribal societies, and yet who does not possess—and could not possibly possess, given the limits of his ability to predict conceptual changes—the concepts of "imperialism" and "socialism." No generalization that he formulates using the terms he has available to him could ever become a general law properly so called because the very nature of tribal politics in the nineteenth and twentieth centuries would be so deeply altered by the development and spread of these notions: His subject matter would change on him, and so his carefully wrought generalizations could never be tested and applied over a wide variety of situations so that they could become more than generalizations.

This hypothetical social scientist is in the same situation as was Marx in trying to formulate the iron laws of capitalist economy—say, the inevitable and immense pauperization of the working-class. Such an attempt was doomed to fail just because capitalist social systems are constantly evolving: For instance, Marx could never have known of the theoretical innovations that would be made by Keynes, innovations which would irrevocably alter the set of institutions, practices, and beliefs about which Marx was trying to theorize. Such unpredictable changes inevitably made Marx's putative general law just that, a *putative* general law.

Nor can the social scientist avoid this situation by arguing that his generalizations can be transformed into law-like statements by recognizing their inherently statistical character. For the statistical generalizations found in the social sciences are not likely to become genuine statistical laws for exactly the same reason that causal generalizations in social science are not, namely, because to become so they must be confirmed in a wide variety of instances, and such confirmation is subject to the same sorts of difficulty I have been discussing. (Actually, the logic of confirmation for statistical laws is exactly the same as that for causal laws, except that in the latter case one is concerned with the occurrence of individual events, whereas in the former one is concerned with the occurrence of sets of events.)

It should be noted before proceeding that there is nothing in what I have said which would be incompatible with the social world being as deterministic as one pleases (deterministic in the sense of being fully law-governed)—or being indeterministic, for that matter. All that is required in order for my argument to work is that social phenomena be unpredictable because they are constituted by the self-understandings of the relevant actors, self-understandings which themselves change in unforetellable ways.

Nor should it be concluded from this that no general statements at all are possible in the social sciences of action. This would be the case if the sorts of changes I have been discussing occurred extremely fast and appeared to be totally random (such a situation would be analogous to our geologist's confronting a world in which the rocks in it changed in irregular ways every month or so). But fortunately this is not the situation in which we find ourselves. The structure of the social world is *relatively* stable, and its changes are usually confined to some roughly definable area; indeed, if this were not the case, it would completely undermine the possibility of sustained social interaction, and hence the possibility of there being some sort of genuine social order at all. There is a kind of regularity and continuity which must be present if there is to be social life; and it is on these facts that the generalizations that we do find in the social sciences rest.

Thus, for example, the sociology of knowledge tries to provide us with a general understanding of the relationship between certain sorts of social structures and certain sorts of belief systems. Moreover, it also tries to provide some understanding of the sorts of intellectual innovations that are likely to find acceptance in societies of a certain description. In so doing, it gives us some understanding of the range of ideas that are likely to gain a foothold in a social order and thereby alter it. And on the basis of such knowledge, one can make certain genuinely testable generalizations about the rate and kind of change in various social systems.

The question is not, therefore, whether generalizations are possible—in the first place, they must be if there is going to be a social order at all, and, in the second, social scientists have already given us a whole slew of them. The question instead is whether or not we can expect these generalizations to be purified and rigorously stated so that they may thereby become genuine general laws. To this question, because of the constitutive role of concepts and beliefs in making human social life what it is, and because of the practical unpredictability of the development of these concepts and beliefs, we have every reason to believe that the answer will be "no." For these generalizations refer to what I hope to have shown to be epistemically anomalous phenomena, and such phenomena are not the sort requisite for formulations of a genuinely nomological character.

IV

My discussion about the possibility of general statements in social science leads directly into a discussion of the nature and role of causal theories in explaining actions, assuming it is the case that the causal generalizations in social science are indeed heteronomic. It is necessary to include this discussion because only then will it be clear what we can expect to be the nature of those sciences that try to give systematic causal explanations of human behavior. I want to conclude by emphasizing that although I believe that general laws properly so called will not emerge from the social sciences—and in this respect they differ from the natural sciences—I do not think it follows from this that a genuinely theoretical science of human behavior is impossible.[26] On the contrary, I believe that until the essentially theoretical character of social scientific explanation is appreciated, no account of the nature of the sciences of behavior will be adequate.

Toward the end of Section II, I mentioned that all causal explanations require the existence of causal generalizations; this is true in the natural as well as the social sciences. The reason for this is that in order to justifiably claim that a particular (kind of) event causes another (kind of) event, one must have good reason to believe that the two events are not merely accidentally related, or even the joint outcomes of a third unknown (kind of) event. That is, one must have evidence that in certain circumstances the first (sort of) event actually is a necessary and/or sufficient condition for the other (sort).

The evidence called for here is of two kinds. In the first place, because the explanation rests, at least implicitly, on a general claim (that, ceteris paribus, the first [type of] event is enough to produce the other, and/ or that the second [type] cannot occur without the first having occurred), the relevant evidence will involve generalizations which report other instances in which the two events are conjoined. In this regard, the more *unlike* the circumstances in which the relation is observed, the stronger the evidence that it is indeed the (type of) event in question, and not some other one in the environment, that is the cause.

But—and this leads to the second sort of evidence—generalizations of covariance alone cannot provide enough weight to support an imputation of a causal relationship. The two events might be causally unrelated to one another, and yet if they were the common effect of another, but unknown event, one would still have a generalization of covariance. This shows that something stronger than this sort of generalization is required. What is needed besides is a generalization which might be said to explain its instances, in the sense that implicit in it is an account of *why* the relationship between the events is indeed one of necessary and/or sufficient conditionship. It is only when one is in possession of this sort of generalization that one can with any degree of confidence make the contrary-to-fact and subjunctive conditionals that one must be able to make in order to claim that in certain circumstances one event is a sufficient and/or necessary condition of the other.

It is precisely at this point that theories are required, for it is from theories that such an account derives. Theories provide a systematic explanation of a diverse set of phenomena by showing that the events in question all result from the operation of a few basic principles. A theory goes beyond generalizations by showing why the generalizations hold, and it does this by specifying the basic entities which constitute the phenomena to be explained, and their modes of interaction, on the basis of which the observed generalizations can be inferred. One might say—with an acknowledgement to the realist theory of science, which I discussed earlier—that theories provide us with knowledge of the causal mechanisms that relate the events in question, and that are the means by which one event brings about the other. It is knowledge of these mechanisms (understood in the broadest sense, such that the having of motives or beliefs might figure in such mechanisms) that supplements mere empirical generalizations and enables them to be evidence that a genuinely causal relationship is involved. It is thus that we are inevitably led from the desire to explain causally a particular (sort of) occurrence to the need for theories.

Of course, as science develops, these theories become much more rigorous and explicit. Moreover, it will naturally attempt to organize and structure the various causal explanations and causal generalizations upon which they rest by systematically interrelating them, and by subjecting them to experimental and other empirical verification. In this process the self-conscious development of "large-scale" theories is absolutely essential.

It is a very odd fact that the most sophisticated statements in the analytic tradition about the nature of social science have consistently failed to mention its essentially theoretical character[27]—a fact which has made much in this tradition appear irrelevant to many of its practioners. I say an odd fact because even a cursory glance reveals the kind of theorizing I am discussing. In neoclassical economic theory, in structural-functional theory in anthropology, in exchange theory in sociology, in structuralist theories of cognitive development in psychology—in these and countless other cases the fact that causal explanations require the development and articulation of large-scale theories is evident.

Of course, such theories have never lived up to the aspirations of Hobbes or Comte; that is, they have never approached the universal scope and precision of theories in the natural sciences. And if what I have argued in this paper is correct, they never will: The causal generalizations that figure in the theories of the social sciences are heteronomic (principally because their objects, human behavior and society, are intentional and historical entities), and consequently these theories are limited. These limits manifest themselves in a number of ways: in the precision of the terminology in these sciences; in the sharpness with which a scientist will be able to specify the conditions in which his theories hold; in the range of application in both space and time of such theories; and in their predictive power, and therefore their testability.

Moreover, there is one last limit on the causal theories of social science which deserves particular mention because of its bearing on the question of the sort of theory that social and psychological phenomena call for. The limit I have in mind is that many of the causal generalizations in a social theory will be restricted to a given cultural context. The reason for this limitation is the constitutive role beliefs play in human life. If, as I have argued, social and psychological phenomena are what they are, and therefore have the causal relations they have, partly because of the beliefs of the actors involved, then these actors coming to have a radically different set of beliefs will likely mean a whole new set of relations among them, and this will consequently require a different set of causal generalizations to explain their social and psychological experience. Thus the causal theories a social scientist develops are likely to be more or less confined to particular cultures or types of culture.

This is an extremely important point, and not just for theoretical reasons alone. For if one interprets the causal generalizations produced by social science as if they were general laws which applied over a whole range of cultures, or even if one thinks that social science is capable of producing such laws, this may have the terribly unfortunate political repercussion of stifling political change. Let me explain, and in the process reveal why I think the theories in social science ought sometimes to be what has been called "critical."[28]

The causal generalizations in social science are about essentially conventional activity just because that activity is partly constituted by the beliefs of those involved. However, if one takes these generalizations to be actual or possible laws, one may be unwittingly reifying the particular conventions one is observing, i.e., treating them as if they were nature-like necessities such that the particular way a group of people interacts is taken to be the way it *must* interact. The reason why a commitment to general laws properly so called inevitably leads to this reification is the generality involved in such laws: If the generalizations one discovers are indeed (potential) general laws, then what might at first appear to be a local or idiosyncratic practice must be seen as an instance of something that is in the nature of things, and thus as something not alterable.

However, from the perspective of this paper, in which I have argued that causal theories in social science are limited in scope to a particular culture, or perhaps to particular sorts of culture, this reification is a form of ideological distortion. For in such cases the social scientist is illicitly transforming the generalizations which account for one particular way of doing things into purported general laws which supposedly govern human life as such. The effect of this concealed ideological transformation can be particularly oppressive, for it can reinforce the social actors' acceptance of a status quo which may be deeply frustrating to them. It can do this both by giving them reason to believe that their social life must be as it is, and by failing to provide them with an analysis of their situation which might help them to change it (and so falsify the causal generalizations which now characterize their behavior!).

I have claimed that ultimately the nature of social-scientific theory (with its heteronomic generalizations, limitations in scope and specificity, and restriction to particular [sorts of] cultural setting) is shaped by the essential historicity of the objects it seeks to explain. And earlier in the paper I suggested that this historicity is itself rooted in the capacity for self-transformation characteristic of human beings. This suggests that any conception of social science which fails to take historicity into proper account will be defective. It will be theoretically defective because it will fail to appreciate the special character of causal theory in social science, and it will be practically defective in the oppression that it can cause in the way I have just indicated.

It is on just this feature of historicity that critical theory focuses. According to it, social-scientific theories not only must self-consciously recognize that they are limited because they are about creatures capable of self-transformation, but they must make this feature play an essential role in their construction. That is, critical theory insists that social science ought to be a means by which such transformation is fostered.

How can social theory do this? By assuming a particular form, namely, one that isolates in the lives of a group of people those causal conditions that depend for their power on the ignorance of those people as to the nature of their collective existence, and that are frustrating them. The intention here is to enlighten this group of people about these causal conditions and the ways in which they are oppressive, so that, *being enlightened, these people might change these conditions and so transform their lives* (and, coincidentally, transcend the original theory). Examples of critical theory are Marx's theory of capitalism and Freud's theory of neurosis.

A critical metatheoretical understanding of social science grows quite naturally out of the account of explanation, cause, action, law, generalization, and theory that I have given in this paper (although obviously it is not entailed by my account). The reason why it does is that both the heteronomic character of causal generalizations in social science and the idea of a critical social theory derive from the same special feature of human beings, namely, what I have called their historicity. It is because humans learn about themselves and their world that they are instrumental in transforming themselves and their relations, thereby defeating the causal generalizations which a social scientist might have used to describe their lives. This is why such generalizations are heteronomic. But it is this very same capacity to be enlightened by these theories about the world and to alter their social arrangements partly on the basis of this enlightenment that makes humans fit subjects for a critical social science.

Moreover, while to a theory of social science that seeks to model it on the natural sciences the heteronomic character of social scientific causal generalizations is a pronounced liability, to a critical social scientist this heteronomy is a virtue. Heteronomy is a virtue for critical theory because it means that humans are capable of self-reflection and self-transformation, and it is just these that a critical social science is meant to foster. Indeed, a critical social scientist actually desires to see his causal generalizations made otiose by a group of actors who, having learned them, alter the way they live. He desires this because it means that he has been successful as a theorist in helping to alter the social world which he is studying.

A consideration of the nature of causal generalizations in explaining human behavior has lead me into a critical theoretic conception of social theory. This, it seems to me, is no accident. In the first place, such a conception is based on the belief that social science must be theoretical, but also on the self-conscious recognition of the heteronomic character of social scientific theories. Moreover, such a conception sees humans as natural creatures in a natural world of cause and effect, and thus as fit subjects for science; but it also sees humans as capable of a kind of initiative which distinguishes them from other natural creatures, and thus it argues that social science must be of a novel form. It is critical theory which understands the basis for the heteronomy of social science (namely, the historicity of human beings) and which builds this understanding into its account of social scientific theory.

PART THREE
Criticism and Advocacy

CHAPTER SIX
The Critical Project
of Jürgen Habermas
David R. Dickens

Jürgen Habermas is undoubtedly the most famous contemporary heir
of the Frankfurt School.[1] As such, his work has become the widespread
object of intense, if sometimes ill-informed, scrutiny. There have been
attempts at presenting an overview of Habermas's work, but many of
these works are as technically formidable as Habermas's original writings.[2] In this paper I shall present the major themes in Habermas's
work in a format which relates them to concerns more familiar to
contemporary social scientists.

The Historical Context

Habermas's work may be best understood in light of the practical
and theoretical developments of Marxian theory since the 1920's. More
particularly, Habermas's thought constitutes a positive critique of the
Frankfurt School of Critical Theory which has itself contributed to a
theoretical reconstruction of Marxism along Hegelian lines.[3] This reconstruction did not begin with the original members of the Frankfurt
School (Max Horkheimer, Leo Lowenthal, Theodor Adorno, et al.) but
instead with two earlier European activist thinkers, Karl Korsch and
Georg Lukàcs.[4] Korsch and Lukàcs had been involved in the worker
council movements in their respective countries. The problematic that
confronted these thinkers was the failure of the revolutionary movements
in Germany and Hungary from 1918–1921. The theory behind these
movements was based on the economistic evolutionary model of classical
Social Democracy, the first political inheritor of Marx's theory.

At the same time as the failure of the revolution in Germany, the
Bolsheviks in Russia were successful in gaining power. As Arato has

pointed out, the Bolsheviks were successful primarily because of tactical revisions of the gradualist strategy of the Social Democrats. Theoretically, their revision of Marxist theory, represented primarily by Lenin, was a move back to the eighteenth-century materialism that Marx himself had already rejected.

In addition to their common political experience in the unsuccessful council movement, Korsch and Lukàcs both had received academic training in the tradition of German idealism. The common practical and intellectual experiences of these thinkers contributed to their formulating the common theoretical claim that "the new socialist society, whatever the necessary historical tendencies of the present, could be predicated only on the conscious and self-conscious actions of human subjects who anticipated in their self-organization and intersubjective relations the structure of the future."[5] In the light of the dramatic decline of revolutionary possibilities in Western and Central Europe after 1923, the primary theoretical problematic became the crisis of revolutionary subjectivity.

The genesis of the Frankfurt School of Critical Theory is situated precisely within this context of Hegelian Marxism with its emphasis on the problem of revolutionary subjectivity. The emancipatory theory of Marx and the Marxism of the Second International was primarily based on an objectivistic crisis theory.[6] Briefly put, the theory states that, due to its internal contradictions as a system of exchange, capitalism was doomed to failure. Revolutionary subjectivity was located in the proletariat or working class. Once the economic contradictions became greater and greater (the market tending toward collapse), the proletariat, already possessing the necessary material prerequisites for human emancipation, would also gain the necessary self-consciousness for the overthrow of capitalism as a system of domination.

Though Lukàcs and Korsch shared with the "official Marxists" the view that the proletariat was the revolutionary subject, they viewed the consciousness of the proletariat as a vital concern which could not simply be deduced from objective conditions. In contrast to the "automatic" conception of official Marxism, Lukàcs and Korsch maintained that while the contradictions in capitalism do indeed precipitate a crisis, this does not necessarily bring about a socialist revolution.[7] Only the active intervention of self-conscious subjects could provide the impetus necessary for the introduction of human liberation: "the blind laws of capitalism lead to a crisis—but not beyond. These are the laws of unfreedom and the laws of bourgeois progress and can guarantee only more of the same. The resolution of the crisis rests ultimately on the consciousness of the actors. On this consciousness depends whether the crisis will issue into barbarism or the laws of unfreedom will cease."[8] Philosophically, the more mechanistic tendencies embodied in the Marxist theory of the Second International and in Engels' works, and implicit in the writings of Marx himself, were rejected in favor of a Hegelian-Marxist dialectical epistemology where the subjectivity of consciousness was just as important for gaining knowledge as the "objectivity" of objects (in nature or history).

The early theoretical and political position of the Frankfurt School, represented at this stage almost exclusively by Max Horkheimer, reflected Lukàcs's Hegelian-Marxist position, with one crucial exception. This exception concerns the immediacy of the relation between revolutionary subjectivity (the proletariat) and correct political practice. Epistemologically, Horkheimer's early essays reflect Lukàcs's characterization of the dialectical relation between subject (knower) and object (known). Politically, Horkheimer, again like Lukàcs, sees the proletariat as the revolutionary subject, but he does not agree with Lukàcs's view of the party as the mediating link between the proletariat and correct political practice. Twenty years after Lukàcs's original invocation of the party as revolutionary organization in *History and Class Consciousness*, Horkheimer in his essay "The Authoritarian State" sees the party as merely another vehicle for domination: "Even if the end of the last phase [of capitalism] will come at an unexpected time or place, it will hardly be brought about by the resurrected mass party, which could only replace the existing rulers. . . . The authoritarian state has to fear the opposing mass parties only as competitors."[9]

Horkheimer's disagreement with Lukàcs concerning the mass party is based on his assessment of capitalism's changed historical situation. According to Horkheimer, the ranks of the bourgeoisie of free market capitalism have been decimated but this has not led to proletarian revolution. Instead, the state has become the "total capitalist," and the El Dorado of bourgeois existence, the market, has been replaced by the state-controlled form of capitalist domination, planned production: "The modern planned economy can feed the masses better, and better be fed by them, than by the vestiges of the market."[10] In light of this development, the fate of working class organizations, such as trade unions and mass parties, is the opposite from that intended by Lukàcs: "The call to unite in trade unions and parties was carried out to the letter, but these organizations carried out not so much the unnatural [to capitalism] tasks of the united proletariat, namely the resistance to class society in general, as that of submitting to the natural conditions of their own development into mass organizations. They integrated themselves into the transformations of the economy."[11]

In this new conception of the changed historical situation of capitalism, the economic or productive sphere remains primary but in an expanded sense. Due to the "totalization of capitalist rationalization" from the productive sphere to society as a whole, ideology and culture now becomes a direct reflection of the productive base, since the previous mediating agencies, such as the bourgeois family, are no longer able to provide a haven for individual development.[12]

This new historical development has profound practical and theoretical consequences, which radically affect the relation between critical theory and the Marx-Lukàcsian emancipatory project. On the practical or political level, the proletariat is no longer seen as the historically grounded revolutionary subject, since the sphere of capitalist domination has been radically altered. Theoretically, while it does not completely rob critical theory of a positive or activist thrust, this new position does tie critical theory's emancipatory hopes more directly to concrete historical factors (rather than to the proletariat, understood as the transcendental emancipatory agent), thus leaving open the possibility that these hopes might prove groundless.[13]

The advent of fascism, and the further consolidation of the authoritarian state, in both the East and West, in the Cold War period following World War II, did indeed bring about an "eclipse of reason," and Horkheimer came to adopt an essentially negative (nonactivist) stance which coincided more closely with that of his fellow member of the Frankfurt School, Theodor Adorno: "If by enlightenment and intellectual progress we mean the freeing of man from superstitious beliefs in evil forces, in demons and fairies, in blind fate—in short, the emancipation from fear—then denunciation of what is currently called reason is the greatest service reason can render."[14]

With the denial of the proletariat as universal revolutionary subject, and its replacement by no other individual, group, or class, critical theory had no active theory of politics and was left only with the notion of immanent critique. The function of immanent critique is essentially negative:

> Spirit, language, and all the realms of the mind necessarily stake universal claims. Even ruling groups, intent above all upon defending their particular interests, must stress universal motifs in religion, morality and science. This originates the contradiction between the existent and ideology, a contradiction that spurs all historical prog-

ress. While conformism presupposes the basic harmony of the two and includes the minor discrepancies in the ideology itself, philosophy makes men conscious of the contradiction between them. On the one hand it appraises society by the light of the very ideas that it recognizes as its highest values; on the other, it is aware that these ideas reflect the taints of reality.[15]

It is at this point that Habermas enters the picture, for (having rejected as historically obsolete the view of the proletariat as revolutionary subject) his work is an attempt to provide a new grounding for critical theory that will restore its active political dimension. Habermas locates this dimension in no particular group or institution of modern society, but in the very structure of human communication. This controversial new claim is at once more radical and more mundane than any previous attempt at grounding emancipatory theory, since it is embedded in the human species and thus extends to everyone. Habermas begins with a critique and reconstruction of Marx's theory in order to lay the foundation for his own communication-based theory.

The Critique of Marx

Habermas begins his critical reconstruction of Marx's theory with an examination of what he sees as a fundamental ambiguity concerning social praxis that is at least partially responsible for the mechanistic tendencies in later Marxist theory. It is to Marx's credit that, without any knowledge of Hegel's early writings, he rediscovered that "interconnection between labor and interaction in the dialectic of the forces of production and the relations of production."[16] This rediscovery is formulated most clearly by Marx in a famous passage from the *Economic and Philosophic Manuscripts of 1844:*

What is great in Hegel's Phenomenology and its final results is that Hegel comprehends the self-generation of man as a process, the objectification as the process of confronting objects, as externalization, that he thus comprehends the essence of labor and conceives objective man, the true because the actual man, as the result of his own labor.[17]

This is the point of view, according to Habermas, from which Marx historically reconstructs the self-formative process of the human species. The mechanism for change in this process is found in the contradiction between the successful domination over nature, gradually secured by means of social labor, and the existing social arrangements (which Habermas calls "the institutional framework of interaction"), that are organized in a "natural" (prerational) way. However, Habermas claims that Marx's analysis, presented in the first part of *The German Ideology*, does not clearly explicate the complex interrelation between labor and interaction. Instead, by employing the ambiguous concept of social praxis Marx reduces the sphere of communicative action (interaction) to that of instrumental action (labor):

> Just as in the Jena *Philosophy of Spirit* the use of tools mediates between the laboring subject and the natural objects, so for Marx instrumental action, the productive activity which regulates the material interchange of the human species with its natural environment, becomes the paradigm for the generation of all the categories; everything is resolved into the self-movement of production.[18]

As Thomas McCarthy points out, this implicit reductionism is not simply a reduction of praxis to *techne*, since Marx uses the term "social labor." However, material production and social interaction (communication) are not clearly delineated as two irreducible dimensions of human life, and this tendency leads to the incorporation of the latter into the former so that in Marx's writings the reproduction of human life is repeatedly characterized solely by the reproduction of the material conditions of life.[19]

Habermas is quick to point out that this is only an implicit reductionism and that in his actual concrete studies Marx is not bound to the mechanistic categorial framework implied in the "Preface" to *A Contribution to the Critique of Political Economy*. The implications of this unresolved ambiguity are enormous, however, for they constitute the central core for Habermas's critical reconstruction of emancipatory theory.

The distinction between these two spheres of human life may be specified at a most fundamental level, according to Habermas, for each is characterized by a different logical criteria of justification. Progress in the sphere of labor is characterized by growth of the productive forces and increased technological efficiency.[20] The form of logic appropriate to this sphere is instrumental or purposive-rational, where decisions are judged according to standards of efficiency. Progress in the communicative or interactive sphere, on the other hand, is characterized by the extension of communication free from domination and is governed by normative consensus as opposed to technical efficiency.

It is grounded in the intersubjectivity of mutual understanding, secured by the general recognition of obligations, which are sanctioned conventionally.[21]

In introducing the distinctive justificatory criteria underlying labor and interaction, Habermas is attempting to provide a more comprehensive theory of what Max Weber called rationalization. On this point Habermas is criticizing not only Marx's implicit reductionism but also the reductionism in the opposite direction of the earlier Frankfurt School theorists, especially Herbert Marcuse, for whom "the very concept of technical reason is perhaps ideological."[22]

Science and Politics

The fundamental distinction between instrumentally organized production and communication based on normative consensus forms the basis for Habermas's critique of the scientization of politics.[23] Habermas identifies three specific aspects of the classical doctrine of politics which have been abandoned in the modern technological approach to politics. First, "politics was understood to be the doctrine of the good and just life; it was the continuation of ethics." Secondly, "the old doctrine of politics referred exclusively to praxis, in the narrow sense of the Greeks. . . . In the final instance, politics was always directed toward the formation and cultivation of character; it proceeded pedagogically and not technically." Finally, "Aristotle emphasized that politics, and practical philosophy in general, cannot be compared in its claim to knowledge with a rigorous science."[24]

In contrast, the modern view of politics, represented in its most extreme form today in behavioristic political science, is based on an entirely different conception, first thematized by Thomas Hobbes in the middle of the seventeenth century. Politics is seen as separate from morality or legality (which were in turn separate from each other). Accepting Francis Bacon's maxim of *scientia propter potentiam* as self-evident, Hobbes maintained that "mankind owes its greatest advances to technology, and above all to the political technique, for the correct establishment of the state." Finally, regarding the epistemological status of political theory, Hobbes wished "to make politics serve to secure knowledge of the essential nature of justice itself," an assertion that "already complies with the ideal of knowledge originating in [his] time, the ideal of the new science, which implies that we only know an object to the extent that we ourselves can produce it."[25]

Viewed as a scientific rather than an ethical enterprise, political decisions are now justified by the instrumental logic of technical reason rather than communicative consensus. It is this illegitimate extension of technological reason into the sphere of politics that Habermas refers to as the scientization of politics. The politically disastrous consequences of this shift are obvious. The democratically decided normative consensus which properly characterizes the political sphere is replaced by an arbitrary (ungrounded) political decisionism carried out by technocratic political "experts." As a result, the self-conscious relation between theory and political practice is severed.

Habermas is not arguing for a romantic return to the classical Greek conception, which would constitute an abstraction. The type of practical philosophy he has in mind is one which developed in the movement of German thought from Kant through Marx, which he characterizes as "an empirical philosophy of history with a practical intent."

The Public Sphere

Habermas concretely situates this development in his book *Strukturwandel der Öffentlichkeit* (*Structural Transformation of the Public Sphere*). As the title indicates, the work is an attempt to define and historically trace the changing structure of the public sphere. The concept of "the public sphere" is important for Habermas because it is the area of social life where communicative interaction can take place: "By the public sphere we mean first of all a realm of our social life in which something approaching public opinion can be formed. Access is guaranteed to all citizens. A portion of the public sphere comes into being in every conversation in which private individuals assemble to form a public body."[26] As Peter Hohendahl points out, the concept of public sphere is not to be equated with that of the public understood merely as a number of individuals who come together. The concept refers instead to the institution that, although it only becomes concrete through the participation of people, cannot be characterized simply as a crowd.[27]

What we commonly call the public sphere emerged during early capitalism as a specific sphere between state and society. Feudal society contained what Habermas calls the representative public sphere, representative in the sense of being directly linked to the concrete existence of a ruler. In contrast, the bourgeois public sphere was a sphere of private individuals joining together as a public body over and against the state. The bourgeois public advanced the principle of public supervision of the state, embodied in the demand that government proceedings be made public (*Publizität*). Rather than merely exchanging one basis of legitimation for another, this principle constitutes for Habermas a means of transforming the nature of political power, for government is no longer merely a matter of executive fiat.

The bourgeois or liberal public sphere was formally guaranteed in the first modern constitutions as a set of fundamental rights which, at the same time, restricted public authority. Even more important:

> Between these two spheres, the constitutions further insured the existence of a realm of private individuals assembled into a public body who as citizens transmit the needs of bourgeois society to the state, in order, ideally, to transform political into "rational" authority within the medium of this public sphere. The general interest, which was the measure of such a rationality, was then guaranteed, according to the presuppositions of a society of free commodity exchange, when the activities of private individuals in the market place were freed from social compulsion and from political pressure in the public sphere.[28]

Daily newspapers played an important role during this time for, with the addition of an editorial component, they became "an institution of the public itself, effective in the manner of a mediator and intensifier of public discussion, no longer a mere organ for the spreading of news (as in feudal times), but not yet the medium of a consumer culture."[29] Through their editorial polemics, the daily newspapers participated in the struggle for freedom and public opinion, and thus for the public sphere as a principle. However, with the establishment of the bourgeois constitutional state, the press was "relieved of the pressure of its convictions," and has since been able to abandon its polemical position and "take advantage of the earning possibilities of a commercial undertaking."[30]

Though he defends the principle behind the bourgeois public sphere, Habermas points out that the historical form in which that principle was embodied is no longer present:

> Although the liberal model of the public sphere is still instructive today with respect to the normative claim that information be accessible to the public, it cannot be applied to the actual conditions of an industrially advanced mass democracy organized in the form of the social welfare state.[31]

With the advent of the Chartist movement in England and the February revolution in France there came a change in the form of the public sphere as the public body expanded beyond the bounds of the bourgeoisie (due to the diffusion of press and propaganda). Furthermore, according to Habermas, this development robbed the public sphere of the coherence created by bourgeois social institutions and a relatively high standard of education. As a result, conflicts which previously characterized the private sphere now intruded into the public sphere. The needs of groups that cannot be met through the self-regulating market economy of the liberal phase now tend toward regulation by the state. The public sphere is no longer the provider of "rational authority" but instead becomes the field for competition of opposing interests.

The increasing regulation by the state leads to what Habermas calls a "refeudalization of the public sphere." Political authorities take over extended functions in the sphere of commodity exchange and private actions assume political functions. Large organizations strike political bargains with the state and each other, excluding the public sphere whenever possible. At the same time, however, these large organizations attempt to secure at least nominal support from the mass of the population through an apparent display of openness.

The key political consequence of this development in the modern welfare state is that the public sphere loses its critical function:

> At one time the process of making proceedings public was intended to subject persons or affairs to public reason, and to make political decisions subject to appeal before the court of public opinion. But often enough today the process of making public simply services the arcane politics of special interests; in the form of "publicity" it wins public prestige for people or affairs, thus making them worthy of acclamation in a climate of non-public opinion. The very words "public relations work" betray the fact that a public sphere must first be arduously constructed case by case, a public sphere which earlier grew out of the social structure.[32]

As the state becomes intertwined with every aspect of the private sector, the notion of a public sphere becomes merely an artifically orchestrated tool for securing legitimation.

There is however a fundamental contradiction inherent in the modern welfare state. The increasing influence of state administration is accompanied by the extension of fundamental rights to private citizens. Because of this countertrend, Habermas sees a possibility for the development of a group which will maintain the principle embodied in the bourgeois public sphere. Though his thoughts here are merely conjectural, and less convincing in my opinion, they do constitute an attempt to indicate what a postbourgeois public sphere would look like. The position is based on the idea that, as freedom of information statutes are extended from agencies of the state to all organizations dealing with the state, "a public body of organized private individuals would take the place of the now-defunct public body of private individuals who relate individually to each other."[33] Habermas claims that only such an organized group of private individuals could take advantage of the channels of communication in the public sphere that have been established to facilitate the dealings of organizations with the state.

Despite the questionable conjectures made at the end of the text, the theoretical analysis found in *Strukturwandel* is of critical importance. The undue neglect of the work is no doubt due to the fact that it has not yet been translated into English, but this does not diminish its significance. The concept of the public sphere is pivotal because it constitutes the institutional embodiment of the notion of communicative interaction central to Habermas's entire theoretical and practical enterprise.

Critical Theory and Methodology

The central theme in Habermas's early work was the fundamental need for self-critical political theory and practice. In the second phase of his work, he attempts to provide a methodological grounding for his claims.[34] In so doing, Habermas's main task is to provide a critique of positivist and hermeneutic models of social science and identify each with a corresponding knowledge–constitutive interest.

The notorious accomplishment of positivist philosophy, according to Habermas, is to make the realm of philosophy coterminous with that of science. In previous times science was dependent upon philosophy for the legitimation of its basic principles, but after Hegel's metacritique of Kant, which subjects epistemology to a critical self-reflection concerning its own basis, philosophy lost its critical relation to science.

Habermas refers to this mistaken conflation of epistemology with scientific methodology as scientism. The critical error in this conception, according to Habermas, is that the replacement of epistemology with methodology rules out the basic question of the grounding for the rules of inquiry themselves.

Modern empirical-analytic sciences based on the neopositivist verification principle exhibit this error in the following form: The basic epistemological principle, observation, is itself a part of the method. In claiming that the method provides data which is free of subjective interpretation, the findings are purported to be interest-free. However, the basic statements that are used to represent the facts are in no sense objective; instead, they are constituted through an a priori organization of our experience which aims at prediction. Thus Habermas claims that the theories constructed by the empirical sciences "disclose reality subject to the constitutive interest in the possible securing and expansion, through information, of feedback-monitored action."[35] The cognitive interest of this enterprise is technical control over objectified processes, be they natural or human.

In a similar fashion, Habermas claims that the historicist-hermeneutic model falls victim to the same illusion, although knowledge here is constituted in a different fashion. Instead of the empirical verification of hypotheses, the goal is the interpretation of a text. The end product, however, is formally the same in the sense that it too partakes of the objectivist illusion of pure theory. By claiming that the interpreter immerses himself in the horizon of the text, hermeneutics supposedly constitutes the facts in relation to the standards that establish them in the same fashion as the empirical sciences do. Further, the entire interpretative process leads to no new knowledge: "The world of traditional meaning discloses itself to the interpreter only to the extent that his own world becomes clarified at the same time."[36] Thus, again like the empirical sciences, hermeneutic inquiry "discloses reality subject to a constitutive interest in the preservation and expansion of the intersubjectivity of possible action-orienting mutual understanding."[37] Habermas's argument here is that the hermeneutic framework leads only to a conservative consensus within the framework of tradition, an issue he takes up more extensively in his debate with Hans-Georg Gadamer.[38] Since the cognitive aim is conservative mutual understanding rather than objectified control, Habermas refers to the cognitive interest of this enterprise as a practical interest.

Habermas's intention in criticizing positivist and historicist models is not to replace them with a more adequate form of presuppositionless metatheory. Rather, he wants to submit them to the scrutiny of a radical self-reflection, as Hegel did with Kant, which he believes reveals a fundamental connection between knowledge and human interests:

The sciences have retained one characteristic of philosophy: the illusion of pure theory. This illusion does not determine the practice of scientific research but only its self-understanding.

This fundamental illusion is not "merely" a philosophical problem, however:

The glory of the sciences is their unswerving application of their methods without reflecting on knowledge-constitutive interests. From knowing not what they do methodologically, they are that much surer of their discipline, that is of methodical progress within an unproblematic framework. . . . For the sciences lack the means of dealing with the risk that appears once the connection of knowledge and human interest has been comprehended on the level of self-reflection.[39]

The common limit of both approaches is that they produce only what Habermas calls homological knowledge and as such are not methodologically self-reflective. In *Zur Logik der Sozialwissenschaften*, written a year before *Knowledge and Human Interests*, Habermas undertakes a similar methodological critique, although his focus is more specifically on the basic distinction between the natural sciences and the human sciences. The argument here is familiar. Habermas claims that, unlike the natural sciences whose object domain is accounted for strictly from the outside, the object domain for the cultural sciences is symbolically structured. Thus a methodology of the cultural sciences would have to concern itself with the meaning of its symbolic objects. Habermas's position here is not simply that cultural science is concerned with the motivations of its subjects. Rather, he is arguing that the domain object (facts) themselves are intersubjective meanings constituted in a socio-cultural matrix which must be interpreted by social actors.

Although in his criticism of the positivists' unified-science approach Habermas is in essential agreement with the hermeneutic position of *verstehende* sociology, his own position is different. This difference is documented methodologically in *Zur Logik* and its corresponding knowledge-constitutive interest is spelled out in *Knowledge and Human Interests*. Together they constitute the approach endorsed by Habermas: critical social science. The methodological approach of *verstehende* sociology is inadequate because it does not go beyond the level of conscious, subjectively intended actions in its account of social behavior. Although the explication of social action based on the actor's subjective interpretation of culturally transmitted meanings is a necessary cor-

143

rective to the overly simplistic account of normative social action found in structural approaches such as Parsonian functionalism and systems theory, it is not sufficient in itself.[40] The objective framework of society, which includes its political and economic organization, involves a system of referents which lie beyond the immediate purview of the social actor. Thus the actor's interpretation of culturally transmitted meanings may not accurately reflect actual political or economic conditions.

In addition to hermeneutic understanding, then, an adequate methodology for the cultural sciences would have to incorporate a critique of ideology. This in turn implies the need for a structural specification of the objective framework itself, along with an historical analysis of the empirical conditions under which this framework develops. Thus a proper methodology for the cultural sciences contains three essential elements: an analysis of social actors' interpretations of culturally transmitted meanings, which characterizes the hermeneutics approach; a specification of the actual structural conditions themselves (the objective framework), along with an account of their historical development; and finally a critique of ideology which reveals the extent to which culturally transmitted meanings reflect (or fail to reflect) the actual structural conditions of life.

The knowledge-constitutive interest that underlies the notion of critical social science is consequently not content to restrict itself merely to the horizon of the given: "It is concerned with going beyond this goal to determine when theoretical statements grasp invariant regularities of social action as such and when they express ideologically frozen relations of dependence that can in principle be transformed."[41] The all-important idea of critical self-reflection is the key to determining the validity of critical theoretic propositions: "The critique of ideology takes into account that information about lawlike connections sets off a process of reflection in the consciousness of those whom the laws are about. Thus the level of unreflected consciousness, which is one of the initial conditions of such laws, can be transformed."[42]

In *Knowledge and Human Interests*, Habermas discusses Freudian psychoanalysis as a "tangible example" of the type of critical model he has in mind.[43] Freud's work, as Habermas sees it, involves both understanding and causal explanation. As a theory of distorted communication, psychoanalysis involves both a hermeneutic explication of the actor-patient's subjective viewpoint and explanatory hypotheses concerning symbolic structures which lie beyond the actor-patient's immediate view. The latter hypotheses refer to the hidden influences of repressed motives, which Habermas describes as a "causality of fate" as opposed to the unchangeable "causality of nature."

The development of explanatory hypotheses which account for the distorted communication are of course based on certain theoretical assumptions, and Freud's limitation is that these claims are not fully developed in his work. The emancipatory interest based on self-reflection which characterizes critical social science is found in the psychoanalytic model, for "the postulated causal connections do not represent an invariance of natural laws but an invariance of life history that operates through 'the symbolic means of the mind' and can thus be analytically dissolved."[44]

In a sense, the rest of Habermas's theoretical corpus up to the present may be understood as an attempt to ground the theoretical assumptions embodied in Freud's emancipatory hermeneutic. Of course the psychoanalytic model is itself only a substantive example of the formal features of the critical theory of society discussed in the epistemological and methodological work, and Habermas's recent work incorporates an astounding variety of philosphical and social theory; but the project remains the same: "to reconstruct the normative foundations of a critical theory."

Language and Communication

As he continually reminds his readers, Habermas's theoretical and methodological critiques up to this point do not constitute a definitive statement of critical social theory. Rather, his work up through 1970 is primarily negative, showing that Marxist dialectical materialism, the attempts of the first generation of the Frankfurt School to articulate a notion of substantive rationality, and any attempts to found a pure philosophy (Husserl being the latest) are all inadequate to the task of providing a positive grounding for critical theory. Instead, as the focus on psychoanalysis suggests, Habermas attempts to provide the solution in a theory of communication.

In proposing a theory of communication as providing a positive grounding, Habermas is claiming that ultimate principles such as freedom, truth, and justice are inherent in the very structures of communication (speech).[45] Such a grandiose claim is based on a theoretical reconstruction[46] of language use which Habermas refers to as "universal pragmatics." In his *Aspects of a Theory of Syntax*, Noam Chomsky distinguishes between linguistic competence and linguistic performance. Linguistic competence refers to the "ideal speaker-hearer's knowledge of his language," whereas linguistic performance denotes "the actual use of language in concrete situations." According to Chomsky, only linguistic competence may be ordered according to a theory of linguistic universals (his "generative grammar"), whereas linguistic performance is irremediably saturated with extralinguistic, empirical contingencies.

Habermas's conception of a universal pragmatics is based on the counter-claim that there are certain features of linguistic performance or speech that may be reconstructed in universal terms. In the same fashion as generative grammar is a formal reconstruction of linguistic competence, universal pragmatics is a formal reconstruction of linguistic performance, or "communicative competence" as Habermas calls it. Universal pragmatics, he declares:

> thematizes the elementary units of speech (utterances) in the same attitude as linguistics does the elementary units of language (sentences). The aim of reconstructive linguistic analysis is the explicit description of the rules that a competent speaker must master in order to form grammatical sentences and to utter them in an acceptable way . . . . The assumption is that communicative competence has just as universal a core as linguistic competence. A general theory of speech acts would thus describe exactly that system of rules adult speakers master insofar as they can satisfy the conditions for a happy employment of sentences in utterance— no matter to which particular language the sentences belong and in which accidental contexts the utterances are embedded.[47]

In arguing that there is an (implicit) formal structure in linguistic performance (speech), Habermas revises the concepts of competence and performance, with the latter referring to contingent aspects of concrete utterances (the personality structure of the speaker/hearer, the role system in force, etc.) and the former to invariable elements of speech situations (the realm of universal pragmatics).[48] With this revision the task then becomes one of specifying the formal features of speech.

To accomplish this task Habermas relies on the theory of speech acts found in the work of J.L. Austin and John Searle. The speech act, according to Searle, is the elementary unit of linguistic communication. It is not a symbol, word, or sentence; it is an utterance. Utterances contain two analytically distinguishable components, a "propositional content" and an "illocutionary force." For clarification purposes these may be represented as consisting of two sentences: a dominating or performative sentence and a sentence of propositional content. The dominating sentence (such as "I promise," "I assert," "I command") "establishes the illocutionary aspect of the utterance, the mode of communication between speaker and hearer, and thus the pragmatic situation of the dependent sentence. The dependent sentence establishes the connection of the communication with the world of objects and events."[49]

In the formal analysis of speech acts, the notion of linguistic competence is subsumed under the more general notion of communicative competence that encompasses:

> not only the ability to produce and understand grammatical sentences [linguistic competence] but also the ability to establish and understand those models of communication and connections with the external world through which speech in ordinary language becomes possible [communicative competence].[50]

The task of Habermas's universal pragmatics becomes one of specifying those formal features of communicative competence, which are in turn "embedded" within every particular utterance. These embedded features, or "rules for situating sentences in any speech act," constitute the "infrastructure of speech situations in general" and are identified by considering the "relations to reality" that are contained in any grammatically well-formed sentence uttered in a particular situation. Every particular utterance, Habermas claims, simultaneously situates the sentence in relation to external reality ("the" world of objects and events about which one can make true or false statements); inner reality (the speaker's "own" world of intentional experiences that can be expressed truthfully or untruthfully); and the normative reality of society ("our" social life-world of shared values and norms). Accordingly, then, a speaker in uttering a sentence puts forth (though usually only implicitly) four types of validity claims. First is the claim that what is uttered is comprehensible (grammatically correct in the linguistic sense); second, the speaker claims that what is stated is true; third, that his manifest expression of intentions is truthful (veracious); and fourth, that the utterance is itself right or appropriate in relation to a recognized normative context (or that the normative context it satisfies is itself legitimate).[51]

Of these four validity claims, only one, that of comprehensibility, is restricted to language itself. The other three claims are related to extralinguistic orders of reality: "the external world," "a particular inner world," and "our social world."[52] The formal infrastructure of speech situations, then, consists of general rules situating the elements of those situations within three extralinguistic orders of reality. Thus, the analysis of communicative competence extends far beyond that of linguistic competence. In addition to providing an account of the speaker's ability to produce grammatical sentences (linguistic competence), communicative competence must also provide an account of his ability:

(1) to select propositional content in such a way that he represents
. . . an experience or fact (so that the hearer can share the knowledge of the speaker);

(2) to express his intentions in such a way that the linguistic expression represents what is intended (so that the hearer can trust the speaker);

(3) to perform the speech act in such a way that it conforms to recognized norms or to accepted self-images (so that the hearer can agree with the speaker on these values).

The theory of communicative competence thus reaches beyond the "merely linguistic," focusing on the ability to "embed" language in a network of relations to the different extralinguistic orders of reality.[53] The expanded scope of the theory of communicative competence correspondingly implies an expansion of the research program of a linguistically grounded critical theory in two directions: individually, toward an empirical investigation into the process of ego development, and, structurally, toward a "reconstruction of historical materialism" in terms of a theory of social evolution.

The Reconstruction of Historical Materialism and Ego Development

In perhaps his boldest move, Habermas claims that the history of human societies may be ordered according to the same developmental logic that characterizes ego development, which is ultimately grounded in the basic structures of communication: "The reproduction of society and the socialization of its members are two aspects of the same process; they are dependent on the same structure."[54] As Habermas points out, this idea is not new in the history of social thought:

From Hegel through Freud to Piaget [and including Mead and Marx], the idea has developed that subject and object are reciprocally constituted, that the subject can grasp hold of itself only in relation to and by way of the construction of an objective world.[55]

What is novel in Habermas's approach is his claim that both processes are dependent upon the development of communicative competence.

The first part of this research program of Habermas is concerned with the process of ego development. According to Habermas, this issue is best approached through an empirical investigation of the process of moral development and the development of interactive competence. Utilizing Lawrence Kohlberg's work on moral development and George Herbert Mead's theory of socialization, Habermas attempts to show that the development of moral consciousness in the individual is dependent upon the development of interactive competence, which in turn is dependent upon the acquisition of communicative competence. He places Kohlberg's descriptive sequence of six stages of moral consciousness into a developmental-logical framework according to a criterion that Habermas claims is characteristic of the entire human species. This criterion, referred to as "interactive competence," is the ability to take part in increasingly complex interactions. Habermas explicates the process of acquisition of interactive competence by employing Mead's theory of social interaction and studies of socialization in terms of stages of role-taking: play, game, and universal discourse.[56]

In these studies, socialization is seen as comprised of two important movements: "The child first becomes a person by growing into the symbolic universe of the family (and the larger society) and later becomes an adult by growing out of it."[57] In the first phase of development, the child "grows into the symbolic universe" by learning to play social roles, first within the family and later in more abstract social groups. The characteristic defining this development is the ability of the child to internalize the role of the other in developing his or her own "role identity."

The second phase of development, which Habermas refers to as "ego identity," appears with the onset of adolescence. At this stage the individual acquires a certain distance from inherited norms, roles, and values (thus "growing out" of the symbolic universe). The reflexivity characterizing the acquisition of role identity is qualitatively extended in the development of ego identity because the adolescent can now do more than only "take the role of the other" (taking himself as a object); he can treat norms themselves as hypothetical claims. Fully developed interactive competence, then, is characterized by the addition of the capacity for a hypothetical attitude toward validity claims in the domain of human interaction.

The question which now arises is, What form of action provides the basis for interaction once the normative consensus which underlies role competence is suspended by the hypothetical attitude? Habermas's answer is "communicative action": that type of action which is orientated toward reciprocal understanding. "Moral consciousness" is seen as a special case of "interactive competence," since it is the ability to make use of interactive competence in discourse for a conscious resolution of morally relevant conflicts.[58] Habermas links these two processes to one another by the concept of reciprocity. The demand for reciprocity is then itself grounded in the very structure of interaction which makes communicative action possible, as is described in Habermas's theory of the ideal speech situation (see the essay by White in the volume at hand).

In order to legitimate the role of communicative competence for societies as well, Habermas undertakes a theory of social evolution or "reconstruction of historical materialism" in which progress is again defined as the increase in communicative rationalization, although in this case in terms of world views.[59] Habermas begins by reiterating his criticism, first expressed in *Knowledge and Human Interests*, of Marx's version of historical materialism. Marx made the mistake of understanding the relations of production as a reflection, more or less, of the forces of production. Because of this confusion, he failed to see that "progress" in the realm of social relations is defined by a different logical criterion than progress in the productive realm.

While technical efficiency defined by instrumental rational action characterizes progress in the productive sphere, linguistic development defined by communicative action characterizes progress in the realm of social relations. This is not to say that the sphere of social relations of production constitutes an autonomous sphere over and against the productive sphere. Habermas remains faithful to the Marxian claim that changes in the realm of forces of production, such as the development of new manufacturing technologies, remain the primary challenges to which a society must respond. But the way in which a society responds to these challenges is not itself governed by technical standards: "The development of productive forces can then be understood as a problem-generating mechanism that *triggers but does not bring about* the overthrow of relations of production."[60]

According to Habermas, the way in which a society responds to crises produced by the development of productive forces depends upon the level of learning achieved by the society. Learning is itself an individual phenomenon, but in order to become a part of society's integrative structure, it must first be translated into world views:

Individually acquired learning abilities and information must be latently available in world views before they can be used in a

150

socially significant way, that is, before they can be transposed into *societal learning processes.*[61]

Whether or not alternative world views may be transformed into new institutional forms depends on the extent to which a society allows for a discussion of these alternatives to take place.

It is this capability, embodied in the normative structures of societies, for rationally discussing alternative world views as possible solutions to system problems that defines "levels of societal learning," and provides the criterion for distinguishing societies in terms of stages of social evolution:

> When I attempt to grasp evolutionary learning processes with the aid of the concept of "institutional embodiment of structures of rationality," it is no longer a question of making orienting *contents* binding but of opening up *structural possibilities for the rationalization of action.*[62]

These stages of social evolution are thus seen by Habermas as homologous with the stages of moral development in the individual since both are characterized by an increasing reflexivity and hypothetical attitude toward norms and competences which are embedded within the structures of communication.

In this way Habermas feels that he has provided a new normative foundation for critical theory on both the individual and social levels. The thread of continuity for this and other aspects of Habermas's project is his expanding analysis of communicative action and its conditions. Communication theory is the new grounding sought by Habermas for critical theory in the Frankfurt tradition. As he carefully qualifies it, it possesses at least the possibility for rational critique and practical action:

> In its validity claims, communication theory can locate a gentle but obstinate, a never silent though seldom redeemed claim to reason, a claim that must be recognized de facto whenever and wherever there is to be consensual action.[63]

Criticisms and Conclusions

The serious reader will no doubt be impressed with the encyclopaedic scope of Habermas's work. Despite his intellectual virtuosity, however, recent critics have raised a variety of questions regarding the plausibility of communication theory as a normative basis for critical theory.[64] For discussion purposes these criticisms may be divided into three inter-related problem-sets: (1) philosophical criticisms of the claim that communications theory provides a nonrelativist basis for critical theory; (2) substantive criticisms of communication theory as failing to link up with concrete issues of social research and political practice; and (3) criticisms of any attempt to provide a normative grounding for critical theory as ill-founded.

The philosophical criticisms raise two related issues. The first is that, contrary to the claims of emancipatory theory since Marx, Habermas invokes metaphysical principles in his claim of universality for com-munication theory. In his earlier work, Habermas claims to have based his model on an "empirically falsifiable philosophy of history," yet in his theory of universal pragmatics he locates a natural basis for truth, freedom, and justice, thus defending a version of the naturalistic fallacy as acceptable.[65] David Held traces this problem back to Habermas's claim for a "quasi-transcendental" interest in emancipation in his earlier work.[66]

The second philosophical criticism is concerned with the extent to which hermeneutic procedures remain in communication theory. In his discussion of the different models of social science, and in his debate with Gadamer, Habermas has stressed the relativist implications of a strictly hermeneutic model of social science remaining, as it does, tied to a particular tradition or life-world. The problem here for Habermas, as his critics see it, is that his own model does not, and indeed cannot, obviate the need for hermeneutic procedures.[67] Misgeld expresses this criticism most forcefully:

> It is claimed that . . . it becomes possible to explain how historically specific modes of communication originate, and how their distor-tions are systematically organized. Yet the ability to decipher them as distorted cannot issue from mere reliance on historical recon-struction or a reconstructionist theory of the pragmatic universals of speech. It also requires, at least, that one risk one's preunder-standing as an act of practical discourse, and that one engage in a communicative action denying, in its accomplishment, its own communal basis. Such a rupture, opening a cleavage in communally shared understandings, cannot be secure of its own groundedness no matter how elaborate the theories instructing it. It remains a practical situated activity.[68]

Despite their internal differences, the criticisms subsumed under the second problem-set address a common issue: Even if one accepts the universalistic claims of communication theory, the theory does not provide adequate guidelines regarding substantive issues of social research and political practice. In regard to social research, Anthony Giddens argues that, as an idealized notion expressing logical relations, communication theory based on the notion of an ideal speech situation is not applicable to concrete social analysis.[69] Put another way, the notion of an ideal speech situation in language is not a sufficient condition for providing a critical assessment of the social structural barriers to fully open discourse.[70]

Similar criticisms are made with regard to the question of political practice. On a concrete level, two related issues are raised here. Who are the potential agents for change (addressees of the theory) and what institutions of modern society are most likely to facilitate such change?[71] To the first question Habermas's reply is, "mankind as such." With this response he is rejecting traditional Marxist notions of emancipatory agents, from the proletariat in the writings of Marx and Engels to Marcuse's more diffuse references to marginal groups in advanced capitalist societies, such as blacks, women, or college students. The problem here again, however, is that the reference to mankind is too general to provide any guidance for political practice.

Habermas also rejects traditional Marxian and social democratic institutions as potential facilitators of transformation, such as mass parties or trade unions. His own preferences since the publication of *Legitimation Crisis* seem to lie in the direction of grass roots interest groups which have organized independently of traditional left parties and unions,[72] yet he fails to show how confidence in this type of political group may be derived from his theory. Thus the criticism that Harbermas's version of critical theory is a case of "politics in search of the political" remains appropriate.[73]

On a more formal level, several critics have pointed out that even in a situation where communication was free from domination, Habermas's theory does not provide an adequate basis for achieving political consensus on social issues.[74] Such a consensus would have to be based on agreement concerning what constitutes genuine human needs. But as J. Donald Moon points out:

> What we take to be a genuine need will depend on our conception of what it is to be a person, our model of man or philosophical anthropology. And while we should always be able to give good reasons for adopting one model of man as against another, I do not see any reason for supposing that a consensus on one particular

model will be reached. This is especially true in an ideal speech situation, where all possible objections can be raised—and so we must expect the discussion to go on indefinitely without reaching consensus.[75]

To his credit, Habermas has in recent years introduced several modifications of his communication theory in light of criticisms such as those discussed above. However, as two commentators have noted, these revisions have only served to further undermine Habermas's original goal of providing a normative grounding for critical theory.[76]

The first modification introduced by Habermas, responding to criticisms that his communication theory implies an overly simplistic view of language, is to posit a distinction between ordinary speech and discourse. It is only within the realm of discourse, he now claims, that the implicit premise of noncoercive communication is located.[77]

The second modification, formed in response to criticisms of applying the psychoanalytic model to society as a whole, is to posit a distinction between reflection and reconstruction. Reflection refers to the act of gaining consciousness of identity-forming processes at the individual level, while reconstruction refers to a similar process at the societal level, concerning "anonymous rule systems."[78]

The problem with these revisions is that both imply the separation of knowledge from processes of enlightenment.[79] Since the fundamental claim of communication theory is to locate an emancipatory potential in the very structure of language itself, this is indeed a serious flaw, for we would now require an account of what moves human beings to try to overcome forms of distortive communication in ordinary speech and enter into a situation of discourse.[80] Relating this dilemma to our earlier criticisms, "What seems to be lacking here is any illumination on the problem of human agency and motivation."[81] As James Schmidt points out, the devastating result of the modifications just discussed is that Habermas's elaborate reconstruction of language in terms of universal pragmatics now fails to link up with the practical domain of communicative interaction, leaving us with only a communicative reformulation of liberal pluralism.[82]

The final, and perhaps most radical, criticism of Habermas's project is the suggestion that any attempt to provide a universal grounding for critical theory is ill-conceived. Paul Connerton refers to the attempt to provide a transhistorical grounding for critical theory as the "myth of enlightenment," where history is seen as an all-embracing process in which a historical subject attains its essence.[83] The problem with such a conception, as Habermas himself points out in criticizing "scientific" Marxism, is that the practical dimension of theory is displaced, since realization of the goal is guaranteed ahead of time. Although this is obviously not Habermas's intent, his inability to link communication theory to concrete practices for the realization of undistorted communication renders his project ultimately inadequate to the great task he has undertaken.

Although we cannot accept Habermas's most ambitious claims for his communication theory, I do believe that his methodological writings are invaluable for the further development of critical social science. Too often critical social scientists have contented themselves with providing critiques of traditional research without engaging in empirical research of their own. Although it is admittedly programmatic, I feel that the model for critical social science, based on the three components discussed above, do provide the basis for a critical protocol for social scientific analysis. Instead of psychoanalysis, which has been rightfully criticized as inappropriate, I would suggest the critical pedagogy of Paolo Freire as an example better suited to the emancipatory aims of critical social science.[84] In addition to traditional structural emphases in Marxian-based studies, concrete ethnographies of everyday life would also be an essential component of critical social science. The import of these studies was emphasized by Allen Hunter in a recent review of two outstanding examples of the kind of work I am suggesting here:

> [Critical social scientists] will be more successful to the degree that they can learn from as well as teach the people they are reaching out to.[85]

Not only is such a recommendation consonant with the obvious political necessity for self-conscious social change, it also provides methodological substance to Habermas's own often repeated dictum that "in a situation of enlightenment there can only be participants."

CHAPTER SEVEN

Habermas on the Foundations of Ethics and Political Theory*

Stephen K. White

Given the fact that natural law theories about the relation of reason and politics have lost much of their force, philosophers and social scientists today generally approach the concept of practical rationality[1] from one of two perspectives: the strategic-rational or the context-rational. The latter may be seen as deriving from Peter Winch's *The Idea of a Social Science*, and entailing some form of ethical relativism.[2] Context rationality refers to understanding an action or judgment in relation to a context of norms.[3] The strategic-rational perspective is of course the more predominant. For present purposes, it can be characterized as combining the view that values are ultimately subjective with a model of self-interested, individual choice.

In the recent work of Jürgen Habermas there is a view of practical rationality that does not fit into either of the foregoing categories. It is developed in the context of his efforts to work out a "theory of communicative competence" or a "universal pragmatics."[4] It is the aim of this paper to introduce Habermas's conception of practical rationality and to indicate some of the ways in which it may be more promising than the other approaches in relation to the problem of justifying basic political norms.[5] The difficulties entailed by the other approaches are well known. The context-rational perspective, based on the Wittgensteinian model of a language game, is ahistorical and offers no way of conceptualizing ideology. And of course its relativism closes off the possibility of any universalist position on the justification of norms,

---

* This essay is a partially revised version of my "Rationality and the Foundations of Political Philosophy: An Introduction to the Recent Work of Jürgen Habermas," which appeared in *The Journal of Politics*, 41: 4 (November 1979), pp. 1156-1171. It appears here with permission of the publishers.

and thus makes a radical break with the tradition of Western political philosophy.[6] While this break may eventually prove to be warranted, the search for ways of avoiding it should not be abandoned too easily. The strategic-rational perspective, on the other hand, has played a historically important role in political philosophy, especially in the forms of contractarianism and utilitarianism. Both of the latter, however, continually run up against the dilemma that calculations of pure self-interest have an unavoidable corrosive effect on the attempt to derive legitimate norms and the obligation to obey them.[7]

I

Critical theorists of the Frankfurt School, such as Horkheimer, Adorno, and Marcuse, have traditionally been interested in the topic of rationality. One of their primary tasks has been the critique of bourgeois society from the viewpoint of a possible "rational society." To what extent such a critique ever could have succeeded is open to debate, since it was never made very clear where the normative foundation for the conception of a more rational society lay. And that such a foundation is necessary seems implicit in critical theory's rejection of orthodox Marxism. For the latter, the determinism of historical materialism makes normative questions relatively unimportant. If critical theory renounces this determinism, though, it must face the task of handling such questions. And it has not, in the past, been very successful with this task. Habermas's concern with rationality grows out of this dilemma, and the recent "linguistic turn" in his thinking should be construed as a search for a new normative foundation. His theory of communicative competence is aimed at clarifying the "normative implications" of "the concept of reaching an understanding."[8]

As a central part of this theory, Habermas has developed the categorical distinction between two types of ordinary language communication: unreflective "communicative action" and critical, reflective "discourse." This distinction appeared in mature form only after his best-known book, *Knowledge and Human Interests*, appeared in German in 1968.[9] The categories are indicative of several changes and shifts of emphasis in Habermas's work. Space limitations do not permit a reconstruction of this intellectual development, nor an explanation of how his recent concern with language fits in with the theory of knowledge-constitutive interests or the proposed "reconstruction of historical materialism."[10] Neglecting these topics in the present context should raise no particular problem, however, because the categories of communicative action and discourse are sufficiently understandable on their own.

With his notion of communicative action, Habermas wishes to explicate the necessary presuppositions of understanding in ongoing language games. His concern is to uncover the linguistic resources and communicative capacities speakers must have if they are to constitute and maintain a set of common meanings which form the unproblematic context of norms and opinions in everyday life and which are taken to be true, real, and legitimate by those who share those meanings.

Communicative action is characterized by the ongoing exchange of speech acts. While Habermas draws here from J.L. Austin, he most closely follows John Searle. The two share a number of views. Both consider speaking a language to be engaging in rule-governed behavior, and thus a theory of language to be part of a theory of action. Further, they consider the basic unit of linguistic communication to be not the word or sentence, but the word or sentence as produced in the performance of a speech act. Both are also interested in exploring the general distinction between the illocutionary force of an utterance and its propositional content, as well as the problem of explicating the pragmatic rules a speaker must master to produce speech acts.[11] Habermas and Searle differ, however, in several ways, most importantly in the particular theoretical use they make of the speech act perspective.

Habermas's point of departure is the idea that ongoing communicative action presupposes that speakers share a "consensus" on four "universal validity claims," which they raise in the performance of speech acts. The four claims are (1) the comprehensibility of the speech act; (2) the speaker's veracity; (3) the truth of the propositional component; and (4) the correctness or normative validity of the performative component.[12] The comprehensibility claim is immediately tested and redeemed, to the degree that the speaker has produced a grammatically well-formed sentence. If a speaker satisfies this first claim, he displays "linguistic competence" in the sense in which Noam Chomsky has used the term. (Speakers manifest this competence by their mastery of an abstract system of linguistic rules, i.e., the rules of transformational grammar.) Habermas, though, thinks that this competence is insufficient to fully explain ordinary language understanding. He posits another universal competence: "communicative competence," which may be tentatively defined as the competence to raise and redeem the three other validity claims.[13]

From the point of view of language theory, it is possible for us to have such a capacity because ordinary language contains certain "pragmatic universals" which allow us to raise the three claims. What Austin called "performative" verbs fall into this category. Habermas modifies Austin's views somewhat and comes up with a classification of performatives based on their ability to permit us to raise validity claims: "Constatives" (e.g., to state, to assert, to maintain) that make possible truth claims; "regulatives" (e.g., to order, to recommend, to proscribe) that make possible the claim of correctness or normative validity; and "representatives" (e.g., to admit, to conceal, to disclose) that make possible the veracity claim. The illocutive force of these different performatives, which is exercised when sentences are uttered, allows us to raise the three claims to validity; by so doing, it establishes the metacommunicative basis for situations of possible speech. What Habermas means by this is that when we perform a speech act, we simultaneously speak about something and do it on the basis of having (in that utterance) occupied one of the universal pragmatic functions of language represented by the three validity claims.[14]

Communicative competence involves more than the capacity for raising and intersubjectively recognizing validity claims; it involves also the capacity to redeem these claims. Each claim has a particular mode of redemption. Veracity is tested by subsequent interaction, in which a speaker's announced motives and intentions will be shown to have been either truthfully or deceptively expressed. The other two claims— truth and normative validity—are not tested in interaction, but rather in discourses; truth in "theoretical discourses" and normative validity in "practical discourses." In discourse we suspend the constraints of ongoing interaction and seek to give cognitive grounds for our validity claims.[15]

In order to understand the distinction between discourse and communicative action, it is necessary to explain what Habermas means by saying that communicative action rests on a "naive" consensus about validity claims.[16] Ongoing communicative action proceeds against an unproblematic background consensus about the veracity of participants' intentions, the truth of shared opinions, and the correctness of dominant norms. Here one can see some parallels between the model of communicative action and the strict language game model. If we think of a subtype of communicative action in which the consensus on opinions and norms not only is not, but *cannot* be, questioned in any radical sense, then one is approaching the game model. Here conflicts among opinions can be resolved only by recourse to an accepted body of knowledge, and disputes over norms can be referred only to more basic norms.

Within the model of communicative action, just as within the language game model, one can operate with the concept of context rationality. For example, when a claim of normative validity is questioned in a particular situation, explanation and justification will proceed by showing how the claim attached to the utterance can be derived from one or more basic norms. Here one can see the limited sense in which Searle's attempt to derive "ought" from "is" is justified. For people *within* a given context of communicative action, what one "ought" to do in a given situation is a question which can be answered by arguing back to what "is" a shared set of norms—something Searle calls "institutional facts."[17] The logic implied in this notion is illustrated by the familiar remark, "They ought not to do that, it's unconstitutional."

While Habermas's concept of communicative action allows some of the same insights provided by the language game model, it would also share some of that model's drawbacks (ethical relativism and the inability to handle the concept of ideology), if it were not supplemented with his notion of discourse. Specifically, Habermas maintains that a capacity for discourse is unavoidably implied in communicative action. Subjects each interact on the basis of a mutual recognition of the other individual and his validity claims; but the very possibility of this interaction rests on each subject's imputing accountability to the other. This supposition of accountability is what differentiates our attitude toward objects (or subjects treated as objects). Supposing that there is such accountability involves two expectations: that the subject ". . . knows what he is doing and why he is doing it, that is, that he intentionally holds the beliefs he does and intentionally follows the norms he does, and that he is capable of discursively justifying them if the question should arise."[18]

Now, Habermas is aware that the fulfillment of the expectation of discursive justification is "counterfactual" and could be completely satisfied only in the ideal case of "pure communicative action." As a social and political theorist, Habermas is particularly interested in how, historically, various world-views (*Weltbilder*), including modern ideologies, have performed a legitimating function in social life by systematically distorting this expectation. These world-views hinder the move from communicative action to discourse, or they restrict the topics of discourse, and thus constitute what Habermas calls structures of "systematically distorted communication."[19] Thomas McCarthy has shown how this notion might apply to belief systems of primitive societies. Using the example of the Azande tribe's belief in witchcraft, he argues that in such societies there is likely to be an absence of any alternative belief system, but even more important an unwillingness or inability to entertain such alternatives. "The situation-dependency of thought, the absence of second-order intellectual activities and the avoidance reactions to any potential challenges to the established consensus amount, in Habermas's terms, to a systematic elimination of the break with the normal context of interaction which is a condition of discourse."[20]

It is precisely to "closed" societies such as these that the language game model with its notion of context rationality seems most appropriate. Unlike this model, however, Habermas's approach through communicative action and discourse leaves intellectual access open to questions of ideology and universal standards for rationality.

Before turning to a fuller explication of the concept of discourse, it is necessary to show how Habermas's theory of action accounts for strategic action and rationality. While there is some terminological variation in Habermas's discussions of this topic, his basic categories are as follows. He distinguishes two types of purposive rational action: "strategic" or social, and "instrumental" or nonsocial (e.g., pushing a lever, building a house). Strategic action shares two characteristics with its nonsocial counterpart: both are taken up with an "objectivating attitude" and both are oriented toward success.[21]

We can examine strategic action in relation to my discussion of the shift from communicative action to discourse. This shift signifies that some element in a common web of opinions and norms has become problematic in a way that cannot be overcome by recourse to some other shared opinions or norms. In other words, a part of the consensus upon which communicative action rests has broken down. When such a breakdown occurs, though, the taking up of a discourse is only one of two courses of action open; the other is to begin acting strategically, which means that action is no longer oriented toward understanding, toward a reciprocal recognition of all four validity claims. The taking up of a strategic attitude constitutes a suspension of two validity claims: (1) veracity—the claim that, e.g., the intentions one expresses in speech acts are one's real intentions; and (2) normative validity—the claim that the norms guiding one's actions are intersubjectively valid. Strategic action is oriented toward the successful maximization of interests, and insofar as the two validity claims interfere with this orientation, they become irrational. From the perspective of communicative action, the interests guiding strategic action are conceived of as emerging from a condition of dissensus in which they are precipitated out of those common values embodied in intersubjectively valid social norms.[22]

Understanding strategic action as a derivative type of social action helps explain why political philosophy cannot be founded solely on the concept of strategic rationality. With this mode of reasoning, Habermas argues, one simply cannot comprehend what is an essential element of intersubjectively valid norms: their "ought" quality, that is, the fact that they often bind individuals even when their interests or external conditions change, making continued conformity to such norms irrational from a strategic perspective.[23] To be useful, the category of strategic action must always be conceptualized against an institutional background; that is, a background understandable only in terms of communicative action in which norms carry a consensus on their intersubjective validity claim and, because of that, can secure an effective motivation to conform to them.

Neither contractarianism nor utilitarianism has any way of conceptualizing such a background, and thus no way of casting doubt on the rationality of individuals who choose to act, say, as free riders or first-person dictators. Leaving these options open will, in the least, undermine any attempt to provide rational foundations for basic norms. And if we take the extreme case of the first-person dictator and generalize it, we end up with a collection of supposedly "rational" individuals who are altogether incapable of social life. This possibility is suggested by Isaiah Berlin's example of an individual who possesses the capacity to reason only in a strictly strategic manner and whose primary pleasure is to stick pins into surfaces with a particular resiliency.[24] And either tennis balls or human skin fill the bill nicely. When questioned about his activity, this individual readily asserts that he would not like others to stick pins in his own skin, but literally cannot understand why he should refrain from sticking them in others as often as circumstances permit. Berlin's immediate concern here is to suggest, on the one hand, that such an individual falls within the bounds of strategic reason, but questions, on the other hand, whether we would feel entirely comfortable calling this man rational. With this query, however, goes the related one as to whether the very notion of a social life among individuals of this ideal type makes any sense. The point here is not that strategic rationality necessarily entails morally repugnant values and actions, but that it does not exclude certain values and actions whose character is such that they cannot serve as part of the foundation of a legitimate political order.

II

Of course, if one now pulls back from attempting to ground political theory in the calculations of individuals acting strategically and turns simply to the category of communicative action, one is faced again with the problems which plague the language game model and context rationality. With an awareness of this dilemma, we are finally in a position to understand the significance of Habermas's notion of discourse. I will be concerned only with "practical discourse" and Habermas's contention that it holds out the possibility of justifying norms without final recourse to either more basic norms (context-rational justification) or to strategic individual choices (strategic-rational justification). At the same time, Habermas's approach does not return to traditional natural law views that rational standards obtain their validity from a transcendent reality. The justification of norms rests ultimately, for Habermas, on the possibility of a rational consensus achieved in discourse.

The notion of discourse, as explained earlier, is implicit in ongoing communicative action. The reciprocal supposition of accountability between participants in communicative action means that they could, if necessary, redeem or "discursively justify" the validity claim attached to any norm they invoke. Such a justification becomes necessary if the "naive consensus" underlying a shared norm breaks down in some way. The central question, of course, is how to reestablish the validity of a contested norm or develop a new one. In the final analysis, Habermas argues, this kind of justification can be adequately explained only in relation to the idea of a "rational" or a "true consensus."[25]

The objection which immediately arises is how Habermas can speak of a "true consensus" without, on the one hand, appealing to a transcendent standard of right or good, or, on the other hand, having the validity of such a consensus be indistinguishable from any given empirical consensus. Habermas avoids these problems by arguing that every competent speaker of a language credits himself with an intuitive knowledge on the basis of which he can distinguish generally between an agreement that is voluntary and one that is coerced.[26] This intuition is developed as we acquire our competence to communicate in ordinary language.

No doubt Habermas is aware that the boundary we perceive in everyday life between what is voluntary and what is coerced is socially conditioned to a substantial degree. He believes, though, that the boundary is not entirely socially determined. If asked to state the characteristics of any voluntary consensus, one might begin with the following predicates: achieved in a way that is "fair," "undeceptive," "free of coercion," "open to revision under changed circumstances." What Habermas intends with his notion of a discursive consensus is to sketch a set of conditions for argumentation such that, if an actual argument fulfilled them, a consensus could be reached and the foregoing predicates could be applied.

Our intuition about what is a voluntary consensus is explained by the thesis that we must always presuppose such a distinction if ordinary language is to be meaningful.[27] The conceptual tie between the understanding achieved in ordinary language communication and the idea of discursive consensus is explained in the following way: The *meaning* of the normative validity claims that we raise in regulative speech acts resides in the possibility of their redemption in discourse. As a rough analogy, Habermas points to the interpretation some philosophers of law give to the notion of a valid legal claim. The validity of a claim to, say, a piece of property means, in the final analysis, that one has effective recourse to a court; in other words, to say that one has a legal right means that one has a legal remedy.[28] Now, what Habermas wants to argue is that the meaningfulness of all normative validity claims we raise in communicative action is tied to the idea of a nonconventional "court" of reason, namely discursive consensus.

When a validity claim is explicitly challenged and justification demanded for it—that is, when we take up an actual discourse—we must "impute" (*unterstellen*) what Habermas calls an "ideal speech situation" (ISS). This mutual imputation among discourse partners is made counterfactually in the same way we suppose individuals to be accountable in communicative action. The ISS is intended to be a theoretical reconstruction of those features of ordinary language communication which allow us to distinguish intuitively a true consensus from a false one. The ISS *must* be imputed in every discourse because, if not, we would be unable to redeem validity claims, and it is on this possibility that their very meaningfulness depends (as indicated in the preceding paragraph). And it is on the meaningfulness of validity claims that the possibility of achieving understanding in communicative action rests.[29]

The features of the ISS require no metaphysical foundation; rather, they are present in our use of natural languages, and each speaker can impute them in discourse because of his communicative competence. Thus, Habermas speaks of this competence as the mastery of certain idealized features of speech situations which allows us to raise and redeem validity claims.[30] This mastery is the source of our intuition about a true consensus; hence the conditions of the ISS constitute a critical standard for any given empirical consensus. The ISS

. . . excludes systematic distortions [of communication] and guarantees especially the freedom of movement between action and discourse, and, within discourse, between the different levels of discourse. Therefore any consensus which has been argumentatively produced under conditions of an ideal speech situation should be seen as the criterion for the redemption of any given thematized validity claim. A rational consensus can, in the final analysis, only be distinguished from a deceptive one through reference to an ideal speech situation.[31]

Such a consensus could be guaranteed only if discourse were freed both from constraints external to the structure of communication (e.g., having to reach an agreement in a limited period of time) and from constraints internal to the structure of communication, which thus cause systematic distortions of discourse. Habermas characterizes the ISS such that these sorts of systematic distortions can no longer operate. Specifically, he argues that communication can be free in this sense only if we assume "for all possible participants a symmetrical distribution (*symmetrische Verteilung*) of chances to choose and carry out speech acts."[32] This general assumption of symmetry means, first, that within discourse, each speaker has an equal opportunity to initiate and continue communication. Second, each has an equal opportunity to make assertions and propose explanations (raise truth claims in constative speech acts), as well as to recommend norms (raise normative validity claims in regulative speech acts); in addition, there is an equal chance to dispute these claims, thus ensuring that no thematized subject matter can have a privileged status with regard to examination and critique. These two assumptions make certain that discussion within the ISS is formally unrestricted. Yet they fail to ensure that participants have not initiated discourse in such a way as to perpetuate patterns of distorted communication (embodied in myths and ideologies) existing in their particular context of communicative action. Nor do these assumptions ensure that discourse is not initiated with a strategic attitude, meaning that the intentions and motives of some participants are concealed.

If these sorts of distortions are not prevented in the ISS, participants could believe that they had attained a valid consensus when, in fact, it was reached under some mode of constraint. In order to preclude this possibility, the symmetry assumption must be extended to the category of communicative action. In other words, the ISS can admit only participants who *as actors* have satisfied the symmetry assumption. This means, as Habermas puts it, that the conditions of unconstrained discourse cannot be conceived apart from the conditions of "pure communicative action." In other words, the validity of reflective discourse can never be guaranteed apart from an ideal form of social life. Pure communicative action exhibits a symmetry of speech acts in two ways. First, there must be a reciprocal openness of participants in relation to their true intentions, motives, and needs, and an equal chance of expressing these in "representative" speech acts. Second, there must be an equal chance to employ "regulative" speech acts so that there are no one-sidedly binding norms; that is, an equal distribution of opportunities "to order and resist orders, to permit and forbid, to make and extract promises, and to be responsible for one's conduct and demand that others are as well."[33] These two symmetries of communicative action will guarantee that discourses are neither initiated for strategic purposes, nor limited in scope to topics predefined as permissible by a dominant set of norms.

When all four of the conditions of symmetry are satisfied, Habermas argues that we have outlined a communicative structure within which an agreement on a norm's validity would warrant the label "rational consensus." The conditions (which can be reformulated as rules) disallow any constraints on discourse which might motivate one to come to a less than fully rational consensus. With these constraints gone, the only "force" exerted in discourse would be the "compulsionless compulsion of better argument" (*zwangloser Zwang des besseren Argumentes*) by which one could be "rationally motivated."[34] With this notion of rational consensus in the ISS, Habermas believes that he has indicated how cognitive grounds for the validity of norms could be established. And it is in this sense that he says that "practical questions admit of truth."[35]

III

With this brief introduction, I have attempted to show how Habermas offers a comprehensive approach to practical rationality. He can account for the insights of both context and strategic rationality, and yet retain a perspective which provides grounds for the universal rational justification of norms. The ambitiousness of Habermas's project is striking, even if one neglects, as I have here, significant aspects of it (for example, his theory of legitimation crisis). To begin a systematic criticism of this project would go beyond the limits of this paper. It may be useful, however, to conclude by examining some of the general implications of Habermas's universalist perspective for ethics and political philosophy.

The notion of a rational consensus achievable under the conditions of the ISS is the core of what Habermas thinks can be developed into a "communicative ethics." Our mastery of the rules for constructing the ISS is what gives us our "ideas of truth, freedom, and justice."[36] Communicative ethics would thus be grounded in what Habermas calls the "fundamental norms of rational speech."[37] This phrase is perhaps unfortunate, since "norms" here do not have their usual connotation, but rather refer to the constitutive rules we must master in order to construct the ISS. Our mastery of these rules allows us to raise and redeem the various validity claims. The rules include those for appropriately using personal pronouns and the different types of performative verbs (regulative, constative, representative) as well as the symmetry rules—these last being the most important for ethics, since they relate to valid procedures for the justification of norms.

An ethical position founded on the rules of rational speech would appear to run afoul of the naturalistic fallacy. Habermas does not think that the basic ethical principle of universalizability needs to be grounded in a nonrational decision. He is able to dispense with the necessity of establishing the universalizability principle in this manner because the function of that principle is performed by the rules of rational speech, in particular the rules of symmetry. But, one might object, does not this theoretical move simply shift the problem back a step? What is the status of these rules? Can they be said to create an "ought" on the part of an individual? Habermas's answer to the first question would be that the mastery of these rules is not to be considered as some essence of human nature, but rather the necessary condition for ongoing understanding in communicative action, which in turn is a condition for the existence of a species which reproduces itself not only materially, but also socially and culturally. As to the second question, Habermas thinks that these rules do involve a type of "ought." Insofar as we participate in a context of communicative action, we have operated according to these rules and have "implicitly recognized" an obligation to the discursive redemption of norms that have become problematic.[38]

Against such an attempt to derive an obligation from descriptive features of human action, a skeptic could present the following question: Could not an individual simply refuse to engage in communicative action and orient himself entirely to strategic action, thus avoiding the immanent obligation of communicative action? Habermas's response to this question is along the lines suggested by the earlier criticism of strategic rationality. If we generalize the individual choice of systematically avoiding communicative action, we end up with a collectivity of individuals who cannot sustain what we understand to be social and cultural life.[39] Among such creatures there could be neither processes of social integration nor individual identity formation.[40] This response, of course, does not really get us over the naturalistic fallacy. To counter Habermas, the skeptic can, without being logically inconsistent, assert that he is under no obligation to preserve the possibility of social and cultural life. Thus, Habermas has not shown us that we can *logically* derive a *necessary* practical obligation for all human beings simply from some descriptive characteristics of action.

The speech act's immanent obligation therefore must be one that we in some sense choose to take on; that is, it has ultimately the logical status of a decision. I say "ultimately" because it seems to me that we are involved here with a type of decision which is quite different from ordinary decisions. By this I mean that the former is of a type which cuts against our concept of rationality, yet without violating any principle of logic. We can interpret the position of Berlin's pin-pusher as manifesting just such a decision; it is not logically inconsistent, but it is a decision categorically different from that of choosing between two types of automobiles or two political parties. The same can be said of the individual who systematically rejects all communicative action. Rejecting the conditions of possible normative interaction is something quite different from rejecting a particular norm or "institutional fact."

This difference might best be described as one between those decisions which cut against a certain conceptual (but not logical) necessity and those which do not do so.[41] Decisions of the latter type are perfectly understandable in terms of our concepts of rationality, man, and social life. Decisions of the former type, on the other hand, take us toward the limits of these concepts, such that we have difficulty comprehending what the structure of individual and social life would be like were these choices made.[42] If Habermas has in fact elucidated a conceptual limit of this sort, then he does have some ground for claiming that there is a necessary connection between communicative action, rationality, and a minimal ethical orientation embodied in the obligation to mutual accountability. Moreover, in exposing this connection, Habermas is giving us an account of that sense of "rationality" we feel is lost when the concept is reduced to the strategic calculations of isolated subjects. Habermas is showing us why rationality is assessable with equal validity from both a subjective and an intersubjective perspective; why the rational individual's judgments and actions may be evaluated not only in relation to his/her values and goals, but also in relation to those of all others to whom that individual's normative claims apply. In making those claims in ongoing interaction, the individual takes on an obligation to others to be accountable for them; that is, to be responsible to others in speech. And to be responsible to others in speech means to be prepared to offer justifications aimed at inducing the agreement of others.[43]

Habermas's argument about the conceptually necessary relation between communicative action, rationality, and a minimal ethical orientation is clearly intended to be universally applicable. It is difficult, however, to avoid the suspicion that there is something peculiarly modern about this analysis. In other words, the necessity Habermas wants to demonstrate may actually be one which holds only within the conceptual horizons of modernity.[44] And if this is so, he may have illuminated something quite significant about the presuppositions of intersubjectivity in the modern world, but he will not have laid the spectre of relativism to rest.

In relation to political theory, one final point needs to be emphasized. It should be at least somewhat clear as a result of my analysis of Habermas's position that he does not intend the ideal speech situation to be some sort of organizational blueprint for a "rational society."[45] Rather, it constitutes a critical standard in terms of which any proposed set of basic social norms can in principle be assessed. In this sense, it is somewhat analogous to John Rawls' notion of the "original position" and the agreement attainable under its requirements.[46] One can think of the original position as embodying the conditions of a possible fair agreement about norms to regulate basic institutions. Habermas has simply taken this mode of questioning further. The ideal speech situation describes the conditions of possible intersubjectivity, and these conditions in turn limit what can be considered rationally justifiable norms.

CHAPTER EIGHT
Political Ethics and Critical Theory
J. Donald Moon

The preceding authors in this volume all share the general view that social and political inquiry should be more "critical" than it now tends to be. They have stressed the reflexivity of social knowledge, and have called for a rethinking of the relationship between social theory and common-sense knowledge, and for the development of new models of social explanation. A central theme in these essays has been the expansion of the role of social theory to include social criticism and the advocacy of new institutions and practices. This emphasis upon the critical dimension of social theory raises crucially important issues regarding the status of value judgments in social science. For if social scientists are to adopt an advocacy role, they must be able to provide some grounding for the values they advance. Otherwise, they will leave themselves open to the charge that they are no longer doing social science, but ideology.

In this essay I will focus on Habermas's conception of critical theory and especially on the role that value judgments play in it. I would like to present some of my own doubts about this argument regarding the cognitive status of the values that are central to his theory. I do not intend to offer a general critique of the idea of a critical theory of society, but only to question one particular version of it. But the questions I raise will, I think, have important implications for critical theory in general.

The Concept of a Critical Theory

The notion of a critical theory of society is one that is not generally familiar to social scientists in this country. Most of us were raised on a conception of social theory that is broadly naturalistic, in the sense that it is modelled on the natural sciences. The dominant understanding of so-called empirical theory in the social sciences today continues to be informed by conceptions of theory, laws, explanation, and concept-formation which were first developed in the philosophy of the natural sciences. In the past ten years or so, this understanding has changed significantly. The prevailing view a decade ago was deeply influenced by positivism, but in recent years many have come to accept those critiques of positivism which have stressed the conceptual presuppositions of scientific work and the inadequacy of straightforward notions of verification or falsification. Nonetheless, even radical post-Kuhnian views of social science continue to accept at least tacitly the naturalist view of scientific explanation in terms of the subsumption of individual events under general laws.

This nomological account of explanation is the keystone to a naturalist account of social science, and it underlies the instrumentalist relationship between theory and practice to which this view of social science gives rise. Social science can be utilized in social life inasmuch as it gives us knowledge of the functional or causal relationships that hold among variables, thereby telling us what variables we must control or manipulate in order to achieve desired values of other variables. A case in point is Keynesian economics, which is a theory that enables us to give more or less adequate explanations of such phenomena as under-employment, the trade cycle, and inflation. At the same time *and precisely because it provides such explanations*, it tells us what we must do in order to control these variables.

A glance at the burgeoning literature in the field of public policy is sufficient to demonstrate that an instrumentalist orientation to political practice is the dominant orientation of this field of political science. Although the explicit concern for value-oriented research may mark a break with at least some of the tenets of behavioral political science, the instrumentalist conception of political practice indicates that the growth of policy analysis by no means marks a new revolution in political science; rather, it is continuous with the dominant behavioral persuasion.

In addition to the instrumentalist, or engineering, model of the relationship between social theory and political practice, there is another model that, like the instrumentalist model, is rooted in a particular account of political and social inquiry. This account might be called the "interpretive," "hermeneutic," or *verstehende* model of social inquiry, and it is one that has come into prominence as a major alternative to behavioralism. Unlike behavioralism, which is indebted to positivist views of the philosophy of natural science, this approach draws heavily on the philosophy of action and language, and on European traditions growing out of the work of Dilthey, Husserl, and Heidegger. It focuses on the intentional character of social phenomena, on the fact that social phenomena are ultimately constituted by the intentional actions of social actors, and must be understood in terms of socially accepted beliefs, purposes, values, and world-views. In the social sciences, according to this model, we are concerned to explain human behavior by grasping its *meaning* or *sense*, and this requires that we understand it from the point of view, and in terms of the concepts and self-understandings, of social actors.

A purely *verstehende* social science gives rise to a particular relationship between theory and practice. An interpretive social theory becomes practical by clarifying the meaning of otherwise unclear or puzzling behavior, by explicating and establishing traditions, and by bringing out the basic assumptions and conceptualizations which underlie a form of life. It does not provide a basis for manipulation and instrumental control, but, rather, by clarifying intentions and expectations, it facilitates mutual understanding and communication.

There is one important point that must be noticed about this interpretive model: it is based upon a postulate of rationality. Because it seeks to explain behavior by bringing out its meaning in terms of the actors' values, beliefs, and world-views, it implicitly assumes the rationality or coherence of the actions or practices in question. If we suppose that an action may not make sense, may not be fully coherent with and appropriate to the actor's situation and his or her beliefs and values, then the possibility of a complete interpretive understanding is denied to us. Moreover, in such situations there will be a number of alternative ways of construing the action in question and, from a purely interpretive perspective, there will be no basis for choosing among them.

An obvious example of such problematic behavior is neurotic behavior, where the person's actions do not make sense at the level of social meaning, or in terms of the actor's avowed or conscious intentions and beliefs. The person who compulsively washes his or her hands is not engaged in instrumentally appropriate action, for the person's hands are already clean. In such cases the actor often cannot provide a reason for his or her action, or the reasons provided are shifting, vague, inconsistent, or in some other ways incoherent.

More controversial examples are actions which make sense in terms of the social norms or practices of the actor's society, but where we cannot give a coherent account of the practices themselves. We cannot simply take it for granted that the belief systems and world-views of each and every society form coherent, well-integrated wholes. But if we confine ourselves to the concepts and self-understandings of social actors, we would have no basis for accounting for and explaining the incoherences which we may find in the traditions of a society. And, more important from the point of view of the relationship between social theory and political practice, we would have no basis from which to criticize these traditions, no standpoint from which to defend changes or reforms in socially accepted self-understandings and practices. Thus, a purely interpretive or *verstehende* social science is necessarily conservative, for it gives rise to a form of political practice that is closely bound to the existing traditions of a society, and that divests itself of any standpoint from which these traditions might themselves be called into question. In Oakeshott's phrase, politics becomes "the activity of exploring and pursuing the intimations of a tradition of behavior."[1]

I have been dwelling on difficulties with the interpretive model of social science, but from the point of view of political practice, the naturalist model is equally deficient. For this model provides us with no basis for deciding on the ends or values which a social theory is to serve. But this is not to say that it leaves the question of ends open, that such a science is value-free or value-neutral. In the first place, as I have argued elsewhere, any social theory of significant scope will be based on a conception of man that will have significant evaluative implications.[2] Second, and more important for my purposes, a social theory that allows only an instrumental relationship to practice is one that drastically restricts the purposes which theory can serve. On the one hand, such a theory increases the power of manipulation and control of those actors and groups who are in a position to use the theory because of their strategic position within a society. On the other hand, such a theory cannot serve to enlighten political actors by criticizing their own self-understandings and revealing to them the ways in which their own beliefs and values may be confused or incoherent. In general, such a social theory reinforces the political realm as an arena of instrumental action, to the exclusion of other possible conceptions of the political.[3]

So far I have presented two alternative conceptions of social theory, the ways in which these conceptions may be applied in practice or become practical, and some of the difficulties of each conception. I have chosen this somewhat roundabout method of getting to my topic because critical social theory takes its point of departure from the inadequacies of these two models, and attempts to overcome them by developing a synthesis of the naturalist and interpretive conceptions of social theory.

Briefly stated, a critical theory of society is a social theory that is developed with practical intent. Critical theory seeks to provide an interpretation of social conditions which begins with the self-understandings of the social actors, but which does not take these self-understandings for granted. Rather, it subjects them to sustained criticism with the objective of uncovering their basic contradictions, incoherences, and ideological distortions. Further, critical theory seeks to explain the power and persistence of such ideological distortions by showing how systematically distorted ideas and belief systems arise, and the role they play in maintaining a system of social interaction. Moreover, it also provides an analysis of the workings of the social system, showing the ways in which a system crisis could arise, thereby providing for the possibility of critical theory's becoming itself a material force leading to system change.

This characterization of critical theory is very abstract, and it must be filled in with examples. Habermas himself offers psychoanalysis and Marxism as examples of critical theory, and his own *Legitimation Crisis* represents an attempt to develop the outlines of a critical theory of advanced capitalist societies. Psychoanalysis, because it is focused on the individual, may be the easiest to describe as a critical theory.

At the risk of serious oversimplification, psychoanalysis may be characterized in the following terms. In the first place, the analyst begins with the utterances and actions of the patient, and identifies those which are incomprehensible at the level of ordinary language and interaction. These are actions to which a clear meaning cannot be given because, for example, there may be a discrepancy between what the patient says and his or her accompanying gestures and manner, or between the patient's statements and actions, or between his or her perceptions and reality. The analyst then interprets the meaning of this behavior by showing how it expresses unacknowledged intentions, desires, or needs, which have arisen usually from some traumatic experience that caused the disturbance. This interpretation is possible only on the basis of a theory of socialization and personality development that the analyst employs, for it is only on the basis of such a theory that we can specify what the effects of the traumatic situation are or could be. The adequacy of the interpretation is confirmed by its coming to be recognized and accepted by the patient in his or her self-reflection on the original episode, and by the patient's ability, on the basis of this recognition, to overcome the symptomatic behavior.[4]

Although this sketch is extremely oversimplified, it is adequate to bring out some of the ways in which critical theory differs from other forms of social theory in terms of its relationship to practice. In the first place, it is tied to an interest in emancipation, in achieving self-clarification or undistorted self-understanding. Secondly, it achieves this purpose at least in part through communicative action, through dialogue leading to self-reflection that transforms the actor's orientation to life, increasing his or her autonomy and powers of self-determination. Unlike interpretive social theories, then, critical theory is not restricted simply to clarifying an actor's self-understandings, or explicating social tradition; rather, it provides a basis for criticizing and altering the social life-world. Unlike naturalist social theories, it is not restricted to an engineering or technical application to practice, and the values or ends it serves are internal to the theory itself, and are not arbitrarily chosen or decided upon.

The Cognitive Status of Value Judgments

Put in this way, the notion of a critical theory comes up against the doctrine of value noncognitivism. For critical theory is based on a particular conception of human emancipation, and unless this value can be justified, it is open to the charge of not being a "theory" at all, but a form of propaganda or persuasion masquerading as science. Indeed, these charges are familiar criticisms of Marxism and psychoanalysis, and they are based on a view of science which sharply distinguishes theory from evaluation. In fact, the choice between critical theory and traditional theory—whether naturalist or interpretive—turns in part on the justifiability of the value claims that critical theory makes. If we cannot provide adequate justifications, then critical theory is in danger of degenerating into a kind of dogmatism that may be successful as a political ideology, but can make no claim to truth.

Jürgen Habermas has attempted to deal with this question explicitly. The argument he has developed has two aims: In the first place, he tries to show that value judgments and normative claims are cognitive, that they can be tested for their correctness, and accepted or rejected accordingly. Secondly, he has incorporated his account of values into his critical theory of modern society in such a way as to show how the development of normative structures of society may be influenced by rational criticism. Although it does some violence to his argument, I will focus only on the first part of his argument. This part is in some ways the more crucial one, for if it fails, then so does his account of crisis tendencies in advanced capitalist society, for that account depends upon the idea that "social evolution transpires . . . within the bounds of a logic of the life-world, the structures of which are determined by linguistically produced intersubjectivity and are based on criticizable validity claims."[5] Thus, if a rational basis for accepting the validity of normative claims cannot be provided, his theory of social evolution and his critical theory of society must also be called into question.

Habermas develops a two-part argument for his contention that "values and norms have an immanent relationship to truth."[6] In the first part, he criticizes decisionistic notions of legitimacy, beginning with Weber's concept of legitimation. He then goes on to develop his own account, centering on the idea of a "rational will" and "generalizable interests." Habermas's critique of noncognitivism turns on the idea that it is always appropriate to ask for reasons to back up a moral judgment, and that this distinguishes genuine value judgments from mere statements of preference or other forms of emotive utterances. Habermas concludes from this that norms do not rest on nonrational decisions, but on at least "the conviction that consensus on a recommended norm could be brought about *with reasons*."[7]

Habermas recognizes that sophisticated noncognitivists could accept this line of argument, holding that while any particular value judgment must be backed up by reasons, there is an irreducible plurality of systems of values and norms, and ultimately a choice of a particular system can only be made as an existential commitment. The problem with this argument, according to Habermas, is that it rests on too narrow a view of argumentation. It recognizes only deductive arguments, while validity claims—claims to truth or to legitimacy—must be settled by what Habermas calls "substantial arguments." Such arguments "have the force to convince the participants in a discourse of a validity claim, that is, to provide rational grounds for the recognition of validity claims." While the rules of argumentation are different in theoretical and in practical discourse, "in both cases the goal is the same: a rationally motivated decision about the recognition (or rejection) of validity claims."[8] Thus, substantial arguments exist in the form of a discourse among people who are seeking a basis for accepting or rejecting a norm or belief. They do not provide a demonstration that a conclusion is necessary, given certain premises, but they lead to a rational consensus on that conclusion among the participants. The consensus is rationally grounded in the sense that all of the objections which have been posed have been answered, and so the participants in discourse have good reason to accept the position in question.

One crucial kind of objection that might be offered to an argument purporting to justify a certain norm or value has to do with the language or conceptual framework in which it is stated. The plausibility—even the possibility—of making a certain argument depends on the system of concepts which the argument employs. In Habermas's words, "There is no mode of experience independent of the language in the frame of which we give our descriptions of what we see or of what we need. The persuasive force of an argument therefore depends on the appropriateness of the language in which we phrase our arguments."[9] This can be seen very easily if we consider the examples of moral argument offered by people like Searle or Foot, which essentially turn on the acceptance of a certain mode of description and certain conventions of usage in order to bridge the gap between descriptive statements and moral evaluations. In Searle's famous example, the fact that someone made a promise to do something is a reason for saying that he or she has a moral obligation to do it, and this inference is licensed by the concept of "promise," which is grounded in a set of conventions specifying a structure of rules and social practices.[10]

The problem with this form of argument is that, by shifting the conceptual framework, the plausibility of the claim in question may be dissolved. Thus questions regarding the appropriateness of a language or framework must also be subject to argumentation, and so the participants in discourse must be free to question and to alter "the descriptive system in the context of which they interpret their experience and needs."[11] Thus the formal properties of the discourse situation must allow for movement from one level of argumentation to another. Communication cannot be impeded either by "external contingent forces," such as political or economic power, or by "constraints arising from the structure itself."[12] This means that there must be "an equal distribution of opportunities for all possible participants to choose and perform speech acts."[13] When these conditions are realized, we have what Habermas calls an ideal speech situation.

Ideal speech situations, then, realize the formal properties of discourse. These properties can be specified more precisely as follows:

> Discourse can be understood as that form of communication that is removed from contexts of experience and action and whose structure assures us: that the bracketed validity claims of assertions, recommendations, or warnings are the exclusive object of discussion; that participants, themes, and contributions are not restricted except with reference to the goal of testing the validity claims in question; that no force except that of the better argument is

exercised; and that, as a result, all motives except that of the cooperative search for truth are excluded.[14]

Given that these conditions are realized, a consensus on a particular norm or value will express a "rational will": Such a norm would be justified or valid. It would be justified because all possible objections to it would have been posed, and answered, by all those affected by it.

The consensus emerging from discourse, or what Habermas calls a "discursively formed will," expresses a *"common* interest ascertained *without deception.* The interest is common because the constraint-free consensus permits only what all can want; it is free of deception because even the interpretations of needs in which each individual must be able to recognize what he wants become the object of discursive will-formation."[15] This second point, that the consensus is ascertained without deception, is crucial because it brings out one of the ways in which discourse is a learning experience for its participants. While a person may enter a discourse situation with a certain conception of what his or her interests or needs are, this conception is itself subject to argumentation. Thus, the interpretive system in accordance with which needs and desires are specified may be revised and the participants come to see their needs—and, I might add, themselves—differently. The interests and needs that a consensus expresses, then, will be generalizable interests, that is, "needs *that can be communicatively shared."*[16] These are needs that can be acknowledged both to oneself and to others.

Habermas recognizes that sometimes disputes will arise that cannot be settled by appeal to generalizable interests because the interests in question are particular. In such cases it is appropriate to settle these issues through compromise, provided the relative power of the contending parties is approximately equal. But the fact that a situation involves only nongeneralizable interests can itself "be tested only through discourse."[17] Thus even in these cases the possibility of a rationally motivated consensus is central to Habermas's argument.

Let me quickly review the argument that has been made so far. I began with the idea that questions of values and norms are distinguished from issues of preference or taste by the fact that they make a claim to validity that must be backed up with reasons. Validity claims, whether regarding empirical or normative questions, cannot be demonstrated deductively, but can only be shown to be rationally grounded through substantial argumentation. Substantial argumentation produces a consensus, but this consensus can be taken as rationally motivated—as carrying a claim to truth or legitimacy—only if the process of argumentation meets certain conditions, namely, those which allow for unrestricted communication among participants. These can be formalized into a set of conditions of discourse. When these conditions are realized, a consensus on norms or values will be based only upon generalizable, common interests, and will express a rational will. It follows from this that social or political norms, to be valid, must rest upon or give expression to generalizable interests.

Before going on to draw out the implications of this argument, I would like to point out that Habermas's "rational will" is very similar to Rousseau's "general will." The general will is general in two senses: It expresses the will of everyone, and it applies to everyone. It is distinguished from the will of all by the fact that the general will regards only common interests, and not private or particular interests, those based on egoism or vanity. The process of formulating the general will—the deliberations of all the citizens, of everyone affected by the decision—is a learning process for the participants, one in which they come to have a different and better understanding of their own wants and needs. The general will, then, is most assuredly a rational will in Habermas's sense.

The role of discourse in Habermas's conception of politics points up another similarity to Rousseau, that is, the centrality of the values of equality, justice, and freedom as self-determination. For if the validation of a norm through discourse is the criterion of political legitimacy, then the conditions of an ideal speech situation become norms which must be realizable or at least not violated within a society. The notion of an ideal speech situation implies a form of life in which equality and reciprocity are realized, and in which people have become clear to themselves and live in accordance with their own consciously understood and articulated values and norms. To the extent that the context of action institutes radical inequalities, then it would be impossible for social actors to express themselves fully in the context of discourse.

The centrality of discourse also provides the touchstone for the activities of the critical theorist. For insofar as norms in our present society are not based on generalizable interests, they are based on force and could not emerge as a rational consensus. These norms, of course, will be given an ideological justification: It will be claimed that they are based on generalizable interests, and they will be formulated in a language or conceptual framework that renders this claim plausible. The critical theorist, then, must begin by answering the question: What norms could be discursively justified, given the limiting conditions which face the society? These norms are then compared to the prevailing normative structures, giving us a model of the suppression of generalizable interests in the society. This model provides an explanation of the way in which an ideology functions to provide apparent legitimation for a structure of domination, while at the same time showing the logical possibility of undermining its claims to normative validity by providing a critique of that ideology.[18]

The critical theorist's critique of ideology, the identification of suppressed generalizable interests, and the development of alternative norms and values constitute the "advocacy role" of critical theory. It must be stressed, however, that a critical theory is not a substitute for discourse. On the contrary, the proposals that the critical theorist advances are hypothetical, they are, in Habermas's memorable phrase, "anticipations of a future consensus." That is to say, they must themselves be tested by public discourse. A critical theory of society can be confirmed only by its free acceptance by the society toward which it is directed. This is, of course, one of the distinctive features of critical theory—its claim to truth or validity as a theory is defined in part in terms of its relationship to practice, in terms of its confirmation in the practical discourse of men and women.

The argument Habermas has made is very appealing. The idea of a critical theory is particularly attractive, for it enables us to clear up all sorts of difficulties in the philosophy and methodology of the social sciences. Even more important, it provides a way to think about social and political theory that is compatible with a respect for human dignity and self-determination, and at the same time is rigorous and demanding in its explanatory aims.

Nonetheless, in the end I find Habermas's account of the cognitive structure of normative discourse to be unconvincing. While I do not accept the noncognitivist account of value judgments, I do not think we can avoid accepting an irreducible plurality of possible value systems. Although the choice of any particular system may be rationally defended, I do not think it possible to show that a consensus on values would necessarily emerge in an ideal speech situation. The basic problem with Habermas's argument turns on the idea of "generalizable interests" as a basis for the validity of norms.

There are two essential problems with the standard of generalizable interests. In the first place, it is inadequate because agreement on basic human interests cannot be expected in an ideal speech situation, and so it cannot provide a criterion of normative validity, nor serve as the basis for the "advocacy role" of critical theory. Second, and more important, many of our deepest and most troubling moral and political disputes do not turn on the opposition of interests, but on fundamentally opposed moral ideals and world-views. Even if we could agree that a certain norm was based upon generalizable human interests, it might still be disputed because it was offensive to our moral ideals, or because it neglected the interests of nonhuman beings. In the next two sections I will present and defend these two criticisms.

Generalizable Interests and Rational Consensus

Assuming that a consensus on a norm were to emerge from an ideal speech situation, it seems fair to say that it would express a rational will, and that such a norm would be valid or binding. But what reason do we have for expecting that such a consensus would necessarily emerge? The formal properties of discourse, which specify that discourse be open, and that participants be free to object to or question any proposed norm, are supposed to guarantee that the only norms which everyone would accept will be those which express or at least are compatible with everyone's interests. This requires that interests or needs of the participants may become the subject of discourse, should someone object to a proposed norm as harmful to his or interests. For people to agree to reject the proposed norm, they would have to recognize that the interest in question reflects a basic or at least genuine human need. However, even in the absence of distortions in communication (due to bad faith, self-deception, or unconscious, unavowed desires), it may be impossible to reach a consensus on what constitutes a genuine human need. What we take to be a genuine need will depend on our conception of what it is to be a person, our model of man, our philosophical anthropology. And while we should always be able to give good reasons for adopting one model of man as against another, I do not see any reason for supposing that a consensus on one particular model will be reached. This is especially true in an ideal speech situation, where all possible objections can be raised—and so we must expect the discussion to go on indefinitely without reaching consensus.

It must be emphasized that this indeterminacy is not peculiar to normative discourse; rather, it follows from the rejection of justificationist views of knowledge. Once we admit that our knowledge claims must be couched in some conceptual framework that is at least in principle subject to criticism and change, then we must admit that each and every statement, no matter how well grounded it appears to be, is open to question. A consensus that exists within any given community at any given time must be seen as transitory, and long-settled disputes may always be reopened. Because the cogency of the claims we advance—whether practical or theoretical—depends upon the language in which they are stated and because an ideal speech situation allows for the possibility of questioning and revising that language, the possibility of consensus is necessarily problematic.

It is instructive, I think, to contrast Habermas with Rousseau in this regard. For Rousseau also expects a general will to emerge from discourse, but not simply because of the formal conditions of discourse, but because of the empirical conditions of a particular form of life—because of the common patterns of socialization, common mores and traditions, a civil religion, and censorship. That is, agreement on the general will is contingent upon the existence of particular social and historical circumstances and, in fact, is impossible to achieve in most societies. Moreover, such consensus is specific to a particular society, and we are left with a kind of social and historical relativism, in which there may well be a plurality of alternative value perspectives corresponding to the plurality of societies and epochs.

To suppose that this is not the case, that a consensus on human needs will actually emerge from an ideal speech situation, would appear to require that one posit that there is only one conception of what it is to be a person that is adequate to our experience as human beings, at least at any given stage of the development of the forces of production. Traditionally, political philosophers have attempted to offer such conceptions, either in essentialist or in historicist guises. On the one hand, human nature can be conceived as fixed, consisting of a given set of needs and capacities, and the human good conceived as the fulfillment of these needs and the exercise of these capacities. On the other hand, human nature can be viewed as teleological, developing over time and changing with our growing insight into the nature of the world and our position in it, or as a consequence of the development of the mode of production. Such views, however, are explicitly rejected by Habermas, and have generally come to be regarded as untenable. Fixed conceptions of human nature can be reconciled with historical and anthropological evidence only with great difficulty, while historicist views are subject to deep philosophical and methodological criticisms. But if we reject such conceptions, on what basis can we assume that people will agree on a common definition of basic human needs?

Generalizable Interests and Political Arguments

My second objection to Habermas's account of legitimation is his acceptance of the standard of "generalizable interests" as the ultimate basis of collective norms and values. Unquestionably, this is an important ground of legitimation, but it is one that is contestable. In fact, it appears that at least some of the conflicts over what are broadly called environmental issues are rooted in a rejection of "generalizable interests" as an adequate standard to govern the relationship between humanity and nature. This is an issue that Karl-Otto Apel has recently addressed in an essay entitled "The Conflicts of Our Time and the Problem of Political Ethics." Briefly, Apel argues that resolving the ecological crisis, which has been brought about in part by the technical capabilities of science, requires a philosophically grounded ethics of collective responsibility. Unfortunately, the possibility of such an ethics has been called into question "because modern science has appropriated and monopolized the notion of rational, intersubjectively binding validation on the level of value-free analysis, with the result that all theoretical structures that are not value-free appear to be mere ideology."[19] Apel claims that the required political ethics can, however, be validated through reflection on the conditions of communication and on the necessary construct of an ideal speech community. According to Apel, such a communicative ethics has direct implications for our present situation, for it entails the imperative "that the survival of the real communications community be secured."[20] This requires political policies to be designed to secure human survival by using the appropriate theories of natural science. The political methods for formulating and implementing these policies, however, must not violate or set aside "those rules of democracy that can be viewed as partial institutional implementation of the ideal communication community."[21]

This rather meager result is, I believe, a reflection of the ultimate formalism of a communicative or discourse-based ethics. But Apel's argument is also interesting because the argument misunderstands the nature of the issues involved in the so-called ecological crisis. For Apel, the crucial problem is one of human survival while maintaining the institutions and rules of democracy. This is a natural perspective for an ethics that focuses upon generalizable interests or genuine human needs. As Hobbes was fond of emphasizing, our first need is to survive.

Of course, to some extent the conflict about our treatment of the natural environment does turn on the problem of human survival. Certainly this is the central concern of the Club of Rome and numerous popular accounts of the problem focusing on the limits to economic activity that are posed by the natural environment. According to these accounts, continued population growth will eventually outstrip the globe's capacity to produce food, or continued economic activity will deplete the fixed stocks of natural resources, such as minerals and fuels, that are available in nature, or growing levels of industrial activity will produce intolerable levels of pollution. Whether the limit we face is starvation, raw materials shortages, or excessive pollution, the result is the same: the impossibility of continuing our present form of life, perhaps even massive starvation and death as the carrying capacity of the planet is degraded.

The scenario is, I think it is safe to say, rejected by most social scientists, particularly economists. They recognize that there are specific problems of environmental degradation, and argue that what we must do is design policies that correct these particular deficiencies in such a way as to maximize the total benefits we acquire from the natural world. This may involve, for example, policies to reduce (or increase) pollution to its optimal level, or policies to change the rate at which we use up some natural resources such as oil. Of course, in evaluating the benefits we get from nature, we must be careful to include such goods as our aesthetic appreciation of natural beauty or wilderness.

What is significant about this dispute is that it is conducted within a common frame of reference. Both the Club of Rome and their critics agree that the issue is one of maximizing the satisfaction of human needs through our interactions with nature. What they disagree about is the impact our actions are likely to have on the ecosystem, which is in part rooted in differing views of the operation of social processes and institutions (such as markets) and in part in different beliefs about natural processes (such as the stability of ecological systems). In large measure, these are essentially technical questions. For both sides, and implicitly for Apel as well, the standard of value is human need, and our relationship to nature, to the world of things, is esentially instrumental.[22]

For many in the ecology movement, however, it is this very conception of the relationship of man to nature that is at issue. Although many of their arguments are couched in terms of environmental constraints on economic activity, these constraints are really secondary. A notable example in this regard is E. J. Schumacher, whose *Small Is Beautiful* has been an essential text of the ecology movement. When Schumacher makes recommendations about how we ought to live, he does not base them upon a scientific understanding of the environment together with the normative goal of maximizing the satisfaction of human needs and wants. In fact, he explicitly and repeatedly rejects this goal, at least as it relates to the achievement of material affluence. What is necessary, he argues, is to develop "a life-style which accords to material things their proper, legitimate place, which is secondary and not primary."[23]

There are two themes that run through Schumacher's argument. The first is an account of human material needs as essentially limited and subordinate to spiritual needs:

> The insights of wisdom enable us to see the hollowness and fundamental unsatisfactoriness of life devoted primarily to the pursuit of material ends, to the neglect of the spiritual. Such a life necessarily sets man against man and nation against nation, because man's needs are infinite and infinitude can be achieved only in the spiritual realm, never in the material.[24]

This conception of human needs is integrally related to a second theme, which is Schumacher's reverential conception of nature and of man's relationship to nature. When Schumacher talks of natural limits on man's activities, and of the need to live peacefully with nature, he is not invoking a scientific view of nature, but an essentially religious view. To make this distinction clear, consider what it means to say that humans are part of nature. On the one hand, it might mean something like: humans are natural beings, who are dependent upon nature in order to satisfy biological needs, and their actions have consequences for various natural processes. This is essentially a causal view, and one that properly underlies the science of ecology. On the other hand, this statement might mean that humans are part of a natural order, that the purpose and meaning of human life depends upon humanity's place in this natural order, and that humans therefore owe a certain respect to nature. This is essentially a moral or religious view of nature; unlike modern science, it sees nature in terms of purpose and meaning, and for those who adopt or, I should say, live this view, the world is not yet disenchanted.

It is because of the fact that Schumacher has an essentially reverential perspective on the relationship between nature and civilization that he is critical of modern industrial society and of the instrumentalist attitude that is its basis. For the instrumentalist, humanity is the measure of all things, and nothing has value apart from our purposes. But from the religious perspective, such an attitude constitutes the sin of pride. From this perspective, humanity and nature both serve purposes beyond themselves, and these purposes restrict the ways we can treat nature and, for that matter, one another.

It is because of this essentially religious perspective that Schumacher can speak of our technology as being violent, and our attitude towards nature as being predatory. From a strictly secular point of view, it is meaningless to talk of being violent towards nature, or having a violent technology, because nonhuman nature is merely a thing, or a collection of things. We can only violate, or be violent towards, objects to which we owe respect, objects which have rights, and to which we have duties. We can, then, be violent towards other people, but not towards mere things. But from the reverential point of view, nature partakes in God's order and purpose, and so when we act in a way that is incompatible with that order, we do violence.

If I am right in arguing that part of what is involved in the disputes over our use of the environment is a fundamental disagreement about what should be our relationship to nature, then these conflicts could not even in principle be settled by an appeal to generalizable interests. This standard begs the question at issue by requiring that we adopt an essentially instrumentalist view toward nature, when that is the very point at issue. The appeal to generalizable interests, then, prejudges a practical issue which is itself to be settled in the context of discourse.[25]

Conclusion

I began this paper by observing that the hope for a more critical social and political theory depends upon our developing an adequate way to ground the political values such a theory requires. Perhaps the most promising work in this direction is that of Habermas, who has argued that a powerful normative standard, what might be called the principle of generalizable interests, is implicit in the structure of communication itself. But in subjecting his argument to close examination, I have found that it is not sufficient to overcome the "pluralism of apparently ultimate value orientations."

While discourse may be able to resolve some value conflicts on the basis of generalizable interests, many conflicts cannot be settled on these grounds. This is because our conception of what is in our interests depends upon our conception of the self, or what it is to be a person, and it is far from obvious that people who do not take a great deal about their lives and the structure of their society for granted could come to agree on such a conception. Even more important, moral conflicts may not simply express conflicts of interest but also involve conflicting moral ideals and world-views; the standard of generalizable interests is too narrow a perspective to resolve such disputes. Thus, the advocacy role of critical theory is apt to be either very narrow, or to rest upon value judgments for which it cannot give a cognitive grounding.

If Habermas's attempt to provide an adequate grounding for normative and evaluative claims fails, this does not mean that critical theory itself is impossible. However, it does mean that our hopes for a radical restructuring of political and social theory must be tempered. Until we have developed an account of practical discourse that shows how values can be discursively justified, the very idea of critical theory will remain problematic.

Notes

Chapter One

1. On the origins and development of this school see especially Martin Jay, *The Dialectical Imagination* (Boston: Little, Brown, 1973). For comprehensive treatments of the thought of the Frankfurt School see David Held, *Introduction to Critical Theory: Horkheimer to Habermas* (Berkeley: University of California Press, 1980) and *On Critical Theory*, ed. John O'Neill (New York: Seabury Press, 1976).

2. The classical statement of the critique of traditional science is Horkheimer's "Traditionelle und Kritische Theorie," translated as "Traditional and Critical Theory" in *Critical Theory*, trans. M. J. O'Connell (New York: Herder and Herder, 1972).

3. For more extended treatments of the thought of Jürgen Habermas, see Part IV of Richard Bernstein, *The Restructuring of Social and Political Theory* (New York: Harcourt Brace Jovanovich, 1976) and Thomas A. McCarthy, *The Critical Theory of Jürgen Habermas* (Cambridge, Mass.: MIT Press, 1978). Also note the many footnote references in the Dickens essay in the volume at hand.

4. For a comprehensive discussion of central figures in these traditions see Josef Bleicher, *Contemporary Hermeneutics* (London: Routledge and Kegan Paul, 1980). Also helpful are collections on interpretation and understanding, such as *Understanding and Social Inquiry*, ed. Fred R. Dallmayr and Thomas A. McCarthy (Notre Dame: University of Notre Dame Press, 1976) and *Interpretive Social Science: A Reader*, ed. Paul Rabinow and William M. Sullivan (Berkeley: University of California Press, 1979).

5. For sociology see, e.g., Alvin W. Gouldner, *The Coming Crisis of Western Sociology* (New York: Avon Equinox, 1970). For political science see, e.g., the essays in *The Post-Behavioral Era*, ed. George Graham and George Carey (New York: McKay, 1972) and Charles Taylor, "Neutrality in Political Science" in *Philosophy, Politics and Society* (Third Series), ed. Peter Laslett and W. G. Runciman (Oxford: Blackwell, 1969).

6. Jürgen Habermas, *Theory and Practice*, trans. John Viertel (Boston: Beacon Press, 1973), p. 254.

7. For an interesting discussion of the vicissitudes in the development of this program see the Chapter "Economics" in *The Social Sciences since the Second World War* by Daniel Bell (New Brunswick, N.J.: Transaction Books, 1982), pp. 66–83.

8. Adam Smith, *The Wealth of Nations* (1776), Book I, Section II, first para.

9. The major works in question are Edmund Husserl's *The Crisis of the European Sciences* (Evanston: Northwestern University Press, 1970) and *Knowledge and Human Interests* by Jürgen Habermas, trans. Jeremy J. Shapiro

(Boston: Beacon Press, 1971). For a comparison of the differing critiques of scientism see Jerald Wallulis, "The Relationship between Theory and Emancipation in Husserl and Habermas," *Analecta Hussserliana*, XV (1982) (forthcoming).

10. For other discussions of the Hobbesian image of naturalist social science see Alan Ryan, *The Philosophy of the Social Sciences* (London: The Macmillan Press, 1970), pp. 102ff and pp. 149ff., and John O'Neill, "The Hobbesian Problem in Marx and Parsons," in his *Sociology as a Skin Trade* (New York: Harper and Row, 1972), pp. 177-208.

11. The phrase is Charles Taylor's, from "Interpretation and the Sciences of Man," *The Review of Metaphysics*, 25 (1971), pp. 17ff.

12. For a more detailed discussion of Schutz's program for phenomenological sociology, see Part III of Bernstein's *The Restructuring of Social and Political Theory*. It is important to add, however, that O'Neill and Bernstein differ in their estimates of Schutz's achievements in crucial ways.

13. J. Donald Moon, "The Logic of Political Inquiry," in the *Handbook of Political Science*, I, ed. Fred Greenstein and Nelson Polsby (Reading, Mass.: Addison-Wesley, 1975), p. 192. See also Martin Hollis, *Models of Man* (New York: Cambridge University Press, 1977) and Brian M. Barry, *Sociologists, Economists and Democracy* (New York: Macmillan, 1970), esp. Ch. VIII.

14. The covering law model is associated with the school of logical empiricism of which Carl Hempel, Herbert Feigl, May Brodbeck, and Ernest Nagel were leading members. Their influences on the social sciences is widely acknowledged (see, e.g., the discussion by Ball in Chapter Two of this volume). It should be noted, however, that some version of this model of explanation has been present in the naturalist tradition since Hobbes. It needs also to be noted that, despite the waning influence of logical empiricism on the social sciences, some version of the model is still retained. As J. Donald Moon writes in Chapter Eight on page 172, "even radical post-Kuhnian views of social science continue to at least tacitly accept the naturalist view of scientific explanation in terms of the subsumption of individual events under general laws."

15. For one recent account of post-empiricism, see David Thomas, *Naturalism and Social Science: A Post Empiricist Philosophy of Social Science* (New York: Cambridge University Press, 1980).

16. For a position similar to Miller's only with respect to natural science, see "Dialectic as Normative Structure: Norms and Counter-Norms in a Select Group of the Apollo Moon Scientists" in Ian I. Mitroff and Richard O. Mason, *Creating a Dialectical Social Science* (Dordrecht: Reidel, 1981), pp. 130-153.

17. See, e.g., Thomas, pp. 148-149.

18. For a discussion of many of these same issues from different and related perspectives by contributors to this volume, see John O'Neill, "Can Phenomenology Be Critical?" in his *Sociology as a Skin Trade*, pp. 221-236; and Brian Fay, "How People Change Themselves," in *Political Theory and Praxis*, ed. Terence Ball (Minneapolis: University of Minnesota Press, 1977), pp. 200-233.

19. This is not to say that critical theorists or other critical inquirers avoid debate about the nature of reflexivity or the goal of critical inquiry. For a most recent example of some direct confrontations on these issues see *Habermas: Critical Debates*, ed. John Thompson and David Held (Cambridge, Mass.: MIT Press, 1982).

20. And also by some of our contributors. Moon argues that if, as an interpretive social science would seem to demand, "we confine ourselves to the concepts and self-understandings of social actors, we would have no basis for accounting for and explaining the incoherences which we may find in the traditions of a society. And, more important from the point of view of the relationship between social theory and political practice, we would have no basis from which to criticize these traditions, no standpoint from which to defend changes or reforms in socially accepted self-understandings and practices. Thus, a purely interpretive . . . social science is necessarily conservative" (p. 174).

Miller also criticizes a purely interpretive approach, on similar grounds. Drawing on the Marxist notion of objective interests, Miller argues that to seek to understand and explain human action solely in terms of the conscious beliefs or reasons people have for acting is to ignore the possiblity that such actions may be due to factors, such as objective interests, of which the actors are ignorant.

Chapter Two

1. Herbert Feigl, "The Origin and Spirit of Logical Positivism," in *The Legacy of Logical Positivism*, ed. Peter Achinstein and Stephen F. Barker (Baltimore: The Johns Hopkins Press, 1969), pp. 3–24; and A.J. Ayer, "Introduction" to *Logical Positivism*, ed. Ayer (New York: Free Press, 1959), p. 3. For discussions of the relation between the early positivism of Comte and Mach and the later positivism of the logical positivists, see Jürgen Habermas, *Knowledge and Human Interests*, trans. Jeremy J. Shapiro (Boston: Beacon Press, 1971), chs. 4–6, and his contributions to *The Positivist Dispute in German Sociology*, trans. G. Adey and D. Frisby (New York: Harper and Row, 1976). See also Gerard Radnitzky, *Contemporary Schools of Metascience*, 3rd edition (Chicago: Regnery, 1973), passim.

2. Robert A. Dahl, "The Behavioral Approach in Political Science: Epitaph for a Monument to a Successful Protest," *American Political Science Review*, 55 (1961), pp. 763–772, at 766; David Easton, "The Current Meaning of 'Behavioralism'," in *Contemporary Political Analysis*, ed. James C. Charlesworth (New York: Free Press, 1967), pp. 11–31; Heinz Eulau, *The Behavioral Persuasion in Politics* (New York: Random House, 1963).

3. David Easton, *A Framework for Political Analysis* (Englewood Cliffs, N.J.: Prentice-Hall, 1965), p. 7.

4. Georg Henrik von Wright, *Explanation and Understanding* (Ithaca: Cornell University Press, 1971), p. 4.

5. See, e.g., John G. Gunnell, *Philosophy, Science and Political Inquiry* (Morristown, N.J.: General Learning Press, 1975).

6. Karl R. Popper, *The Logic of Scientific Discovery*, first published in German in 1934 (New York: Harper and Row, 1963), p. 59.

7. Carl G. Hempel, *Aspects of Scientific Explanation* (New York: Free Press, 1965), e.g., p. 249.

8. All quotations are from George E. G. Catlin, *Principles of Politics* (London: Allen and Unwin, 1930), pp. 87, 27, and 39, respectively.

9. David B. Truman, "The Impact on Political Science of the Revolution in the Behavioral Sciences," Brookings Lectures (1955), reprinted in *Readings in the Philosophy of the Social Sciences*, ed. May Brodbeck (New York: Macmillan, 1968), pp. 541-560, at 549; cf. also pp. 550-552.

10. Easton, "The Current Meaning of 'Behavioralism'," p. 16; and *A Framework for Political Analysis*, p. 7. Scarcely two years had passed before Professor Easton announced, in his Presidential Address to the American Political Science Association, the dawning of the "post-behavioral" era (*American Political Science Review*, 63 (Dec. 1969), pp. 1051-1061). Easton's proposed move was two-fold: first, to abandon the behavioralist *label*—offensive to many younger scholars— while effectively abandoning none of its tenets; and second, recognizing the legitimate place of "moral concern" in scholarly research. Since then those few political scientists who bother to pay lip service to the "post-behavioral credo" carry on pretty much as before. *Plus ça change . . . .*

11. Quoted in Bruce Mazlish, *The Riddle of History* (New York: Harper and Row, 1966), p. 57.

12. Karl Marx, *Grundrisse*, trans. Martin Nicolaus (New York: Penguin, 1973), p. 244; cf. also pp. 255, 468, and *Capital*, I (New York: International Publishers, 1967), p. 44.

13. See Alan Gewirth, "Can Men Change the Laws of Social Science?," *Philosophy of Science*, 21 (1954), and Habermas's account of the "subversive" and emancipatory role of Critical Theory in *Knowledge and Human Interests*, esp. the Appendix entitled "Knowledge and Human Interests: A General Perspective," pp. 301-317.

14. Kenneth Keniston, *The Uncommitted* (New York: Dell, 1970), p. 274.

15. Ibid.

16. Robert A. Dahl, *Who Governs?* (New Haven: Yale University Press, 1961), pp. 279, 280-281.

17. Robert A. Dahl, *Modern Political Analysis* (Englewood Cliffs, N.J.: Prentice-Hall, 1965), p. 59. It should be noted that Aristotle never in fact claimed that man is "instinctively" a political animal: one's *bios politikos* is constituted by what one has learned in the course of playing the role of citizen. One is not, that is to say, born with political "instinct"; political sensibility exists as a potential which can only be realized through acting with one's fellow-citizens in the setting provided by the *polis*.

18. In Professor Dahl's defense it must be said that he at least knows who Aristotle was, and is therefore a more worthy opponent than a bright young political scientist I know, who dismissed Aristotle with the remark that the Romans (!) didn't know as much as we know about political behavior.

19. Lest one think that Arendt's distinction between labor and work is an arbitrary one of her own devising, one should note that English (along with French and German) usage recognizes the distinction. After all, our language contains two words, not one, and we do in fact fastidiously honor the distinction between them. For example, we speak of a "work of art," not a labor of art; of a woman about to give birth as "going into labor," not going into work!

20. See Thucydides, *The Peloponnesian War* (New York: Modern Library, 1951), p. 79.

21. Bertrand de Jouvenel, *Sovereignty*, trans. J.F. Huntington (Chicago: University of Chicago Press, 1963), p. 304.

22. See Jürgen Habermas, "On Systematically Distorted Communication," *Inquiry*, 13 (1970), pp. 205-218; and—for a critique of Arendt with which I am sympathetic— "Hannah Arendt's Communications Concept of Power," *Social Research*, 44 (1977), pp. 3-24.

23. Hannah Arendt, *The Human Condition* (Chicago: University of Chicago Press, 1958), p. 23; see also Jürgen Habermas, *Theory and Practice*, trans. John Viertel (Boston: Beacon Press, 1973), pp. 47-48.

24. Thomas Hobbes, *Leviathan* (Oxford: Oxford University Press, 1909), Part III, ch. 17, p. 128.

25. John Locke, *Second Treatise of Government*, ed. Peter Laslett (Cambridge: Cambridge University Press, 1960), § 124.

26. Arendt, pp. 41-42.

27. Ibid., p. 42. Arendt rather overstates her case here, I think, for ordinary, everyday deeds also have "meaning" for those who perform and witness them. But it is not this sort of rule-governed conventional meaning that Arendt means (sic) to mark here. For a critique and a corrective, see Richard J. Bernstein, "Hannah Arendt: The Ambiguities of Theory and Practice," in *Political Theory and Praxis*, ed. Terence Ball (Minneapolis: University of Minnesota Press, 1977), pp. 141-158, esp. 154 ff.

28. Arendt, pp. 42-43. It should be noted that Arendt's point about the law of large numbers is not necessarily conservative or aristocratic, for Gramsci makes exactly the same point. See Antonio Gramsci, *Prison Notebooks*, trans. and ed. Quinton Hoare and Geoffrey Nowell Smith (New York: International Publishers, 1971), pp. 410-412, 428-429.

29. Arendt, p. 43.

30. Quoted in Albert O. Hirschman, *The Passions and the Interests* (Princeton: Princeton University Press, 1974), p. 50. See, further, J.A.W. Gunn, "'Interest Will Not Lie': A Seventeenth-Century Maxim," *Journal of the History of Ideas*, 29 (October-December 1968), pp. 551-564, and *Politics and the Public Interest in the Seventeenth Century* (London: Routledge and Kegan Paul, 1969); and J.G.A. Pocock, *The Machiavellian Moment* (Princeton: Princeton University Press, 1975), passim.

31. See Garry Wills, *Inventing America* (New York: Vintage Books, 1979).

32. James Madison, "Federalist, Number 51," in Alexander Hamilton, Madison and John Jay, *The Federalist Papers*, ed. Clinton Rossiter (New York: Mentor Books, 1961), p. 322.

33. Hamilton, "Federalist, Number 9," p. 72.

34. Alexander Hamilton, "Letters from Phocion, Number I" (1784), in *The Works of Alexander Hamilton*, II, ed. John C. Hamilton (New York: Charles S. Francis, 1851), p. 298.

35. Hamilton, "Federalist, Number 9," p. 73; Hamilton's emphasis.

36. Madison, "Federalist, Number 51," p. 322.

37. Hamilton, "Federalist, Number 9," p. 73.

38. J. Hector St. John Crèvecoeur, *Letters from an American Farmer*, published 1782 (New York: Dutton, 1957), p. 70. Here Crevecoeur is speaking specifically of religious zeal; but his point applies to zeal of any kind and from any source.

39. Richard Hofstadter, *The Progressive Historians* (New York: Knopf, 1969), p. 5.

40. Madison, "Federalist Number 10," p. 83.
41. Madison, "Federalist Number 51," p. 324.
42. Alexis de Tocqueville, *Democracy in America*, ed. J.P. Mayer and Max Lerner (New York: Harper and Row, 1966), p. 6; I have altered the translation slightly.
43. John Stuart Mill, *On Liberty* (New York: Dutton, 1951), p. 88.
44. See Louis Hartz, *The Liberal Tradition in America* (New York: Harcourt, Brace, 1955), passim; and Norman Jacobson, "Political Science and Political Education," *American Political Science Review*, 57 (September 1963), pp. 561–569. My debt to Jacobson's article—and to his teaching—is considerable.
45. Arendt, p. 187.
46. Tocqueville, p. 461.
47. Ibid., p. 462; emphasis added.
48. Ibid., p. 463.
49. Ibid., p. 462.
50. Ibid., p. 463.
51. Ibid.
52. Ibid., pp. 463–464.
53. Ibid., p. 464.
54. Arendt, p. 322.
55. Max Weber, "Politics as a Vocation," in *From Max Weber: Essays in Sociology*, trans. and ed. H.H. Gerth and C. Wright Mills (New York: Oxford University Press, 1958), p. 128.

Chapter Three

1. Anthony Giddens, *New Rules of Sociological Method* (London: Hutchinson University Library, 1976). This project is dependent upon his previous volume, *Capitalism and Modern Social Theory* (Cambridge: Cambridge University Press, 1971), and his *Studies in Social and Political Theory* (London: Hutchinson, 1977).
2. John O'Neill, "The Mutuality of Accounts: An Essay on Trust," in *Theoretical Perspectives in Sociology*, ed. Scott G. McNall (New York: St. Martin's Press, 1979), pp. 369–380.
3. Giddens, *New Rules of Sociological Method*. p. 8. These propositions are set down as the "new" rules of sociological method in Giddens' concluding chapter. What is worse, his bald formulation of these propositions is unlikely to please even those within the field of interpretative sociology who take these propositions as something more than shibboleths and are by now involved with much more intricate issues of methodological procedure in their daily work as sociologists. For these practitioners, Giddens' critical comments merely summarize the normal troubles of sociological work that cannot be escaped even in the resolutely quantitative practice of sociology.
4. John O'Neill, "From Phenomenology to Ethnomethodology: Some Radical 'Misreadings'," in *Current Perspectives in Social Theory*, I, ed. Scott G. McNall and Gary Howe (Greenwich, Conn.: JAI Press, 1980), pp. 7–20.
5. Giddens, *New Rules*, p. 161.
6. John O'Neill, "Can Phenomenology Be Critical?," *Philosophy of the Social Sciences*, 2 (March 1972), pp. 1–13; reprinted in *Phenomenology and Sociology:*

194

Selected Readings, ed. Thomas Luckmann (New York: Penguin, 1978), pp. 200–216.

7. Peter L. Berger and Thomas Luckmann, *The Social Construction of Reality* (New York: Doubleday, 1967), p. 15.

8. George H. Mead, *Mind, Self, and Society*, ed. and intro. Charles W. Morris (Chicago: University of Chicago Press, 1967), pp. 155–156.

9. Georg Simmel, "How Is Society Possible?," in *Essays on Sociology, Philosophy and Aesthetics*, trans. and ed. Kurt H. Wolff (New York: Harper and Row, 1965), p. 344. See also John O'Neill, "On Simmel's 'Sociological Apriorities'," in *Phenomenological Studies: Issues and Applications*, ed. George Psathas (New York: Wiley, 1973), pp. 91–106.

10. Peter Winch, *The Idea of a Social Science* (London: Routledge and Kegan Paul, 1958), p. 119. For an excellent discussion of Winch, see Stephen P. Turner, *Sociological Explanation as Translation* (Cambridge: Cambridge University Press, 1980).

11. John O'Neill, "Self-Prescription and Social Machiavellianism," in his *Sociology as a Skin Trade* (New York: Harper and Row, 1972), pp. 11–19.

12. Erving Goffman, *Interaction Ritual: Essays on Face-to-Face Behavior* (New York: Doubleday Anchor, 1967), p. 31.

13. Edmund Husserl, *The Crisis of European Sciences and Transcendental Phenomenology: An Introduction to Phenomenological Philosophy*, trans. David Carr (Evanston, Ill.: Northwestern University Press, 1970), p. 122.

14. Yehoshua Bar-Hillel, "Indexical Expressions," in his *Aspects of Language* (Jerusalem: The Magnes Press, 1970), pp. 69–88.

15. Harold Garfinkel, *Studies in Ethnomethodology* (Englewood Cliffs, N.J.: Prentice-Hall, 1967), p. 34.

16. Jürgen Habermas, "What Is Universal Pragmatics?," in his *Communication and the Evolution of Society*, trans. Thomas A. McCarthy (Boston: Beacon Press, 1979), pp. 1–68.

17. Jürgen Habermas, "The Scientization of Politics and Public Opinion," in his *Toward a Rational Society*, trans. Jeremy J. Shapiro (Boston: Beacon Press, 1970), pp. 68–69.

18. Harold Garfinkel, "A Concept of, and Experiment with, 'Trust' as a Condition of Stable Concerted Action," in *Motivation and Social Interaction*, ed. J. O. Harvey (New York: Ronald Press, 1963), pp. 187–238.

19. Max Weber, "Science as a Vocation," in *From Max Weber: Essays in Sociology*, trans. and ed. H.H. Gerth and C. Wright Mills (New York: Oxford University Press, 1958), pp. 129–156. Cf. Herminio Martins, "The Kuhnian 'Revolution' and Its Implications for Sociology," in *Imagination and Precision in the Social Sciences*, ed. T. J. Nossiter, A. H. Hanson, and Stein Rokkan (London: Faber and Faber, 1972), pp. 13–58.

20. Alfred Schutz, "Concept and Theory Formation in the Social Sciences," *Collected Papers*, I, ed. Maurice Natanson (The Hague: Martinus Nijhoff, 1964), pp. 41–42.

21. Alfred Schutz, "The Problem of Rationality in the Social World," *Collected Papers*, II, ed. and intro. Arvid Brodersen (The Hague: Mouton, 1964), pp. 85–86.

22. See Giddens' remarks on the problem of adequacy in his *New Rules*, pp. 148-154, and in his *Central Problems in Social Theory* (London: Macmillan, 1979), pp. 245-253.

23. Giddens, *New Rules*, p. 79.

24. Ibid., p. 104.

25. See John O'Neill, "Part II: On Language and the Body Politic," in his *Sociology as a Skin Trade*.

26. The problem of the nature of violence in liberal society and the criteria for the use of violence in a socialist revolution is treated at length, from a phenomenological perspective, in John O'Neill, "Merleau-Ponty's Critique of Marxist Scientism," *Canadian Journal of Social and Political Theory*, 2 (Winter 1977-1978), pp. 33-62.

27. Giddens, *New Rules*, pp. 121-122.

28. For an analysis of the notions of objectification, reification, and estrangement, see John O'Neill, "The Concept of Estrangement in the Early and Later Writings of Karl Marx," in his *Sociology as a Skin Trade*, pp. 113-136.

29. Giddens, *New Rules*, p. 115; my emphasis.

30. Alfred Schutz and Thomas Luckmann, *The Structures of the Life World*, trans. Richard M. Zaner and H. Tristram Engelhardt, Jr. (London: Heinemann, 1974).

31. Alfred Schutz, "The Well-Informed Citizen: An Essay on the Social Distribution of Knowledge," *Collected Papers*, II, pp. 120-134. Cf. Roger Jehensen, "The Social Distribution of Knowledge in Formal Organizations: A Critical Theoretical Perspective," *Human Studies*, 2 (April 1979), pp. 111-129.

32. Schutz, "The Well-Informed Citizen," p. 134.

33. Habermas, "The Scientization of Politics and Public Opinion," pp. 62-80.

34. John O'Neill, "Le langage et la décolonisation: Fanon et Freire," *Sociologie et Sociétés*, VI., pp. 53-65.

35. John O'Neill, "The Literary Production of Natural and Social Science Inquiry," *The Canadian Journal of Sociology*, 6 (Spring 1981), pp. 105-120.

36. S. B. Barnes, "Sociological Explanation and Natural Science: A Kuhnian Reappraisal," *Archives Européennes de Sociologie*, XIII (1972), pp. 373-391.

37. Michael Oakeshott, "The Tower of Babel," *Cambridge Journal*, 2, as quoted in Winch, *The Idea of a Social Science*, pp. 62-63.

38. John O'Neill, *Making Sense Together* (New York: Harper and Row, 1974).

39. Alvin W. Gouldner, "Sociology and the Everyday Life," in *The Uses of Controversy in Sociology*, ed. Lewis A. Coser and O. N. Larsen (New York: Macmillan, 1976), pp. 417-433.

Chapter Four

1. "Causal analysis provides absolutely no value judgment and a value judgment is absolutely not a causal explanation," contends Weber in "Critical Studies in the Logic of the Cultural Sciences," *The Methodology of the Social Sciences*, ed. and trans. Edward A. Shils and Henry A. Finch (Glencoe, Ill.: Free Press, 1949), p. 123. And in "The Meaning of 'Ethical Neutrality' in Sociology and Economics," ibid., p. 33, he contends: "[T]he treatment of one of these types of problems with the means afforded by science or by logic is meaningful, but . . . the same procedure is impossible in the case of the other.

A careful examination of historical works quickly shows that when the historian begins to 'evaluate', causal analysis almost always ceases—to the prejudice of the scientific results."

2. In "The Meaning of 'Ethical Neutrality' in Sociology and Economics," p. 5, Weber argues: "Every professional task has its own 'inherent norms' and should be fulfilled accordingly. In the execution of his professional responsibility, a man should confine himself to it alone, and should exclude whatever is not strictly proper to it—particularly his own loves and hates." And in "'Objectivity' in Social Science and Social Policy," ibid., p. 60, he maintains: "In the social sciences, personal value-judgments have tended to influence scientific arguments without being explicitly admitted. They have brought about continual confusion and have caused various interpretations to be placed on scientific arguments even in the sphere of simple causal connections among facts, according to whether the results increased or decreased the chances of realizing one's personal ideals. . . ."

3. Indeed, Weber's most extensive and vigorous discussion of value freedom is largely occupied with the explanation and illustration of the role of "value-relevance" in the choice of questions and in the stipulation of definitions for the vague terms which social science borrows from ordinary usage. See ibid., pp. 72-112.

4. See, for example, ibid., pp. 58ff.

5. See, for example, ibid., pp. 3, 18 and 58. Also "Science as a Vocation," in *From Max Weber*, ed. H. H. Gerth and C. Wright Mills (New York: Oxford University Press, 1958), pp. 148, 156.

6. Weber, " 'Objectivity' in Social Science and Social Policy," p. 58, and "Politics as a Vocation," in *From Max Weber*, pp. 121ff.

7. "Reason and Commitment in the Social Sciences," *Philosophy and Public Affairs*, 8 (1979), pp. 241-266.

8. Theodore J. Lowi, *The End of Liberalism* (New York: Norton, 1969), p. 159.

9. For example, Alvin W. Gouldner, "Anti-Minotaur: The Myth of a Value-Free Sociology," in *Sociology on Trial*, ed. Maurice Stein and Arthur Vidich (Englewood Cliffs, N. J.: Prentice-Hall, 1963).

10. For example, Leo Strauss, "The Social Science of Max Weber," *Measure*, 2 (Spring 1951), pp. 204-230.

11. See George W. Stocking, *Race, Culture and Evolution* (New York: Free Press, 1968).

12. "An Anthropologist's Credo," in *I Believe*, ed. Clifton Fadiman (New York: Simon and Schuster, 1939), p. 19.

13. On the political views of workers in the contemporary United States see Richard Hamilton, *Class and Politics in the United States* (New York: Wiley, 1972), and Robert Gilmour and Robert Lamb, *Political Alienation in Contemporary America* (New York: St. Martin's Press, 1975); on the economics of racism see Robert Cherry, "Economic Theories of Racism," and Michael Reich, "The Economics of Racism," both in *Problems in Political Economy: An Urban Perspective*, ed. David Gordon (Lexington, Mass.: Heath, 1977 ed.). I am not, of course, suggesting that these writings definitively establish the falsehood of dominant assumptions about class, politics, and ideology. However, depending as they do on widely accepted data and standard analytical techniques, they

show, by implication, that conservative social forces, not rational inference or mere misinformation, remove the burden of argument from those who assume that blue-collar workers are conservative or that white workers, rather than their employers, benefit from racism. By right, these safe and standard propositions should be controversial in the extreme.

14. See Karl R. Popper, *The Open Society*, II (Princeton: Princeton University Press, 1963); J. W. N. Watkins, "Historical Explanation in the Social Sciences," *British Journal for the Philosophy of Science*, 9 (1957), pp. 104–117; George Homans, "Bringing Men Back In," *American Sociological Review*, 29 (1964), pp. 809–818.

15. G. M. Wilson, "A New Look at the Problem of 'Japanese Fascism'," in *Reappraisals of Fascism*, ed. Henry A. Turner (New York: Watts, 1975), p. 202.

16. Peter Bachrach and Morton Baratz, *Power and Poverty* (New York: Oxford University Press, 1970), p. 49.

17. See Watkins, pp. 104–117.

18. See Steven Lukes, "Methodological Individualism Reconsidered," *British Journal of Sociology*, 29 (1968), pp. 119–129, and M. Mandelbaum, "Societal Facts," *British Journal of Sociology*, 6 (1955), pp. 305–317, both reprinted in *The Philosophy of Social Explanation*, ed. Alan Ryan (New York: Oxford University Press, 1973).

19. His initial, highly influential statement is "The Function of General Laws in History," *The Journal of Philosophy*, 39 (1942), pp. 35–48. His more-or-less final elaboration, refinement, and defense is the title essay of *Aspects of Scientific Explanation* (New York: Free Press, 1965).

20. See, for example, Jürgen Habermas, *Knowledge and Human Interests*, trans. Jeremy J. Shapiro (Boston: Beacon Press, 1971), pp. 308–311.

21. The covering-law model requires, for good reason, that the laws in question employ only general, qualitative predicates, referring to no particular time, place, or person, for example, "male," "plantation-owner," "intelligent," but not "Confederate" or "nineteenth-century." After all, the model would be neither valid nor informative if "Whoever is Napoleon Bonaparte becomes Emperor of France" is counted as a law. But, among purely logical constraints, only the requirement of generality distinguishes that pseudo-law from real ones. Thus, the relevant covering-law connecting despair with surrender must be valid throughout the universe of military leaders, applying to Etruscan warrior-kings and Iroquois war chiefs, quite as much as Lee's compeers. At present, it is mere wishful thinking to suppose that such a law exists. On the requirement of qualitativeness, see Carl G. Hempel and P. Oppenheim, "Studies in the Logic of Explanation," originally written in 1948, in Hempel, *Aspects of Scientific Explanation*, pp. 268ff.

22. See Thomas S. Kuhn, "Concepts of Cause in the Development of Physics," in his *The Essential Tension* (Chicago: University of Chicago Press, 1977), pp. 21–30.

Chapter Five

1. See A. R. Louch, *Explanation and Human Action* (Berkeley: University of California Press, 1966), passim; R. Peters, *The Concept of Motivation* (New York: Humanities Press, 1958), ch. 1; D. Hamlyn, "Behavior," in *Philosophy*,

28 (1953); H. L. A. Hart and A. M. Honore, *Causation and the Law* (Oxford: Oxford University Press, 1959), esp. pp. 48-55; and William Dray, *Laws and Explanation in History* (Oxford: Clarendon Press, 1957), ch. 5.

2. Hart and Honore, p. 21.

3. This is the central thesis of Louch's book, for example.

4. Dray, ch. 5, part 4. Also cf. Hart and Honore, p. 52.

5. In *Philosophy, Politics and Society* (Second Series), ed. Peter Laslett and W. G. Runciman (Oxford: Blackwell, 1962), pp. 48-70.

6. Ibid., p. 55.

7. I have defended this distinction in detail in my "Practical Reasoning, Rationality, and the Explanation of Action," *Journal for the Theory of Social Behavior*, 8 (1978), pp. 77-101.

8. The Realist position has been developed by Rom Harre. See, for example, Harre and Peter Secord, *The Explanation of Social Behavior* (Oxford: Blackwell, 1972). See also Russell Keat and John Urrey, *Social Theory as Science* (London: Routledge and Kegan Paul, 1975).

9. I learned a great deal on this matter from David Miller of Warwick University. See Miller's review of Rom Harre's *The Principles of Scientific Thinking* (London: MacMillan, 1970), entitled "Back to Aristotle?" in the *British Journal of the Philosophy of Science*, 23 (1972), pp. 69-78.

10. This is just the sort of debate that developed over Weber's thesis. See, for example, the essays by Robertson, Samuelson, and Hansen, in *Protestantism, Capitalism, and Social Science*, ed. Robert Green (Lexington, Mass.: Heath, 1973).

11. *The Explanation of Behavior* (London: Routledge and Kegan Paul, 1964), pp. 21-25. There Taylor claims that the fact "that the system achieves this (normal) result-condition neither calls for nor admits of explanation" (p. 22).

12. Ibid., p. 24.

13. In the case of practical reasoning processes, I take it that this is just what developmental psychologists do; for example, see Jean Piaget, *The Origins of Intelligence in Children* (New York: Norton, 1963), particularly Part II.

14. Of course, in order for this to be so one must be able to distinguish between *causal generalizations* and *causal laws* properly so called. For this paper, general laws properly so called are universal well-confirmed empirical hypotheses of conditional form capable of supporting counterfactuals. They state that under certain specified boundary conditions every case in which events of the type N occur an event of the type E will occur, ceteris paribus. Causal generalizations, on the other hand, although of essentially the same form as that of general laws, are much more rough-and-ready: they are not universal, nor well confirmed; their boundary conditions are not well articulated; and their capacity to support counterfactuals is limited to a quantifiably unspecified range of events.

15. This part is a direct borrowing from Donald Davidson's "Causal Relations" in the *Journal of Philosophy*, LXIV (November 9, 1967), pp. 691-703.

16. Hart and Honore, pp. 13-14.

17. Reprinted in Carl G. Hempel, *Aspects of Scientific Explanation* (New York: Free Press, 1965), p. 232 and p. 236 (italics mine).

18. In the first half of his article, "Theory in History" (*Philosophy of Science*, 34 (1967), pp. 23-40), Leon Goldstein gives other instances of this doctrine to be found in the work of the philosophers Patrick Gardner (in *The Nature of*

Historical Explanation, pp. 57-89), Ernest Nagel (in "Determination in History," *Philosophy and Phenomenological Research*, 20 (1967), p. 307), and Karl Popper (in *The Open Society*, p. 448).

19. See, for example, Louch, chs. 1, 2.

20. See Donald Davidson, "Mental Events," reprinted in L. Foster and J. Swanson, *Experience and Theory* (Amherst: University of Mass. Press, 1970), pp. 79-101. See also William Alston, "Do Actions Have Causes?" in the *Proceedings of the Seventh Inter-American Congress of Philosophy* (Quebec: Laval University Press, 1970), pp. 256-276.

21. One might be tempted to interpret this as an excessively idealist account of social life because it seems to make ideas the crucial factor in social change. Such an interpretation would be a mistake, however. As "materialist" a theory of social change as one likes is compatible with what I say here, provided that this theory includes the assertion that social practices and psychological states are partly constituted by the self-understandings of the actors involved. (Marxism is such a materialist theory, for instance.)

22. The argument in this section was suggested by Karl R. Popper, *The Poverty of Historicism* (London: Routledge and Kegan Paul, 1957); and by Louis Mink, "Philosophical Analysis and Historical Understanding," *Review of Metaphysics*, XXI (June 1968), pp. 667-698.

23. Maurice Cranston, *Freedom* (London: Longmans, 1953), p. 118.

24. In *The Poverty of Historicism*, passim.

25. See Alasdair MacIntyre, "Predictability and Explanation in Social Science," *Philosophic Exchange*, 1 (Summer 1972), pp. 5-13. In chapter 8 of *After Virtue* (Notre Dame: University of Notre Dame Press, 1981) MacIntyre develops an argument quite like the one I am making in this paper.

26. This is in contrast to the views of MacIntyre, for example, who, after having shown that the particulars characteristically studied by social scientists are not predictable, claims to have shown thereby "that the aspiration to construct theories of scientific or a quasi-scientific sort in this area *must* fail" ("Predictability and Explanation in the Social Sciences," *Philosophic Exchange*, 1 (Summer 1972), p. 12). He makes the same claim in "Ideology, Social Science, and Revolution," *Comparative Politics*, 5 (April 1973), p. 336.

27. For example: Georg Henrik von Wright, *Explanation and Understanding* (Ithaca: Cornell University Press, 1972); A. R. Louch; Peter Winch, *The Idea of a Social Science* (London: Routledge and Kegan Paul, 1958).

28. See Jürgen Habermas, *Knowledge and Human Interests*, trans. Jeremy J. Shapiro (Boston: Beacon Press, 1972), chs. 10-12, and *Theory and Practice*, trans. John Viertel (Boston: Beacon Press, 1973), essay 7; and Brian Fay, *Social Theory and Political Practice* (London: Allen and Unwin, 1976), esp. ch. 5.

Chapter Six

1. Most notable among lesser known contemporary critical theorists are Alfred Schmidt, *The Concept of Nature in Marx* (London: New Left Books, 1971); Oskar Negt, *Öffentlichkeit und Erfahrung* (Frankfurt: Suhrkamp, 1972) (coauthor with Alexander Kluge); and Albrecht Wellmer, *Critical Theory of Society* (New York: Seabury Press, 1971).

2. Thomas A. McCarthy, *The Critical Theory of Jürgen Habermas* (Cambridge, Mass.: MIT Press, 1978) is an outstanding accomplishment, excellent in breadth and detail, but at times technically cumbersome, as is Trent Schroyer, *The Critique of Domination* (Boston: Beacon Press, 1973). Brief, accessible commentaries of Habermas's work written in English include Fred Dallmayr, "Reason and Emancipation," *Man and World*, 5 (1972): 79-109; Richard Bernstein, *The Restructuring of Social and Political Theory* (Philadelphia: University of Pennsylvania Press, 1978), pp. 171-236; Anthony Giddens, *Studies in Social and Political Theory* (New York: Basic Books, 1977), pp. 135-164; David Held, *Introduction to Critical Theory* (Berkeley: University of California Press, 1980), pp. 249-352; and Dick Howard, *The Marxian Legacy* (New York: Urizen Press, 1977), pp. 118-152.

3. Andrew Arato, "Political Sociology and Critique of Politics," in *The Essential Frankfurt School Reader*, ed. Andrew Arato and Eike Gebhardt (New York: Urizen Press, 1978), p. 15.

4. The Italian Antonio Gramsci was equally important in forging the reconstruction of Marxist theory along Hegelian lines, but his work was not as directly influential on the development of critical theory as that of Lukàcs and Korsch.

5. Arato, "Political Sociology and Critique of Politics," p. 6.

6. See Russell Jacoby, "Politics of the Crisis Theory," *Telos*, 23 (1975): 3-52.

7. While Marx himself was certainly ambivalent regarding this matter, the very presence of this ambivalence should be cause for concern among critical thinkers.

8. Russell Jacoby, "Toward a Critique of Automatic Marxism," *Telos*, 10 (1971), p. 145.

9. Max Horkheimer, "The Authoritarian State," *Telos*, 15 (1973), p. 9. In place of mass parties, Horkheimer in this essay endorses the workers' councils as the appropriate forms of revolutionary organization, although he shortly abandoned this position.

10. Ibid., p. 4.

11. Ibid.

12. See Dick Howard, p. 102.

13. James Miller, "Review of J. Habermas, *Legitimation Crisis*," *Telos*, 25 (1975), p. 214.

14. Max Horkheimer, *The Eclipse of Reason* (New York: Oxford University Press, 1947), p. 187.

15. Ibid., p. 178. Adorno expresses essentially the same point with reference to the gap between concepts and the reality they represent: "Reciprocal criticism of the universal and of the particular does justice to what it covers, and whether the particular fulfills the concepts." Theodor Adorno, *Negative Dialectics*, trans. E.B. Ashton (New York: Seabury Press, 1973), p. 146.

16. Marx quoted in Jürgen Habermas, *Theory and Practice*, trans. John Viertel (Boston: Beacon Press, 1973), p. 168.

17. Quoted ibid.

18. Ibid., p. 169.

19. See McCarthy, *The Critical Theory of Jürgen Habermas*, p. 147.

20. Habermas, p. 47.

21. Jürgen Habermas, *Toward a Rational Society*, trans. Jeremy J. Shapiro (Boston: Beacon Press, 1970), pp. 91–92.

22. Habermas's criticism here is supported by his claim that instrumental efficacy is the appropriate criteria for rationalization in the productive sphere. The criticism would also apply to Adorno and Horkheimer in their *Dialectic of Enlightenment*, trans. John Cumming (London: Allen Lane, 1973).

23. See Habermas, *Toward a Rational Society*; and Habermas, *Theory and Practice*.

24. Habermas, *Theory and Practice*, p. 42.

25. Ibid.

26. Jürgen Habermas, "The Public Sphere," trans. Sara Lennox and Frank Lennox, *New German Critique*, 1 (1974), p. 49. Since *Strukturwandel der Öffentlichkeit* has not been translated into English, I have referred wherever possible to this article on the public sphere rather than to the book.

27. Peter Hohendahl, "An Introduction to Habermas' 'Public Sphere'," trans. Patricia Russian, *New German Critique*, 1 (1974): 45–48.

28. Habermas, "The Public Sphere," p. 53.

29. Ibid.

30. Ibid., p. 54.

31. Ibid.

32. Ibid., p. 55.

33. Ibid.

34. Jürgen Habermas, *Zur Logik der Sozialwissenschaften* (Frankfurt: Suhrkamp, 1970); and Jürgen Habermas, *Knowledge and Human Interests*, trans. Jeremy J. Shapiro (Boston: Beacon Press, 1971).

35. Habermas, *Knowledge and Human Interests*, p. 309.

36. Ibid., p. 310.

37. Ibid.

38. See Jürgen Habermas, "Der Universalitätsanspruch der Hermeneutik," in *Hermeneutik und Ideologiekritik*, ed. Karl-Otto Apel (Frankfurt: Suhrkamp, 1975), pp. 120–159; and Habermas, "Zu Gadamer's *Wahrheit und Methode*," in ibid., pp. 25–26. Habermas's point here is that hermeneutic knowledge, like knowledge gained from the empirical-analytic sciences, remains essentially tied to the given. Critical social science, on the other hand, leads beyond the present social arrangements.

39. Habermas, *Knowledge and Human Interests*, p. 315.

40. For an excellent discussion of Habermas's critique of functionalism and systems theory see McCarthy, *The Critical Theory of Jürgen Habermas*, pp. 213–222. In Habermas's own work, see *Zur Logik der Sozialwissenschaften*, pp. 164–184; and Jürgen Habermas and Niklas Luhmann, *Theorie der Gesellschaft oder Sozialtechnologie* (Frankfurt: Suhrkamp, 1976), pp. 142–270.

41. Habermas, *Knowledge and Human Interests*, p. 310.

42. Ibid.

43. For this account of Habermas's usage of psychoanalysis, I have relied heavily on Thomas McCarthy's excellent discussion in his introduction to the English edition of Habermas's most recent work: Thomas A. McCarthy, "Translator's Introduction" to *Communication and the Evolution of Society* (Boston: Beacon Press, 1979), vii–xxiv.

44. Ibid., p. xiii.

45. For this discussion of Habermas's communication theory I have again borrowed heavily from the work of Thomas McCarthy, this time his discussion in *The Critical Theory of Jürgen Habermas,* pp. 271-291.

46. For an explanation of Habermas's notion of a reconstructive science see ibid., pp. 276-279.

47. Jürgen Habermas, "Was heisst Universalpragmatik?" in *Sprachpragmatik und Philosophie,* ed. Karl-Otto Apel (Frankfurt: Suhrkamp, 1976), p. 205. Quoted in translation in McCarthy, *The Critical Theory of Jürgen Habermas,* pp. 274-275.

48. McCarthy, *The Critical Theory of Jürgen Habermas,* p. 425.

49. Ibid., p. 275.

50. Ibid., p. 276.

51. Ibid., p. 280.

52. Habermas, *Communication and the Evolution of Society,* p. 67.

53. McCarthy, *The Critical Theory of Jürgen Habermas,* pp. 280-282.

54. Habermas, *Communication and the Evolution of Society,* p. 99.

55. Ibid., p. 100.

56. McCarthy, *The Critical Theory of Jürgen Habermas,* pp. 345-351.

57. Ibid., p. 342.

58. Ibid., p. 350.

59. Habermas actually characterizes social evolution as a "bidimensional learning process" involving development in the forces of production as well as the relations of production. He focuses primarily on development in the sphere of relations of production since he wants to claim that normative structures constitute the "pacemaker" of social evolution. See ibid., pp. 248-249; Habermas, *Communication and the Evolution of Society,* pp. 120-121.

60. Habermas, *Communication and the Evolution of Society,* p. 146.

61. Ibid., p. 121.

62. Ibid., p. 122.

63. Ibid., p. 97.

64. C. Fred Alford, "Review of J. Habermas, *Communication and the Evolution of Society,*" *New German Critique,* 18 (1979), pp. 176-180; Bernstein; Paul Connerton, *The Tragedy of Enlightenment* (New York: Cambridge University Press, 1980); Giddens; Held; Peter Hohendahl, "Critical Theory, Public Sphere, and Culture," *New German Critique,* 16 (1979), pp. 89-118; Howard; Garbis Kortian, *Metacritique: The Philosophical Argument of Jürgen Habermas* (New York: Cambridge University Press, 1980); McCarthy; Dieter Misgeld, "Critical Theory and Hermeneutics," in *On Critical Theory,* ed. John O'Neill (New York: Seabury Press, 1976), pp. 164-183; John O'Neill, "Critique and Remembrance," in *On Critical Theory,* pp. 1-11; James Schmidt, "Offensive Critical Theory?" *Telos,* 39 (1979), pp. 62-70. See also the papers by J. Donald Moon and Stephen White in the present volume.

65. Alford, "Review of J. Habermas, *Communication and the Evolution of Society,*" p. 180; Habermas, *Communication and the Evolution of Society,* pp. 175-177; and White's essay, Chapter Seven, the present volume.

66. Held, p. 393.

67. Giddens, pp. 162-163; McCarthy, *The Critical Theory of Jürgen Habermas,* p. 355; Misgeld, pp. 182-183.

68. Misgeld, p. 182.

69. Giddens, p. 160.

70. Held, p. 396; Hohendahl, "Critical Theory, Public Sphere, and Culture," p. 117.

71. Bernstein, p. 224; Giddens, p. 156; Held, p. 395; Howard, pp. 148, 151; McCarthy, *The Critical Theory of Jürgen Habermas*, pp. 379, 381, 383, 384-385.

72. Hohendahl, "Critical Theory, Public Sphere, and Culture," p. 117.

73. Howard, p. 148.

74. See the paper by J. Donald Moon in the present volume; Held, pp. 395-396; and Schmidt, p. 69.

75. Moon, p. 182, in the present volume.

76. McCarthy, *The Critical Theory of Jürgen Habermas*, p. 379, and Schmidt, p. 68.

77. Schmidt, pp. 68-69; Jürgen Habermas, "Postscript to *Knowledge and Human Interests*," *Philosophy of the Social Sciences*, 3 (1973), p. 168; Habermas, *Theory and Practice*, p. 18.

78. Habermas, *Theory and Practice*, pp. 23-24.

79. Schmidt, p. 69.

80. Ibid.; Bernstein, pp. 223-224.

81. Bernstein, p. 224.

82. Schmidt, p. 70.

83. Connerton, p. 131. See also related criticisms that view communication theory as Kantian in form: Bernstein, pp. 224-225; Kortian, *Metacritique: The Philosophical Argument of Jürgen Habermas*, p. 128; McCarthy, *The Critical Theory of Jürgen Habermas*, pp. 379-380.

84. The suggestion of Freire's work as a more appropriate example, and the corresponding call for concrete ethnographies, was first suggested by John O'Neill, "Critique and Remembrance," pp. 1-11.

85. Allen Hunter, "Review of *Resistance Through Rituals*, ed. Stuart Hall, Tony Jefferson, and Paul Willis, *Profane Culture*," *Radical America* 13 (1979), pp. 76-79.

Chapter Seven

1. I will follow S. I. Benn and G. W. Mortimore, "Introduction" to *Rationality and the Social Sciences*, ed. Benn and Mortimore (London: Routledge & Kegan Paul, 1976) pp. 4-5, in distinguishing "epistemic" rationality, which refers to beliefs and theories, from "practical" rationality, which refers to actions and what constitutes good reasons for them.

2. Peter Winch, *The Idea of a Social Science* (New York: Humanities Press, 1958); and "Understanding a Primitive Society," in *Rationality*, ed. Brian Wilson (New York: Harper and Row, 1970).

3. The term "context rationality" is used by Steven Lukes, "Some Problems about Rationality," in Wilson, pp. 203ff.

4. Jürgen Habermas, "Vorbereitende Bemerkungen zu einer Theorie der kommunikativen Kompetenz," in Habermas and Niklas Luhmann, *Theorie der Gesellschaft oder Sozialtechnologie* (Frankfurt: Suhrkamp, 1971); and Habermas, "What is Universal Pragmatics?" in *Communication and the Evolution of Society*, trans. Thomas A. McCarthy (Boston: Beacon Press, 1979).

5. There is now a good study of Habermas's work as a whole: Thomas A. McCarthy, *The Critical Theory of Jürgen Habermas* (Cambridge, Mass.: MIT Press, 1978).

6. Karl-Otto Apel, *Analytic Philosophy of Language and the Geisteswissenschaften* (New York: Humanities Press, 1967), p. 56; Alasdair MacIntyre, "The Idea of a Social Science," in Wilson, p. 118. For a thoughtful defense of ethical relativism, see Steven Lukes, "Relativism: Cognitive and Moral," *Essays in Social Theory* (London: Macmillan, 1977).

7. Making use of recent work in rational-choice theory, David Braybrooke has convincingly shown that self-interested maximizers will not agree to a social contract unless some special assumptions are made, such as the validity of promise-keeping, "The Insoluble Problem of the Social Contract," *Dialogue*, 1 (March 1976), pp. 3–37. The utilitarian tradition has an analogous difficulty with its standard of public policy, the greatest happiness of the greatest number. The problem is not a new one, but it has been given no generally satisfactory solution by utilitarianism's defenders. As Alasdair MacIntyre argues, the greatest happiness criterion yields morally acceptable results only if we presuppose that a given society already accepts certain "non-utilitarian norms of decent behavior"; otherwise this criterion could justify, for example, the mass execution of Jews, if the greatest number happened to favor it. *A Short History of Ethics* (New York: Macmillan, 1966), p. 238. Thus, to be successful, both contractarianism and utilitarianism require strategically *non*rational thought and action. Legitimacy and obligation rest finally, then, on an element of nonrationality. The attempt to skirt this dilemma by simply expanding the scope of strategic rationality to encompass nonself-interested action is criticized by S. I. Benn, "Rationality and Political Behavior," in Benn and Mortimore, *Rationality and the Social Sciences*, pp. 255–260. For a recent proponent of the view that legitimate norms can be derived solely from strategic choices, see David Gauthier, "Reason and Maximization," *Canadian Journal of Philosophy*, 4 (March 1975), pp. 411–434.

8. Jürgen Habermas, *Theory and Practice*, trans. John Viertel (Boston: Beacon Press, 1973), pp. 16–17. Cf. Albrecht Wellmer, "Communication and Emancipation: Reflections on the 'Linguistic Turn' in Critical Theory," in *On Critical Theory*, ed. John O'Neill (New York: Seabury, 1976).

9. Jürgen Habermas, *Knowledge and Human Interests*, trans. Jeremy J. Shapiro (Boston: Beacon Press, 1971).

10. A good discussion of these topics is in McCarthy, *The Critical Theory*, chs. 2–3.

11. Habermas, "Vorbereitende Bemerkungen," p. 102; John Searle, *Speech Acts* (Cambridge: Cambridge University Press, 1969), pp. 16–17, 22–31.

12. Habermas, *Theory and Practice*, p. 18. This idea is most extensively developed in his "What is Universal Pragmatics?," esp. pp. 1–5.

13. Habermas, "What is Universal Pragmatics?", pp. 26–34; "Toward a Theory of Communicative Competence," *Inquiry*, 13 (1970), pp. 360–375.

14. Habermas, "What is Universal Pragmatics?", pp. 27-29; 65-68; "Thoughts on the Foundation of Sociology in the Philosophy of Language: Six Lectures," Christian Gauss Lectures at Princeton University, Spring 1971 (unpublished), Lecture III, p. 25.

15. Habermas, *Theory and Practice*, pp. 17-18; "Wahrheitstheorien," in *Wirklichkeit und Reflexion: Walter Schulz zum 60, Geburtstag* (Pfullingen: Neske, 1973), pp. 219-229.

16. Habermas, "Vorbereitende Bemerkungen," pp. 115-116.

17. Searle, pp. 175-198.

18. Thomas McCarthy, "A Theory of Communicative Competence," *Philosophy of the Social Sciences*, 3 (1973), p. 140; see Habermas, "Vorbereitende Bemerkungen," pp. 114-120.

19. Habermas, "Vorbereitende Bemerkungen," p. 120.

20. Thomas McCarthy, "The Problem of Rationality in Social Anthropology," *Stony Brook Studies in Philosophy*, I (Stony Brook, N.Y.: 1974), p. 17.

21. Jürgen Habermas, "Überlegungen zum evolutionären Stellenwert des modernen Rechts," in *Zur Rekonstruktion des Historischen Materialismus* (Frankfurt: Suhrkamp, 1976), pp. 260-262; "What is Universal Pragmatics?", pp. 40-41; "Historical Materialism and the Development of Normative Structures," in *Communication and the Evolution of Society*, pp. 117-118.

22. Habermas, "Historical Materialism and the Development of Normative Structures," pp. 118-119; "Theorie der Gesellschaft oder Socialtechnologie? Eine Auseinandersetzung mit Niklas Luhmann," in Habermas and Luhmann, *Theorie der Gesellschaft*, p. 252.

23. Jürgen Habermas, *Legitimation Crisis*, trans. Thomas McCarthy (Boston: Beacon Press, 1975), pp. 102-105.

24. Isaiah Berlin, "Rationality of Value Judgments," in *Rational Decision (Nomos*, VII), ed. Carl J. Friedrich (New York: Atherton, 1964), pp. 221-223.

25. Habermas, "Wahrheitstheorien," pp. 240-257.

26. Habermas, "Vorbereitende Bemerkungen," pp. 121, 123.

27. Ibid., p. 122.

28. Habermas, "Wahrheitstheorien," p. 239.

29. Habermas, "Vorbereitende Bemerkungen," p. 122.

30. Habermas, "Toward a Theory of Communicative Competence," p. 372.

31. Habermas, "Wahrheitstheorien," p. 257.

32. Habermas, "Vorbereitende Bemerkungen," p. 137; "Wahrheitstheorien," pp. 255-256.

33. Habermas, "Wahrheitstheorien," p. 256; "Vorbereitende Bemerkungen," pp. 136-139.

34. Habermas, "Vorbereitende Bemerkungen," p. 137.

35. Habermas, *Legitimation Crisis*, pp. 111, 97-110.

36. Habermas, "Toward a Theory of Communicative Competence," p. 372.

37. Habermas, *Legitimation Crisis*, p. 110.

38. Jürgen Habermas, "Zwei Bemerkungen zum praktischen Diskurs," in *Zur Rekonstruktion*, p. 339.

39. Ibid., pp. 340–341.

40. Habermas, *Legitimation Crisis*, p. 110, fn. 16.

41. See the discussion of conceptual necessity in Kant and Hegel, in Charles Taylor, *Hegel* (Cambridge University Press, 1975), pp. 95–96.

42. Ibid. shows how conceptual necessity in this sense is not simply a question of the meanings of words.

43. I have tried to explain Habermas's ideas on these topics in "On the Normative Structure of Action: Gewirth and Habermas," *The Review of Politics* (April 1982), pp. 282–301.

44. John Rawls recently appears to have abandoned his universalistic claims expressed in *A Theory of Justice* (Cambridge, Mass.: Harvard University Press, 1971), in response to similar considerations. See his "Kantian Constructivism in Moral Theory," The John Dewey Lectures, The *Journal of Philosophy*, 9 (September 1980), pp. 515–572.

45. See Habermas's remarks in "A Reply to my Critics," in *Habermas: Critical Debates*, John Thompson and David Held (Cambridge, Mass.: MIT Press, 1982), pp. 219–283; and Stephen K. White, "Reason and Authority in Habermas: A Critique of the Critics," *American Political Science Review*, 74 (December 1980), pp. 1007–1018.

46. Habermas has suggested such a similarity, in "Wahrheitstheorien," p. 258, fn. 45; cf. "Legitimation Problems in the Modern State," in *Communication and the Evolution of Society*, pp. 204–205. It might appear that Rawls' appeal to the contractarian tradition and his employment of "the concept of rationality . . . standard in economic theory" make such a comparison farfetched. The Rawlsian argument works, however, because he *limits* the use of strategic rationality to choice within the "original position" and the "formal constraints of the concept of right"; he invokes, but does not systematically explain, quite different criteria of rationality or "reasonableness." John Rawls, *A Theory of Justice*, pp. 14, 16, and secs. 9 and 23, esp. pp. 130–131. In his most recent work, Rawls has given more attention to the problem of the relationship of "the Rational" and "the Reasonable." See "Kantian Constructivism in Moral Theory."

Chapter Eight

1. Michael Oakeshott, "Political Education," in his *Rationalism in Politics* (London: Methuen, 1962), pp. 125–126.

2. "Values and Political Theory," *Journal of Politics*, 39 (November 1977), pp. 877–903.

3. See Brian Fay, *Social Theory and Political Practice* (London: Allen and Unwin, 1975).

4. See Jürgen Habermas, "On Systematically Distorted Communication," *Inquiry*, 13 (1970), pp. 205-218, for such an account of psychoanalysis.

5. See Jürgen Habermas, *Legitimation Crisis*, trans. Thomas McCarthy (Boston: Beacon Press, 1975), p. 14. See also his "Historical Materialism and the Development of Normative Structures" and "Towards Reconstruction of Historical Materialism," in Jürgen Habermas, *Communication and the Evolution of Society*, trans. Thomas McCarthy (Boston: Beacon Press, 1979).

6. *Legitimation Crisis*, p. 95.

7. Ibid., p. 105. It should be noted that in this essay I am following Habermas's account in *Legitimation Crisis*. In his other work he has developed these ideas much further, arguing that any act of linguistic communication presupposes that "the speaker must have at his disposal, in addition to his linguistic competence, basic qualifications of speech and symbolic interaction (role-behavior), which we may call communicative competence. This communicative competence means the mastery of an ideal speech situation." (Jürgen Habermas, "Towards a Theory of Communicative Competence," *Inquiry*, 13 (1970), p. 367.) That is, the necessity of discourse and the conception of an ideal speech situation (and the norms which constitute it) are already implicit in communicative action. It is, then, always appropriate to ask for reasons for a moral judgment (or a factual assertion), because "the expectation of discursive redemption of normative validity claims is already contained in the structure of intersubjectivity" (*Legitimation Crisis*, p. 110). See also Karl-Otto Apel, "The A Priori of the Communication Community and the Foundations of Ethics," in his *Towards a Transformation of Philosophy*, trans. G. Adey and D. Frisby (London: Routledge and Kegan Paul, 1980).

8. Habermas, *Legitimation Crisis*, p. 107.

9. Jürgen Habermas, "Theories of Truth," unpublished ms., p. 29.

10. John Searle, *Speech Acts* (Cambridge: Cambridge University Press, 1969), ch. 8.

11. Habermas, "Theories of Truth," p. 30.

12. Ibid., p. 31.

13. Ibid.

14. *Legitimation Crisis*, pp. 107-108.

15. Ibid., p. 108.

16. Ibid.

17. Ibid., p. 111.

18. Ibid., Part III, ch. 3.

19. Karl-Otto Apel, "The Conflicts of Our Time and the Problem of Political Ethics," in *From Contract to Community*, ed. Fred Dallmayr (New York: Marcel Dekker, 1970), p. 82.

20. Ibid., p. 99.

21. Ibid., p. 100.

22. It should be pointed out that for Habermas an instrumental attitude towards nature is a basic human interest, an interest in possible technical control over objectified processes, which is constitutive of scientific knowledge. If we can think of technology as a "project," it could only be "a 'project' of the human species *as a whole*, and not . . . one that could be historically surpassed." (Jürgen Habermas, "Technology and Science as 'Ideology'," in his *Toward a Rational Society* (Boston: Beacon Press, 1970), p. 87, emphasis in

the original). Thus an instrumental attitude towards nature is one of the most fundamental assumptions of Habermas's theory. See also, Norman Stockman, "Habermas, Marcuse, and the *Aufhebung* of Science and Technology," *Philosophy of Social Science*, 8 (March 1978), pp. 15-25.

23. E. J. Schumacher, *Small Is Beautiful* (New York: Harper, 1973), p. 294.

24. Ibid., p. 38.

25. It should not be thought that this is an area where, consensus not being forthcoming, we might attempt to settle disputes regarding the environment by means of compromise. For compromise to be appropriate, we must be able to reach a consensus that the interests involved are particular, and that this is a fit subject for compromise. But what is involved here are not conflicting *particular* interests, but conflicting moral ideals and world-views. And just because it does not involve one's interests, a person holding a reverentialist view of nature is not likely to consider compromise to be appropriate at all.

Author Index

211

Subject Index

Action: Arendt on, 38, 41, 47-49; behavior, unlike, 12, 40-41, 47-49, 116; and causal explanation, 18-21, 34-36, 44, 47, 87-88, 104-28; and causal theory, 123-28; and context rationality, 157-58, 161-62; Habermas's theory of communicative, 23, 136, 149-51, 159-70; hermeneutics and rational, 173-74; and institutions, 35-37, 40-47, 59, 116, 120, 126-28; and language, 13, 54, 59, 173; and meaning, 12-14, 61, 116, 120-22, 126-28, 173; and objective interests, 83-84; and praxis, 61, 136-37; as rational and reflexive, 54, 62-63, 117, 122, 127-28; and science, 31-32, 41; singularity thesis of human, 103-15; and strategic rationality, 157-58, 162-63, 167-69

Anthropology: and covering-law model, 85; physical, 79; and racism, 79-80; structural-functional theory in, 125

Behavioralism. See Political Science

Capitalism: and democracy, 7; Habermas on, 133-34, 138-41; Marxism on, 132-35; and modern politics, 7, 9, 39, 43; and rationalization, 7, 134; Weber on rise of, 76, 104-5, 107

Causal explanation. See Explanation; Generalizations

Causal theory. See Theory, social scientific

Causality: and adequate explanations, 91-100, 103-28; v. covariance, 122; and covering-law model, 15-21, 84-87; depth and sufficiency, relationship to, 18, 91-92, 93-95, 97; Habermas on, 144-45; and human action, 18-19, 104-15; Humean view of, 84, 105-9; mechanistic, 106-8, 124-25; problem of, 6, 15-21, 84-100; realist view of, 106-9, 124; and technical control, 5, 172

Club of Rome, 184-85

Commonsense knowledge: and expert knowledge, 58, 64; and Habermas's ideal speech community, 59-60; mutuality of, 62; poverty of, alleged, 67-70; primacy of, 14, 56; reflexivity of, 28-29, 55, 62-63, 68; relativization of, 55; and social scientific knowledge, 53-56, 60-70, 171; structures of, 55; unarticulated, 56; and values, 55, 62-63

Communication, Habermas's theory of, 23-24, 135, 137-38, 141, 145-48, 154, 157-64

Conceptual history, 8, 27-29, 37-38

Consensus: background, 23, 159-60, 162; background, breakdown of, 162, 164; and behavior, 35; future, 181; naive, 160, 164; normative, communication based on, 136-37; normative, and democracy, 138; normative, suspension of, 149-51; political, 82, 153-54; rational, as goal of discourse, 24, 164-67, 177-81; rational, achieving questioned, 25-26, 181-88, 209n.; voluntary, 164-65

Constitutive meanings, 116, 122, 126. See also Meaning

Contractarianism, 158, 163, 205n.

215